MURDER ON FAMOUS GROUNDS
A Mary Wandwalker Mystery

By
Susan Rowland

CHIRON PUBLICATIONS • ASHEVILLE, NORTH CAROLINA

© 2024 by Chiron Publications. All rights reserved. No part of this publication may be reproduced, stored in a retrieval system, or transmitted, in any form by any means, electronic, mechanical, photocopying, recording, or otherwise, without the prior written permission of the publisher, Chiron Publications, P.O. Box 19690, Asheville, N.C. 28815-1690.

www.ChironPublications.com

Interior and cover design by Danijela Mijailovic
Printed primarily in the United States of America.

ISBN 978-1-68503-209-8 paperback
ISBN 978-1-68503-210-4 hardcover
ISBN 978-1-68503-211-1 electronic
ISBN 978-1-68503-212-8 limited edition paperback

Library of Congress Cataloging-in-Publication Data Pending

Names: Rowland, Susan, 1962- author.
Title: Murder on family grounds / Susan Rowland.
Description: Asheville, North Carolina : Chiron Publications, 2024. |
   Series: A Mary Wandwalker mystery ; volume 3 | Summary: "Back in 1979, Mary wrote to the Falconers and was rejected. Now forty years later, key phrases from her letter appear in the faked suicide note of Perdita Falconer. Neither Perdita nor her killer had access to Mary's document.
   Too exact for coincidence, the link is the pseudonym of the drug dealer who supplied her fatal dose. He or she is known as "the Kestrel." When Mary was romanced by David Falconer in the 1970s, "the Kestrel" was codename for a Russian spy entertained at Falconer House. Could the resurrection of the nom de plume be connected to Viktor Solokov, the Russian oligarch renting the Falconer estate with his beautiful wife, Anna? For the Falconers have dark secrets, some centuries old. When George Jones's wife Caroline begs Mary to save her husband from treacherous Anna, and the murderous talons of the Kestrel, Mary must act"-
   - Provided by publisher.
Identifiers: LCCN 2024002191 (print) | LCCN 2024002192 (ebook) | ISBN 9781685032098 (paperback) | ISBN 9781685032104 (hardcover) | ISBN 9781685032128 (limited edition paperback) | ISBN 9781685032111 (electronic)
Subjects: LCGFT: Detective and mystery fiction. | Novels.
Classification: LCC PS3618.O8815 M87 2024 (print) | LCC PS3618.O8815 (ebook) | DDC 813/.6--dc23/eng/20240122
LC record available at https://lccn.loc.gov/2024002191
LC ebook record available at https://lccn.loc.gov/2024002192

FOR JOEL WEISHAUS,
ALWAYS BELOVED.

The Mary Wandwalker
Mystery Series by Susan Rowland:

#1 - *The Sacred Well Murders*
#2 - *The Alchemy Fire Murder*
#3 - *Murder on Family Grounds*

ACKNOWLEDGEMENTS AND HISTORICAL NOTE

I would like first to thank my longsuffering and dedicated critique group, the mystery writers, Gay Toltl Kinman and Meredith Taylor. I owe them so much. Writing a novel is like making a jigsaw in four dimensions. It takes everyone, which means special thanks are due to family and friends. In particular Cathy Rowland, John Rowland, our parents, and all who know me at Pacifica Graduate Institute, and Greenwich University, London.

Much gratitude is due to to Christine Saunders, Leslie Gardner, Evan Davis and Guillaume Batz, Claire Dyson, Ailsa Camm, Caroline Barker and Ailsa Montagu, Kathryn Le Grice, Ida Covi, Roula-Maria Dib, Lori Pye, and Jacqueline Feather and many more who contributed tea and sympathy, not to mention coffee and wine. Kudos also to the Jungian Society for Scholarly Studies for encouragement.

I add special thanks to wonderful Jungian analyst Julia Paton. This one is for you.

Murder on Family Grounds is a work of fiction, and no character is based on a real person, nor did any of the events depicted take place. Indeed, Oxford University is yet to erect a Cardinal or Sumer Colleges. On the other hand, during the many years of writing this book, British institutions and some stately homes have begun the painful task of owning up to past involvement with African slavery. Notable among these is the way portraiture has gotten involved.

In September 2023 a portrait of actor David Harewood joined the permanent art collection at Harewood House, home of the Earls of Harewood. David Harewood's ancestors were among the slaves whose exploitation produced the profits that built Harewood House. The actor contributes his portrait today as a way of representing what has been repressed or downplayed in the historical record. He says on his Wikipedia page that he hopes that people seeing his portrait will:

"[S]ee a picture of a black person that they may recognise from the television, they will enquire as to why his picture is there, and then they'll understand… all of the unpaid work that my ancestors did, and the brutality of what they suffered… helped build this house." https://en.wikipedia.org/wiki/David_Harewood

I mention this remarkable step because *Murder on Family Grounds* contains portrait painters and a project for bringing the labor and suffering of slaves into "the picture." As with the earlier novels, this book stems from Jungian arts-based research as a way in which the alchemical properties of art transform who we are, and how our relation to the cosmos can be.

FURTHER READING

Gerzina, G. (1995/2022) *Black England: A Forgotten Georgian History.* Great Britain: John Murray.

Rowland and Weishaus (2021) *Jungian Arts-Based Research and the Nuclear Enchantment of New Mexico.* Hove and New York: Routledge.

DRAMATIS PERSONAE

From the Archive

Mary Wandwalker: a loyal archivist replaced by a computer

Mr. Jeffreys: her Civil Service boss, with connections to the Security Services

The Falconers, Spouses and Exes

Sir Daniel Falconer: deceased, patriarch and part-time spy, d. 1978

Margaret Falconer: deceased, wife of Daniel, mother to David and Arthur, d. 2015

Arthur Falconer: elder son of above, still living

Ingrid Falconer: Arthur's long suffering wife

David Falconer: deceased, second son and Mary's fiancé, d. 1978

Simon Falconer: son to Arthur and ex-addict.

Patrick McCarthy: Simon's husband, painter

Belinda Choudhry MP: Simon's ex-wife and mother to Perdita Falconer, married to…

Richard Bishop: history professor at Sumer College, Oxford, married and separated from Belinda.

DRAMATIS PERSONAE

Mike McCarthy: father to Patrick, a portrait painter who sold out

Perdita Falconer: deceased daughter of Simon and Belinda, student at Cardinal College, Oxford, d. 2018.

The Solokovs

Viktor Solokov: Russian oligarch, cozy with Government Party

Anna Solokov: his young wife, with big file at Interpol.

Kyrill Solokov: deceased, KGB spy, known as the Kestrel, d. 2011

Rosalind Forrest: deceased, American actor, mother to Viktor and wife of Kyrill, d. 1987.

Police, Students, Other Relatives

George Jones: undercover detective sergeant, son to Mary Wandwalker who gave him up for adoption shortly after his birth. Father: David Falconer.

Caroline Jones: his wife of twenty years, former teacher, suffers from chronic clinical depression.

Jamie Sanders: Cardinal College nurse.

Helga and Johann: Hungarian twins sponsored by Viktor Solokov at Oxford University.

Chief Inspector Bert Reynolds: has heard all the jokes.

Rameses and Summers: his constables.

CONTENTS

CHAPTER 1: How It Began – with the End   3

CHAPTER 2: Lunch, You Said   9

CHAPTER 3: Not Family?   13

CHAPTER 4: An Apartment in the Barbican   21

CHAPTER 5: Two Letters, Forty Years Apart   29

CHAPTER 6: A Meeting at Cardinal College   35

CHAPTER 7: Encounter in the Chapel   45

CHAPTER 8: At the Jones Cottage   55

CHAPTER 9: George and Anna   61

CHAPTER 10: Party Games   65

CHAPTER 11: Mary's Quest   73

CHAPTER 12: A Summer Garden in 1978   79

CHAPTER 13: Not Accident Prone?   93

CHAPTER 14: The Mysteries of Anna Solokov   99

CHAPTER 15: Trap, Not a Nest   107

CHAPTER 16: The Kestrel Then and Now   115

CHAPTER 17: Three Falconers   121

CHAPTER 18: Afternoon Tea at Falconer House   125

CHAPTER 19: From Falconer House to Oxford   137

CHAPTER 20: Dinner in Sumer College   141

CHAPTER 21: After Love   147

CHAPTER 22: Those Damn Students   155

CHAPTER 23: Mary at Falconer House	159
CHAPTER 24: In Service of the Living and the Dead	167
CHAPTER 25: George and Mary	173
CHAPTER 26: The Accused	177
CHAPTER 27: An Assortment of Red Herrings	185
CHAPTER 28: An Old-Fashioned House Party	195
CHAPTER 29: Nighttime Conversation	201
CHAPTER 30: Staircase	207
CHAPTER 31: House Party on Family Ground	213
CHAPTER 32: Best Laid Plans	217
CHAPTER 33: Not the Kestrel File	225
CHAPTER 34: David Falconer	229
CHAPTER 35: Pregnant Conversations	235
CHAPTER 36: Giving Thanks	241
CHAPTER 37: Mike McCarthy	249
CHAPTER 38: Ready for Dinner?	257
CHAPTER 39: Thanksgiving	261
CHAPTER 40: Regroup at the Randolph Hotel, Oxford	271
CHAPTER 41: Mothers	281
CHAPTER 42: Young and in Love	287
CHAPTER 43: Helga's Choice	293
CHAPTER 44: Family	303
CHAPTER 45: We Who Have Loved	309
CHAPTER 46: The Depth Enquiry Agency	319

CHAPTER 1
HOW IT BEGAN – WITH THE END

Mary Wandwalker's office smelled of November — earth mixed with dead leaves from damp shoes. Tonight, there will be fireworks in Hyde Park. *That's what I want*, she reflected, *to explode into a final shower of light because I am losing what matters most.*

For weeks Mary refused to accept defeat. After nearly 40 years of service, surely she could dig up reasons to remain Chief Archivist. She loved her work in the National Archive, felt at home in its vaults beneath London.

"At least you've no family to worry about," said her longtime boss, Mr. Jeffreys, with unnecessary emphasis, she felt.

After what felt like the 10th recitation of his "I'm letting you go" speech, he'd remained at her office door, watching.

You need your work, and not just for the money, came that annoying voice from inside her.

"Shut up," said Mary, not entirely silently, as Mr. Jeffreys raised his eyebrows. She expected him to leave. He did not.

Mary's gray eyes widened. Unlike Mr. Jeffreys to loom. He probably wasn't waiting for her to admire his pearl gray suit. He liked to disconcert Mary. In the middle of some budget battle, he'd present a sensitive task for a troublesome spy or get her to track down documents that, if made public, would destroy a government minister. These missions and yes, caring for her underpaid staff, were what she lived for.

Today everything about him was taut. His face, the color of black flint, was immobile.

There's something he's not telling me. This was not Mr. Jeffreys of old. She sensed he enjoyed her strategies to obtain pay rises for her staff. Today her longtime boss had an agenda she could not fathom. More than simply sending her away, she was sure. Even though he kept harping on it.

Mr. Jeffreys flicked a bit of dust from his sleeve and repeated. "It's done, Miss Wandwalker. I won't, can't, reassign you. Your involuntary retirement starts today. Pack your personal possessions, if you have any."

He scanned her office, then folded his arms. No framed photographs, no inappropriate gifts cluttering her desk. She'd taken her books home the previous week. Mr. Jeffreys's gaze landed on that half-dead plant from a departed intern. She never remembered to bring water for it, the plant that is.

In the pause, Mary's mouth dried. That dying plant is me without the Archive, she thought. Mr. Jeffreys pressed his lips together. Mary caught a hint of a suppressed grin. There is more, she prayed to the gods of this, her safe cave.

Somewhere at the bottom of his bureaucratic soul, the man she'd answered to for decades must be on her side. He *must*.

I'm resilient, she told herself. I'm Mary Wandwalker. Mary gulped. Damn you, Mr. Jeffreys. You know what the Archive means to me.

My home, she wanted to howl at him. These are my stone vaults and brick tunnels. *You're kicking me out of the place where I feel safe.* Mary shut her eyes, surprised that she was surprised. Face it, Mary, she told herself. Despite the rows and appeals, part of you still thought it would never happen. Well, it happened. I built my life around this job, and it's gone.

Mary straightened in her chair. She had her pride. Her neat figure appeared to advantage in her favorite vintage suit. Today might be the day, she'd said to herself, dressing that morning. I'll not go quietly. She lifted her chin and gave him the look that skewered her interns.

Let him speak first. Let him make the first move on whatever he's plotting. The silence between them swelled, became pregnant. At last, Mr. Jeffreys walked over and took the chair facing her.

HOW IT BEGAN – WITH THE END

"Mary," he began, as the wood groaned under his bulk. "Miss Wandwalker, we've never discussed your unique qualities." He gave a wry smile. "Without doubt, you are, were, the most remarkable archivist, probably in the four centuries of this institution."

Mary opened her mouth. He put his hand up. "Unfortunately, your secret is why you must leave the Archive. It's not something I could put on a dismissal notice."

She could not help herself. "You saw the mess in the Archive when I arrived? No one could find anything before 1960. I created…" Mr. Jeffreys raised an eyebrow. "Okay, *we* created, a thriving research resource."

She hated the appeal in her voice. "The Archive is my home."

Even that word elicited only a flicker. Ah, this is new, thought Mary. This is bigger than previous times he's held back. She shivered.

"What's this nonsense about a secret?" she blurted out. "There's no secret. If I can't retrain as a digital archivist, surely, I can assist the scholars. Most of them *know* me. Some of them even like me."

Self-depreciation and humor were tools in her personal survival kit.

Mr. Jeffreys gave a strangled sound. He shook his head.

"Yes, that overpriced course, Introduction to Digital Archives. Your professor rang to complain. He'd never had a student challenge the philosophy while being unable to complete basic coding. Your stormy eyes frightened him."

Mary cleared her throat. "I'm highly skilled," she retorted. "Self-trained, but I've managed crisis after crisis down here. There must be something you can offer me." She shut her eyes briefly. "Even if it's not in the Archive."

There, the admission that she would leave her subterranean office and not return.

Mr. Jeffreys eyes gleamed before their impassivity returned. Mary wanted to growl. Yes, she'd given him the opening he wanted.

"*Not* in the Archive is a good place to start, Miss Wandwalker," he said gently. "I do have a task, something only you can accomplish. It's connected to that secret I mentioned."

He put his hand up. "Hear me out." His chair creaked again. "You see, I know what you are hiding, Miss Wandwalker. Simply this: You have something grand about you."

Mary shook her head, outraged. "I'm no snob."

"You mistake me. I mean ... well, let's call it a connection to a larger thing, a vision or spirit. Making the repository of the nation's dirty linen into your domain is a clue. Your secret is even in your name. Remember that Anglo-Saxon scholar explaining that 'Wandwalker' is a corruption of 'windtalker': old women who talked to the gods." He leaned forward to emphasize his next words. "That gift is locked up inside you."

He paused. She sniffed, yet noticed Mr. Jeffreys was choosing his words with unusual care. His voice rose until she felt a thrill inside.

"Your secret is a gift and a curse. For you will never be satisfied unless providing service that brings out the extraordinary in you. Once the Archive required your unique qualities. No longer. Digitization banishes you. And it also frees you."

Mary's head rose to protest. Mr. Jeffreys refused to be interrupted.

"People like you are rare. Forty years ago, I did not know how much you would re-create the Archive for the 20th century. Unfortunately, we are now ..." He spread out his hands.

She opened her mouth then closed it. Could Mr. Jeffreys be right? She loathed compassion. His expression had lost the flinty quality. She missed it. Her no longer boss rose to leave.

"I have an opening for another kind of life, and I must warn you, it could be dangerous. It means seeking your own ground, Miss Wandwalker."

The finality in his tone fueled the anger she was barely controlling.

"Dangerous? So, what is it, this new thing?" she forced herself to mutter. "Now that computers have replaced me."

Mr. Jeffreys coughed. Mary shot him a suspicious glance. If he laughed, she wouldn't stand for it.

"Miss Wandwalker, you undersell yourself. Your insight found those lost letters from Henry VIII's court for that radical artist ... McCarthy, wasn't it?"

She nodded, too full to speak.

"Yesterday I heard from another fan of yours. Professor Richard Bishop reminded me of that stash of telegrams from the 1890s that you dug up. It became the book that made his career."

Mary gulped. She'd had an affair with Richard Bishop. Indeed, all her lovers had been connected to the Archive. Mr. Jeffreys did not know that. Or did he?

He sighed and rose his bulk from the chair. "To put it plain, Miss Wandwalker, you've been down here too long. People out there need you. You just haven't found them yet."

An iron grid squeezed Mary's heart. Find your own ground, he'd said. Well, she would, somehow. Losing my job is not the end, she reassured herself.

As if he read her mind, Mr. Jeffreys became brisk. He clapped his hands, becoming the Mr. Jeffreys she knew.

"Miss Wandwalker, your adventures await. Join me for lunch tomorrow at the Barbican Centre. Some people are very keen to meet you. Insistent actually." Mr. Jeffreys mouth twisted at his own change the mood.

Mary stared at him. She could not believe what she had heard.

"Lunch?" You won't tell me now about this mysterious job?"

Her jaw dropped; a crimson flush began. "I've just lost my... I have to find a future... and you're inviting me to *lunch*."

"That's it," said Mr. Jeffreys. He slapped his knees and began to leave, filling the doorway with hideous cheerfulness.

"Get angry, Miss Wandwalker. You should. None of this is fair. I'd be…" he paused for inspiration … "seriously perturbed," he concluded. He turned back once more. "Tomorrow at 1 p.m. at the Waterside Restaurant. Do not fail. It's a matter of life and death."

The door clicked behind him, leaving Mary dumbfounded in an empty room.

*****

Minutes later, the dazed ex-archivist checked her desk drawers for any last personal items. Pulling out a long-lost handkerchief, Mary recalled another Mr. Jeffreys; the youth she had met long ago, before the Archives. Back then, he was the only Black student at her Oxford college. One October night she woke to ugly drunken chants. The all-male, all-white Rugby Club, she realized. Pulling the thin pillow over her head failed to block the racist taunts. It was when she recognized the sound of fists on flesh that she swung her cold feet out of bed.

Throwing on a dressing gown and shoes she descended the staircase to the quad and peered out. Six of the Club staggered around singing and throwing punches at a dark figure in the center fountain. They melted away when Mary rattled the bolts of the door. Any hint of a College porter investigating cleared them away. Cowards, she thought as she tiptoed out.

The Black student was wet all over. He attempted to wash his bloody nose with a swollen hand. Mutely she offered a handkerchief from the pocket of her dressing gown. She remembered the roughness of his chin when she dipped the cloth in water then wiped his face.

Mary helped the young Jeffreys out of the fountain and gave him an arm to his own staircase. No words were exchanged then, or since, over the incident. Mary knew he did not forget. When she had been desperate for a job, he responded with a shelf-stacking position at the long-neglected Archive. It was she, not he, who made the job into her life. Now that life had ended.

CHAPTER 2
LUNCH, YOU SAID

Arriving at Barbican Tube station, Mary strode into the temple of architectural modernism. Its relentless concrete reminded her of past occasions going to see Shakespeare, and once, with a French lover, to a season of the European Avant Garde at the Barbican Cinema. At no time had she become a fan of these gray towers. Now her shoes echoed on its brick walkways the color of withered plums.

Mary preferred her London pre-1900, or at least to have the grace to pretend so.

"The 20th century is overrated," she would say to new recruits to the Archive. "And don't get me started on the 21st."

True, it was an exaggeration. Mary deliberately sculpted her authority from cultivated eccentricity. Yet over the years she'd become comfortable stuck in the past. *Too comfortable,* she realized walking purposefully.

Inside the Barbican's chief restaurant, Mr. Jeffreys waited in the dazzle of sun piercing plate glass windows. Across from him busy tables met his impassive scrutiny. He stood to greet her.

"This is family ground for you, Miss Wandwalker," said Mr. Jeffreys.

She took a step back, shocked to her core. Mr. Jeffreys knew she had no family, what with her parents dying just before she attended Oxford, no siblings, and over the years refusing several marriage proposals. Mr. Jeffreys ignored her reaction and addressed the impossibly thin waiter. "Take Miss Wandwalker's coat and bring four menus. Please."

"Is this some kind of game?" she said as she let the waiter seat her. "I have no family ground."

All she had was her dignity. Mr. Jeffreys met her expression with gravity. Mary looked away. Wasn't yesterday enough? Resentment stiffened her spine. She ignored her host by scrutinizing the elegant restaurant clientele.

Ah, those exaggerated colors on toned bodies went with the peculiar animation of the other diners. Of course, she was among actors and artists from the Barbican's Theatre and Galleries. The buzz was unlike the city's watering holes Mr. Jeffreys used to choose. In the old days, as she'd have to learn to think of them, he'd offer lunch when budget negotiations got heated.

Today there was no Archive between them, only a cream menu card. She picked it up. Words blurred in front of her swollen eyelids. Today she would refuse provocations. She lifted her chin.

"Ah, here's Patrick," said Mr. Jeffreys, signaling an approach from behind. "He's alone. I was expecting both."

"Who?" said Mary, not looking up. Footsteps, then a figure sat himself at the round table. She glanced over the top of her menu. A man of around 40 with a brown goatee shook Mr. Jeffreys's hand with a strained smile. He wore a nondescript suit that gave off a whiff of… oh, paint fumes. Glancing nervously at Mary, she thought him vaguely familiar. Some Civil Service colleague, no doubt.

"Miss Wandwalker, Patrick McCarthy. Introductions quite unnecessary, I'm sure," announced Mr. Jeffreys. "Let's order before we talk. I'll have the soup and the duck. Plus, we'll take a bottle of your best claret."

The waiter was already tapping into his machine, not giving anyone a chance to get away, Mary reflected. "The same," she muttered.

"Make that three," said Patrick with such forced brightness that the waiter looked up, meeting Mary's sore eyes. Then he vanished, reappearing almost instantly with large glasses of purplish wine and a basket of bread cradled under one arm. Tip earned, noted Mary.

"Miss Wandwalker, I cannot tell you how grateful I am to see you."

The new lines around Patrick's mouth made him look haunted, not grateful at all, Mary thought. Patrick's hair showed gray at the temples and could do with a trim. Mary found it easier to look at the paint stains on his hands. These, she remembered.

"It's kind of you to thank me, Mr. McCarthy. I saw your exhibition. You did remarkable work with the Anne of Cleves Letters that I located for you."

Patrick McCarthy turned to Mr. Jeffreys. "You haven't told her?"

"I thought it best coming from you."

"Told me what?" Mary tensed in response to Patrick's tormented expression. He was going to say something bad. Surely today of all days she should be spared.

"You know I'm married to Simon Falconer."

Falconer, not that! Of all the names in the world, yes, only that name could cut through the fog of losing the Archive.

"Simon Falconer," she said slowly, a man from an ancient minefield. "Yes, I did know you were married. You mentioned it when you came to the Archive. But I'd forgotten."

She glanced again at his pallor, and then memory stabbed her. She'd forgotten, being buried in her own troubles. Not only was the terrible thing fodder for the Sunday papers, but Mary had sent flowers, anonymously.

"Oh, Mr. McCarthy, I'm sorry. The Oxford girl who overdosed. She was Simon Falconer's daughter." Mary stumbled into cliché, hoping her feelings would come through. "I'm so sorry for your loss," she said.

"You sent a wreath to the funeral," broke in Mr. Jeffreys amiably. 'From an old friend of the family.' Nice touch, Miss Wandwalker." To her perplexed look, he added: "The thing is, Patrick inquired, and got your name. How is Simon, by the way?" He nodded at Patrick who was reducing his bread to bullets.

"Devastated, as you'd expect. Of course, he's drinking too much. It's only been a couple of months. We're all... well, the family finds it hard to believe. Perdita was ... a beloved daughter. And the death, so, so insane. No one dreamed she would ever take psychotropic mushrooms. No one in the family."

"It happened at her Oxford college?" Mr. Jeffreys darted glances at Mary, giving her time to adjust.

Patrick swallowed. This was hard for him. "Yes, they found Perdy dead in her room at Cardinal. Too much partying, they said." He took a deep breath and flung the next words at the other man. "You know what I think, Jeffreys. It was not like Perdita to experiment, especially not with drugs like magic mushrooms. She was so quiet, so keen on her studies. Not even 20. We all adored her ..."

Patrick gripped the table. He looked up at Mary. "I apologize, Miss Wandwalker. You see, even though Simon and I have only been married since it was legal, the truth is he, Belinda and I have known each other from school. Perdita Falconer was my child, too."

"Belinda?"

"Perdita's mother, Simon's ex-wife. Now a Conservative MP. We remained close despite Belinda's fury when Simon left her for me. After the divorce, Perdita lived with Belinda and her new husband, Richard Bishop."

Mary glared at Mr. Jeffreys and reached for her water glass. What a setup, she thought, Mr. Jeffrey's dropping names like Richard Bishop oh so casually into our conversation yesterday. I will not be dragged into his schemes. Mr. Jeffreys was watching Patrick gearing up to say whatever it was he wanted.

"As you are family, Miss Wandwalker, we thought..."

"I am not family!"

Someone had shouted. It must have been her because all heads in the restaurant were turned to their table. The mallards paddling on the Barbican manmade lake swerved toward the picture window. Mary shivered. It must have been her because the stunned expressions of the diners converged on her dry lips.

CHAPTER 3
NOT FAMILY?

Not family? Denial hurt Mary's jaw. Yes, she'd shouted at Patrick's absurd proposition, that she, Mary Wandwalker, was one of the Falconer family. Just because, because. ... Mary pressed her lips into a line despite what it would do to her lipstick.

Mr. Jeffreys applied his magisterial nod to the diners and frozen waiters. As one, the waiters turned their backs, the diners buried their heads in their food or menus. Mary's nose filled with savory steam. Her tight stomach relaxed at the bowl of soup that appeared on the table, in which big slices mushrooms floated like lily pads in puddles of cream.

"Ah yes, the Waterside is famous for its soups," said Mr. Jeffreys. "Do dig in. How appropriate. These mushrooms are not hallucinogenic, of course."

With a shudder, Mary picked up her spoon. The spoon wobbled until she grabbed her wrist with her left hand. After a few sips she could concentrate on chewing the mushrooms and holding the spoon to cool the rich broth. For a while silence circled the table in the hum of the dining room.

Twenty minutes later, Mary sawed through her duck and potatoes with grim efficiency. Finally, Patrick ventured a few words.

"Miss Wandwalker, I did not mean to offend you."

Mary wasn't offended, she was outraged, stabbed. She stared at Patrick for a whole minute before recalling that his loss was recent. He deserved a reply. If only she could organize her words about that terrible time. She jabbed a fork into an over roasted potato.

"Mr. McCarthy," she began. "A long time ago I wrote to the Falconers about family." Her throat produced a rasp. It appeared to shock Patrick. She took a gulp of water before going on. "I wrote," she repeated, "and the reply came from the Falconer solicitors. They made it clear that I was never going to be part of the Falconer family." To Mary's surprise, Patrick looked relieved. He knew.

"That was 40 years ago, wasn't it?" he said gently.

She nodded.

"After David Falconer's death, you wrote to Lady Margaret about the baby."

Mary dropped her knife. It splashed orange sauce on her suit cuff. She could not look up.

"Don't. Not that, not ever," she croaked to the tablecloth. She never, ever, talked about the baby. She looked away, careful to avoid both men. What was the best route around the tables to the door?

"Don't go," Mr. Jeffreys said softly. He shot a hand to her wrist. "You can't go. Listen, Mary. There are things you must know."

He rarely called her Mary. In her mind she was sprinting out of the concrete labyrinth of the Barbican Center and into the dust and fumes of the siren-haunted city. Damn Mr. Jeffreys for reading her thoughts. Meanwhile, Patrick bit his knuckles. He glanced alternately at Jeffreys or Mary.

"I'm really sorry, Miss Wandwalker," said Patrick. "We must talk about the Falconers. For Simon's sake. It's a matter of life and death. We have that letter, your letter to the family." Mary glanced at him. "When Lady Margaret died in 2015, well, before she died of course, she summoned Simon and me. She wanted us to return the letter to you. It has a handwritten apology on the back."

"I don't want it."

NOT FAMILY?

Mr. Jeffreys had finished his food. He nodded at Patrick, as if to say, 'I'll try now.'

"Miss Wandwalker, let me put the problem in the fewest possible words. Despite the gap of 40 years, your letter is directly connected to the death of Perdita Falconer."

Mary's jaw dropped. "Impossible. Perdita can't have been born until …"

Patrick broke in. "My husband, Simon, her father, was not even born in early 1979 when you wrote that letter. Simon was born in October 1979. Look, I did a family tree for you."

He took out a square of white paper from his top pocket and unfolded it on the tablecloth.

Falconer Family Tree (motto: *Service through Family*)

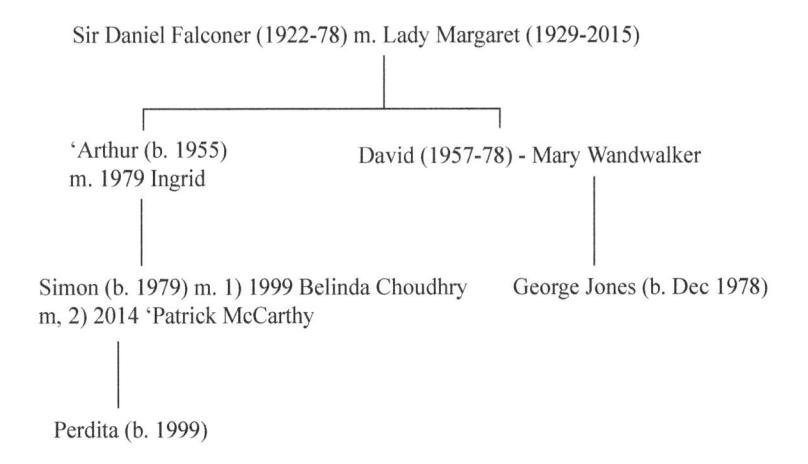

Sir Daniel Falconer (1922-78) m. Lady Margaret (1929-2015)

'Arthur (b. 1955) m. 1979 Ingrid

David (1957-78) - Mary Wandwalker

Simon (b. 1979) m. 1) 1999 Belinda Choudhry m, 2) 2014 'Patrick McCarthy

George Jones (b. Dec 1978)

Perdita (b. 1999)

"So, it was Simon's father I saw at the funeral," said Mary. "I knew there was a brother."

"Funeral?" Patrick wanted more.

Mary pushed her plate away and turned to the window. She made herself notice the water, the anxious ducks tracking passersby, the geraniums dying of cold in concrete tubs. How to escape this conversation?

Only once, decades ago, had a female friend guessed her secret. She'd tried to insist that Mary talk about the baby, even get therapy. The woman meant well. Mary ripped the page out of her address book with the woman's details. She threw away her Christmas cards unopened. Now this excruciating lunch.

"Miss Wandwalker refers to David Falconer's funeral in November of '78," said Mr. Jeffreys, unrelenting.

"Yes, of course." Patrick's voice faded into the tapestry of buzzing voices. Even so, Mary could hear the next words. "He would be ..."

"The baby's father." Mary was stiff as stone. Her voice seemed to be coming from a long way off. "I gave the baby up for adoption."

It was clear from Mr. Jeffreys' face that he would not stop. There was more to this meeting. Mary's eyes flicked toward the window again. Maybe, just maybe, she could make a run for the exit.

"You have to keep going, Mary," said Mr. Jeffreys.

She shook her head. *No, I don't.*

He cleared his throat. "Very well. Eat your duck while I fill Patrick in."

"You see Patrick, when Mary and I were at Oxford, we shared a history tutor, although I was two years ahead. He was Sir Daniel Falconer, father to two sons. The elder, Arthur, went on to produce Simon, your husband. Mary met his second son, David, when he interrupted a tutorial. Unfortunately," Mr. Jeffreys paused to scrutinize Mary, "Sir Daniel's death came just a month after David's fatal accident. I attended the second funeral, Miss Wandwalker did not."

Mary's eyes flashed. "By that time the Falconers had made it clear they wanted nothing to do with me. ... They did not want David's child." She grabbed her wine glass and downed the lot, followed by the remains of her water. Mr. Jeffreys signaled to the waiter for more wine.

"We were engaged," Mary said. Wherever she was, it was bleak. She directed her words to the table.

Patrick made as if to speak before Mr. Jeffreys frowned him down.

"When I was forbidden to attend David's funeral, I snuck in. Arthur saw me. Lady Margaret did not. I was surprised at Sir Daniel. He'd been kind, welcomed me to Falconer House on that one visit." Mary put down her napkin and struggled to stand. "Of course, I'm sorry about Perdita, but as I never knew her ..."

"Your son did." Mr. Jeffreys words were brutal. Dark understanding eyes met Mary's shock. She sank back into her chair. This was too much to bear.

Her keen hearing caught a melancholy wail from outside. It must be a seagull from the River Thames. Yesterday, Mr. Jeffreys had been preparing her for today. She had not seen her baby for 40 years. Glancing at Patrick, she saw no escape; he knew this also.

"The baby was adopted," she repeated.

The past was dead. She knew that because she'd buried it in the deepest vaults of the Archive. From the first moment she'd entered, huge and sore from giving birth, she'd collected the pains of her labor, the tiny cries of her baby, and shut them away. She'd thought never to feel that ache again. She'd been wrong.

Mary Wandwalker shut her eyes. No, she would not recall that impossible time of grief, pregnancy, and rejection. Yet she'd not been defeated, she realized. Alone yes, and staring at walls, she nevertheless determined to survive — to do the right thing — as she then believed, in giving up the baby. Until one day she descended into the Archive, a woman, not a girl. Having fought her inner demons, she became confident dealing with those in the Archive's dusty tunnels.

"Yes," confirmed Mr. Jeffreys. "The baby was adopted by a nice childless couple called Jones. He was in the Metropolitan police. Both dead now. George Jones got in touch with me at a few months ago. He met his cousin Perdita shortly before she died."

Mary blinked. "Wait, did you say his name's George, George Jones?"

"His name's on the family tree," said Patrick.

"I didn't look," said Mary feeling foolish, no exposed, horribly exposed. She turned to the other man. "You, Mr. Jeffreys? He got in touch with you. Why?"

"I'm not surprised you forgot I helped you with the adoption paperwork. My name was on the documents. Until we met, I think George had some idea I was his father." Mr. Jeffreys gave a bark of laughter. "Then he asked after you."

Mary began to breathe too quickly. "I cannot see him. I can't."

Patrick grabbed the water jug and topped up her glass. She took a big gulp.

"No one is going to force you into anything," said Mr. Jeffreys, frowning at Patrick, who gave her a sickly smile. The drumming in Mary's chest quietened.

"Can we get back to Simon, Perdita's father," said Patrick. "Please, please, Miss Wandwalker, come and talk to him. You see, there's more to her death than the police will admit. Right now you are the only clue we have to the truth. Not knowing how or why she died is driving us insane. It's been three months, and Si's getting worse. Please, please, come to the flat. Hear it from Simon."

Mary forced her tormented expression to meet Mr. Jeffreys' firm one. He nodded.

"Miss Wandwalker, you may remember that it was Sir Daniel who recruited me into the Security Services. After his death in France — I chose to move sideways to the Archive, where I found you a position."

Mr. Jeffreys seized Mary's half-full wine glass, poured it into his own and swallowed it all. Mary was shocked. Mr. Jeffreys never broke the rules of polite intercourse. He savored fine claret. Never would he knock back alcohol as if it would quench an unbearable thirst. He's very upset, Mary thought. There is more than he is saying. She waited.

NOT FAMILY?

"Sir Daniel tutored both of us," Mr. Jeffreys said.

Mary sniffed.

"He was good to one of Oxford's first Black British students. For that reason, among others, I've retained an interest in the Falconer family. There aren't that many of them left. After David died, Arthur married and produced Simon. Perdita Falconer is ..." He paused for a sigh, "*was* Simon's only child, the youngest Falconer heir." His voice deepened. "Recently, I've suspected a pattern, a very old and very deadly pattern. The Falconers are a little too accident prone."

Mary began to breathe faster.

"You see Miss Wandwalker, we want you to help us discover if someone is killing them off."

CHAPTER 4
AN APARTMENT IN THE BARBICAN

In a daze, Mary followed Patrick and Mr. Jeffreys along the brick walkway. They were heading into the heart of the Barbican labyrinth. Unlike Mary's previous visits to high culture, this time she would enter someone's home. The Falconer family tree, with her son's name on it, had somehow been planted in her handbag. She recalled that "Barbican" referred to the Roman watchtower that once stood on this muddy ground.

This history gave the convoluted Barbican Complex a more meaningful shape in her fevered imagination. She recalled reading in the Sunday papers that a few Barbican inhabitants had been spooked by actual spooks: the ghosts of Roman guards. Could they still be on patrol?

I am inside a modern fortress, she mused. Not unlike the Archive, except for being built in the sky rather than underground. To her surprise, letting her mind touch on the Archive was not so bad. She directed her thoughts to wondering why the Barbican planners would hark back to Roman London of slaves and soldiers.

Less of a mystery was why Patrick, the artist, would have an ultrafashionable, ultraexpensive flat in the Barbican with Simon Falconer. Family ground, Mr. Jeffreys had called it. Drat him. Her connection to the Falconers could hardly be characterized that way.

"Simon and I rent from my father," Patrick tossed at her with forced cheer as they walked along the landing. "Mike McCarthy snapped up the apartment back when this was affordable housing. These days, what with those design awards, it's major kudos to live here. Rich artists or architects go nuts anytime anything is for sale."

"Mike McCarthy the portrait painter? He's your father?" queried Mary.

Patrick gestured her toward a bright blue front door. Each entrance on this landing glowed in a different primary color. Although it could have been garish, the palette worked to soften the relentless concrete.

"Oh yeah, my dad. He's *that* portrait painter," said Patrick, unlocking the door and ushering them into a small room. It was dusk inside, from closed window blinds. Patrick's tone was bitter. "Mike McCarthy, portrait painter to the stars. My father will flatter anyone in paint who throws him enough dosh. Doesn't matter how dodgy or corrupt they are."

"He's very popular," said Mr. Jeffreys, diplomatically.

"He's an arsehole."

The voice came from the furthest corner in the small space, while Patrick strode forward, pulling up the blinds.

"Total arsehole," he agreed. "My dad's portraits imitate the Old Masters to flatter his subjects. That's why they are so sought-after. Naturally, he hates my work. My portraits reveal what power really is, his celebrate it."

He pointed at seats for Mary and Mr. Jeffreys before continuing. "The great Mike McCarthy never wanted me to leave stockbroking. Now my dad charges us top rent for this bijou apartment. And he won't lower himself to examine my work."

Mary expected a Barbican flat, one housing a painter no less, to be unusual. In fact, despite having helped Patrick with archive sources, this afternoon was the first time she had seen his work. She was astonished and moved by how Patrick's radical approach challenged the viewer's expectations.

Gone was the imitation of life. In place of the frozen face, these portraits flickered, changed, as ingredients from their past forced their way onto the canvas. Such was the riot of color, disassembly, and multimedia quality of Patrick's vision that Mary temporarily forgot her reluctance to be in the same space as someone named Falconer.

Patrick created innovative portraits of historic personages he considered unjustly neglected. He used paper scraps of the period such as recipes, torn up letters, bills of sale, interspersed with layers of oil pigment. Parts of faces and/or bodies appeared on translucent watercolor washes. Mary stood very still, hardly breathing. Her body thrummed to experiences, agonies, and joys from lives she knew nothing of.

It was as if each portrait were in fact multiple tiny hands reaching out to pull the viewer into a different story. Intense and animated, concluded Mary. The work deserves time to truly appreciate it.

She shot a last longing glance at the Anne of Cleves. Yes, there were the letters that she tracked down for Patrick, back in the Archive. Not the original documents, of course. As astonishing finds, they had been rushed off for preservation. No, Patrick had jumped in the air when Mary handed over the photocopies. Delicately folded to make the Queen's ruff and gown, the hard-to-decipher writing demanded attention. Staring at the most uncelebrated of Henry VIII's queens, Mary felt kinship.

"Miss Wandwalker," said Mr. Jeffreys reprovingly.

She could no longer avoid it. Turning, she saw Simon Falconer, the nephew of her dead lover, David, lounging on a chaise, watching her. Patrick knelt beside him and removed the whisky bottle from Simon's hand.

"Mr. Falconer." Mary set down her handbag at her feet.

"Simon, please." He slurred the words as if it was a great effort to speak.

Simon struggled to sit upright. Mary realized that he must have been drinking for hours. He was used to it, judging by the veins decorating his nose. Blonde fuzz covered his skull from what would once have been the fashionable shaven head. His blue eyes were equal parts tormented and curious. They certainly tormented her.

"You look like ... someone I used to know, your uncle David. Your eyes are the same shade." She coughed to stop more words spilling out.

He stared at her. "I never knew him. My father did, of course. He said the same. Perdita's eyes were blue violet. Falconer blue with a touch of sunset, we used to say. With her mother's midnight hair, she is ...she was ... beautiful. Each morning I expect her text or phone message. It's been weeks ..." He choked.

"Three months," said Patrick, gently.

Mary could smell despair on Simon. It was part his unwashed jeans, part old sweat. Tears as endless as the sea, she thought, reminded of David. No good, she had to say something.

"I'm really sorry about your daughter, but I don't know why I'm here."

Patrick threw an anguished glance at Mr. Jeffreys, then struggled to his feet.

"Where are my manners?" he exclaimed. "Miss Wandwalker, Jeffreys, sit down, please. I promise the chairs are more comfortable than they look. I'll get coffee. Si, don't look at me like that. No more whisky. You know what the doctor said."

Patrick vanished through a door concealed by being the middle section of a triptych of portraits. Soon a metallic roar and the scent of chocolate-and-applewood from coffee brought relief. Mary's tight shoulders relaxed. She took a plastic chair she recognized as a design classic. Mr. Jeffreys grunted into a steel device that groaned under his weight.

"You don't know why you're here, Miss Wandwalker?" said Simon. He sniffed his empty glass before setting it down. "Didn't Patrick tell you about the letter? Well, the *two* letters, one supposedly from our darling girl. Jeffreys says only you can tell us more."

AN APARTMENT IN THE BARBICAN

Mary looked at Mr. Jeffreys, who smiled blandly. "We'll wait for Patrick and the coffee," he said. She could not read him. It would have surprised her if she could.

You've got guts, Mary Wandwalker, my most creative ex-employee, Mr. Jeffreys said to himself. *Guts and compassion. The latter you try to hide. I know you got that Archive employee with a mental breakdown into therapy. You took on extra work to cover his absences. That way he kept his job. And you visited that young woman with cancer and stopped me advertising for her replacement until she could return. It cost you. Maybe it also helped with your loneliness.*

Aware of Mary's scrutiny, Mr. Jeffreys took out a tiny diary from his jacket pocket and pretended to consult it. He liked to make notes the old-fashioned way.

Yes, I did know about Richard Bishop and your other lovers. You never let anyone get close after David Falconer's death. It's time that changed. Maybe only the Falconers can fix what the Falconers broke.

While Mr. Jeffreys ruminated, Mary suspected him of prolonging the encounter with Simon Falconer. The man on the couch might resemble David, but he looked like his troubles were beyond anything she could do.

Bad living had added a layer of fat to Simon's moderate frame. Compared to lines of strain on lean Patrick, Simon Falconer's suffering was out of control. For the first time Mary Wandwalker acknowledged a grief equal to her own 40 years ago.

"Would you like to talk about Perdita?"

Mary knew she wasn't a people person. She could see that reflected in the painful twist of Simon's lips. *I would have known him,* she realized. *If I'd married his uncle, I would have been family. Perdita's parents are divorced, yet they are a family through her. I would have been inside the circle.*

"Can't talk about Perdita. So ironic, her name. Our lost child … our little girl." He stared purposefully at Mary for the first time. There was an unbearable intimacy between them.

"Why don't *you* tell me about Uncle David?" he said. "He was my Pa — Arthur's, younger brother. Pa says the family never recovered from his death."

Nor have I, Mary wanted to say. This is the truth she did not want to give these strangers, David's family. Briefly she shut her eyes.

"Miss Wandwalker?"

Was that malice in Simon's expression? Mary found her dignity.

"No, Mr. Falconer" she said. I will not talk about David."

"Even after 40 years?" Simon looked incredulous. "Is that because of the …"

"*Simon.*"

Patrick stood at the door with a tray upon which trembled a French press and mugs. He wrenched his frown from Simon and lowered his burden onto the coffee table. "Si, darling," he said with a visible struggle. "Please get the letters out for Miss Wandwalker."

"Perhaps I won't stay for coffee," said Mary, standing up. She knew that Simon had been about to refer to the baby.

Patrick threw himself into a chair and held up his hands to Mary. "Please don't punish us, Miss Wandwalker. You're our last hope. Our last hope of finding out what really happened to Perdita."

Punish? Mary realized he was right. She picked up her handbag.

"Give it a rest, Patrick," said Simon. "Miss Wandwalker is not interested. There is nothing we can say to make her look at the letters. As I keep telling you, knowing means more pain. We can't get our darling girl back."

Mary sat down again, torn between outrage and sympathy. Some creature inside her sat up while Patrick raked his hair with his hands and Simon slumped back on the couch.

Back in the restaurant Patrick said that questions over Perdita's death were driving them insane. Not true, she realized.

Only he, Patrick, was desperate for the truth. Husband Simon wanted to retreat into a cave of booze. She sniffed.

"Tell me about the letters," said Mary Wandwalker.

CHAPTER 5
TWO LETTERS, FORTY YEARS APART

That afternoon in the Barbican apartment, Mary Wandwalker sipped coffee while her male companions waited for her to examine the letters. After a second cup, she decided they passed the test. Simon stopped drumming his fingers when Mary held out her hand. Patrick almost fell over in eagerness to hand her a photocopy of what the police deemed a suicide note. On paper ripped from a notebook, she saw a childish hand in blue biro.

> Dearest Mother, Papa, Dick, and Patrick, I have to do this, I'm sorry. The Kestrel told me that one golden day I'd see that the Falconer family is a trap not a nest. It is true. Your Perdy.

Although Mary was reading silently, the words summoned a girl's voice. It grew louder in the crowded room. She looked up. Patrick groped for Simon's hand. It was shaken off by his sweating husband. Only Mr. Jeffreys gazed at Mary, intent.
"The Kestrel?" she queried.
"Yes, that's the problem," said Patrick quickly. "You'll see from your letter."
Patrick took Perdita's note from Mary. He put it to bed between the cardboard on his lap, then offered Mary an envelope. This was a real letter on Basildon Bond notepaper, stamp, postmark, and folded inside. Yes, she really had written letters like this, Mary recalled. Although not like *this,* the letter to the Falconers after David's death. It contained news of her

pregnancy. She had expunged from her memory that hateful reply from the Falconer lawyer.

Mary held the envelope as if it might explode. Finally, she turned it over to see the scrawl of a very old woman who insisted on a fountain pen. "Tell Mary Wandwalker I am sorry, Margaret Falconer."

Mary's jaw tightened. Margaret, she'd forgotten the name of David's formidable mother. After flicking a glance at Mr. Jeffreys, she pulled out her letter from 1978. She had no intention of reading it. Everyone else in the room was leaning forward as if they could smell old sad words. Unfolding the paper torn from a pad sold in every W.H. Smiths in the 1970s, the fragment swam into her vision.

...When I was at Falconer House that time, I heard a voice saying that after one golden day anyone could see that Falconer family is a trap, not a nest. Even so, I'm asking you to offer the welcome of a nest to David's and my..."

No, she would not continue.

"Don't Miss Wandwalker, please."

Patrick sounded strangled. Mary looked down and saw that her clenched fist had scrunched up the letter.

"Sorry, I didn't realize," she said. An archivist damaging a document. She was shocked. Or rather, shocked that she was not shocked.

"I forgot. Yes, I did write those things about the Falconer family being a trap, not a nest. Just like Perdita all these years later. What a coincidence. She must have seen my letter."

"Not possible, Miss Wandwalker," said Patrick. "We went through Lady Margaret's letters when she died, in 2015. I remember saying to Si that we should contact you. He convinced me not to. Said it would drag up painful memories for everyone. We put everything in a trunk in our lockup in Ealing. Perdita was away at school at the time. She had zero chance to see your letter."

"Face it, Mary. Miss Falconer attributes the trap and the nest to a source named the Kestrel," said Mr. Jeffreys in his biting voice. "The problem is this — the police say that the Kestrel is the criminal behind the dangerous psilocybin being sold at the university, the drug of the fatal overdose. We know that Perdita Falconer had contact with the Kestrel's drug ring. That is where she got the name."

Mary nodded. She began to see what he was working up to. Patrick held his breath while Simon slumped.

Mr. Jeffreys coughed again. "Miss Wandwalker, this Kestrel is a bird of extraordinary range. Back in 1978, there was a man, an er ... associate of Sir Daniel's, known as the Kestrel. I knew about him. He was often entertained at Falconer House. You must have encountered him on your one visit ... In fact, Patrick believes ..." Rarely was Mr. Jeffreys interrupted, so Mary jumped when Patrick's words tumbled out.

He was loud. "You, Miss Wandwalker, overheard the Kestrel in 1978 on Falconers, nests, and traps. Just like Perdy."

Mary leapt in. "Wait a minute. How can someone called the Kestrel in 1978 be the person supplying drugs 40 years later? He'd be old."

"He'd be dead," said Simon.

"I have no memory of such a person," insisted Mary.

"You did write that letter?" asked Simon, now very quiet. "Including that part about the trap, not a nest?"

Mary nodded.

"You see, we are pretty sure Perdita didn't. Write that suicide note."

Mary looked at Mr. Jeffreys who had been rubbing his knees. He did that when judging how much to reveal, she recalled. After a glance at Simon, he continued.

"The police struggled to find samples of Miss Falconer's handwriting. The youth of today do not use pens, it seems. Their expert could not decide about the note, and therefore, the official record is death by misadventure. They think the magic mushroom drug caused her to choke, blocking her airways. The coroner agreed."

"Suicide is out of the question." Patrick banged down his coffee mug on the glass tabletop. "So is misadventure. Perdita did not do drugs. Even this drug. You of all people know that, Si. Years ago, we warned her about the extra strong mushrooms on the estate."

Mary was puzzled. "Magic mushrooms are that dangerous? I thought …"

"That they are relatively risk-free," continued Mr. Jeffreys. "Usually, the case if you eat the whole mushrooms. However, there is a disturbing fashion for extracting and distilling the psychedelic substance. The result is hallucinations, often leading to vomiting, diarrhea, and seizures. I remember Sir Daniel instructing visitors to keep out of Falcon Wood because the mushrooms there are particularly potent."

"You said the police inclined to treating it as a suicide," repeated Mary. "Hallucinations, seizures, and whatever might not mean death. If she choked on her own vomit … horrible of course, but why not an accident?"

Simon groaned. Patrick made to bang his fist, caught Mary's expression, and stopped.

"Miss Wandwalker, that's precisely it. Magic mushrooms, or their distillate, psilocybin, are no way to take your life. The police think she willingly ingested the liquid, like her pals at Cardinal College taking risks for kicks. The fashion is to disguise the taste in port wine. Our Perdita didn't even like port." Patrick groaned. "Darling Perdy would never have agreed to doctored port. To her, even one mushroom would be a no-go."

Simon Falconer intercepted Mary's stare.

"I'm druggie in the family," he said with a certain amount of pride. "That is, I used to be. I started on 'shrooms as they're known. Then I graduated to coke and pills. It was while I was sowing my wild oats in my 20s."

"And 30s," said Patrick with a mixture of affection and long suffering. "You see, we made sure that Perdita knew the danger of illegal drugs. When she was 15, she used to go with Si to NA."

Mary blinked. "Narcotics Anonymous," murmured Mr. Jeffreys. "Let us not stray too far from updating Miss Wandwalker. The handwriting professional I recommended doubted that this note was written by Miss Falconer. What remains," and he swiveled his chair to face Mary, "is the wording straight from your own letter of 40 years ago."

"Coincidence," said Mary, determined to detach herself from anyone named Falconer.

"Coincidence?" echoed Mr. Jeffreys. "This from the best archivist in this country? Remember that letter of commendation? It was because you discovered lost Second World War files with the gravesites of convicted spies. A very tricky situation with the Russian Embassy came to an end thanks to your remarkable perspicacity. Not to mention it was you who dug up the 17th-century deeds to the land on which stands the Houses of Parliament. No one else had your intuition and tenacity. That saved His Majesty's Treasury a ton of money. And then ..."

Mr. Jeffreys stopped, seeing Mary about to interject.

"No, you *have* moved on, Miss Wandwalker. Your future is here and now. The name Wandwalker is known in high places. It has been suggested more than once that your investigative skills should be put to better use."

He leaned toward her. "Mary, you are more of a detective than you know. Even within the Archive, it was *you* who prevented the falsifying of legal documents, *you* who ended the anonymous bullying, *you* who solved that theft. Shall I go on?" He paused.

Mary struggled, but no words came. Mr. Jeffreys folded his arms.

"You've been a sleuth for decades, Miss Wandwalker. So, try this. Say you catalogued this note about the Falconers, with its nests and traps. With your incisive mind, would you cross-reference both letters?"

"Of course."

A sigh of relief rippled around the room. Mary answered automatically as Miss Wandwalker, Chief Archivist. The Archivist in her saw what she did not want to admit. Damn! Damn Mr. Jeffreys, who knew her too well. Caught by the very job she'd been ejected from, she fumed.

CHAPTER 6
A MEETING AT CARDINAL COLLEGE

Bloody Falconers are indeed a trap, not a nest, Mary said to herself. Lured first by Patrick's pallor, Simon Falconer's resemblance to his dead uncle, Mary's lost beloved, floored her. His suffering in David's bones opened a door. She'd buried her past behind that door. There was also her baby, a Falconer too. Both drove a wedge into Mary's heart. Easier to say yes than to excavate old ground. Yes, to the ludicrous idea of going to another party at the Falconer estate.

Unable to remember the details of her visit to Falconer House in 1978, Mary Wandwalker, despite misgivings, agreed to a plan concocted by Patrick McCarthy and Mr. Jeffreys. I do want a new life, she reflected. Perdita's letter and mine are undoubtedly connected. This thread is mine to follow.

She began to plan a way forward. Mr. Jeffreys has a point — drat him, Mary said to herself. I've detected before. Perdita Falconer, I want to hear about her from outside the charmed circle. Since I will be in Oxford anyway, I can inquire at Cardinal College.

When Patrick explained that the College, not to mention Perdita's friends, were sworn to silence by their lawyers, Mary merely inclined her head. Rarely defeated by officialdom, and never cowed, she'd worked out the one person who might speak.

All right, Archivist Wandwalker, she muttered. *You got me into this. I'm doing this for you, I mean me.*

Patrick visibly gleamed at Mary's plan.

"Fantastic notion to have a chat with that nurse at Perdita's college. We family are forbidden to bother Cardinal while the police are tracking down the psilocybin."

He went on. "Although the cops insist Perdy must have taken it voluntarily, they're after the big cheese supplier, the Kestrel. That nurse might know something. Perdita thought highly of him. Text me when you are done. I'll pick you up in the car."

It was midmorning when the fast train from London deposited Mary on chilly Oxford Station. To acclimatize to the town she used to know so well, she decided to walk to Cardinal College. "I won't be defeated by the cold," she said to herself, swinging her arms to get her blood pulsing. By the time she stood under Cardinal's huge belltower, her chilled extremities remembered the iron of an Oxford winter. She prayed for a warm office.

First, however, she had to traverse the angry wind blowing across Cardinal's vast quads. With the determination of a mountain climber, Mary fought every step until she reached the corner that housed the Infirmary. Directions to the Consulting Office pointed upward.

Mary groaned. Fortunately, she was early for her appointment, so she had time to catch her breath. The college nurse better be worth the effort, Mary told herself. She hoped he could help her get a sense of Perdita as a person. Until then she would not abandon the possibility of suicide or accidental overdose. After all, she'd been a student herself, one that had known despair. Pausing at the foot of a stone staircase, Mary shivered.

Even less inviting was the prospect of being Patrick's plus-one at tonight's evening party at Falconer House. Some Russian oligarch renting the entire estate demanded the great and the good gather over champagne and canapes to admire his new portrait. Of course, Patrick would be included, as his father was the celebrated artist.

Mary began to mount the circular staircase that would take her to the top of a tower. Richer than God, the College should have installed an elevator years ago, she grumbled silently. Although her legs ached from the physical exertion, she knew her the blade in her stomach could be traced to the prospect of Falconer House. *Not now, Mary*, she said to the pain. *This is an adventure, isn't it?*

So high was the nurse's office that the number of stairs seemed to increase with every turn. Mary's student memories of Cardinal were of acres of lawn and grand arches on every super-cleaned range. Cardinal's walls had an uncanny reflective quality she remembered from an all-night ball with David. Blonde at noon, they soaked up any bit of moon and glowed in the dark.

Since most of Cardinal's undergraduates were wealthy or well connected, Grammar school Mary had seldom visited as an undergraduate. Even after meeting Cardinal student David Falconer, the sheer scale intimidated. The ball was an exception. David had danced with her until dawn.

Two weeks afterward, she waited for David Falconer in her unassuming college off the High Street. He never made it. A porter told her that his car had plunged into a stretch of Cardinal wall encrusted with spikes. The wall was just fine. A stone gargoyle grinned wickedly at a shard of windscreen slicing into David's neck.

Mary pushed away the old wound as she reached the office door. *I'm here for David's nephew Simon*, she told herself. Yes, there's the slot for the nurse's name: Jamie Sanders. Before she could knock, the door swung open.

"Well, I've heard of mature students, but you're not what I expected."

Nor was Jamie. For a start, Mary rarely encountered nurses. She'd been careful with her health and never been a patient in hospital. Moreover, even today it was unusual to see a Black person in the richer colleges, even as an employee. *Now, that really is shocking*, she reflected.

"I'm Miss Wandwalker," she said stiffly. "We had an appointment. I believe I am on time."

"That you are, and I'd forget my head if it were not the best part of me. And there goes that d... dratted bell in Tom Tower. Come in, come in, Miss um ... what was it now?"

With a broad smile and friendly London tones, he waved Mary to the chairs placed beside his desk, not in front. He would sit with patients, not behind a desk in judgment of them. Mary approved.

"Wandwalker, Mr. Sanders. My name is Wandwalker. It's from old English, 'windtalker.' They were old women who talked to the gods."

"Blimey, you've come to the right place for that," agreed the young man. He leaned forward with elbows on his knees. His muscled forearms eased out from his blue uniform top over jeans. She liked the way he'd tied his dreadlocks behind his head; a concession to a medical role that did not diminish him. Then Mary caught on to his wry tones. Irony, she appreciated that.

"Well, I'd imagine Cardinal College ... contains those who think well of themselves," she said with a small smile.

He sighed. "Half the problems I deal with come from students thinking themselves immortal. No," he corrected himself, "not thinking, behaving as they have always done, as spoiled children, now playing with grown-up toys."

"Like drugs," said Mary, happy to get to the point. "As I said in my call, that's what I am researching."

"Yeah, well it's no secret that universities are rife with drugs," said Jamie. "You said there was something specific about this College?"

"Perdita Falconer," said Mary. Surprise was about all she had. Sanders clenched his fists, stared, then relaxed them. His face shut down like a computer screen.

"She died. Overdose of extra-strong psilocybin from mushrooms. It was in all the papers, lots of social media threads."

"I know," said Mary. "I've spoken to her family. In fact, I'm working for them."

"You're a Private Investigator?" His incredulity was not flattering.

"Sort of. Tell me more about the psychotropic mushrooms. I'm particularly interested in their liquid form. Do you know where it's coming from?"

Sanders got up abruptly and went to the window. Mary didn't believe he was seriously staring at the wheeling rooks beyond the paned glass. They seemed to be dismantling a nest in the big plane tree. It was near enough to stretch bare twigs to tap on the window.

"You met her, didn't you?" Mary heard herself saying. "You wouldn't be this upset if she was just another statistic." The young man tensed.

"No Cardinal student is a statistic, Miss Wandwalker," said Sanders, looking down where Mary imagined he could see students running late for noon lectures. There was a scraping sound, and he was back on the opposite chair, fixing Mary with pained brown eyes.

"Why are you really here, Miss Wandwalker?"

The direct question struck Mary like a slap in the face. There was so much on her mind that she did not want to say.

"I'm sorry," said Sanders, wearily, leaning back on the chair. "That's what I ask every student who sits where you are now. They come up here talking about runny noses and eyestrain from their bloody computer screens. It saves time if I can get them to come out with the request for the pill, or condoms, or that funny rash in an embarrassing place. However," he shot her a grimace, "I'm guessing those worries don't apply to you."

Mary smiled, then took the plunge. "What do you know about distilled psilocybin?"

Jamie sighed. "Yeah, months ago I heard whispers about a new psilocybin, very dangerous because concentrated. Someone's offering it to rich students. Not too much of it, so it has cachet. It goes for twice the price of three grams of coke, or so I'm told."

"That's interesting," said Mary. Again, the suggestion that Perdita could have been targeted. "You know her family says she never took drugs."

Jamie grinned. "Miss Wandwalker, every parent says that about their beloved offspring."

"Well ... yes but ... Have you heard anyone refer to 'the Kestrel'?"

"Some kind of bird? Seriously, I never heard of it before the police grilled me. They said it was the code name of the dealer."

"Don't the students confide in you?"

Sanders looked sharply at Mary.

"Are you implying that the gently bred lords and ladies of Cardinal assume I'm a drug dealer? Because I'm Black?"

"No, I. I mean it never occurred ..." Mary was horrified. And yet, a small voice whispered, *Wouldn't you wonder too, just for a moment?* Mary pushed away the insight into her prejudices.

"Mr. Sanders, I did not mean to imply…"

"The students did."

"What?"

"Imply. More than imply. When I started here at Cardinal, I got regularly asked for weed. A few times for harder drugs. It's how the gilded youth see people like me."

"I'm so sorry," said Mary, subdued. Sanders looked at her. He relaxed. His face was sad.

"No need to give you a hard time, Miss Wandwalker. The students are learning that a Black family can have a daughter who is a professional violinist and a son who plans to train to be a surgeon when he's saved up enough dosh from working rich gigs like this one."

He shot her a grin. "For now, I don't get dazzled by their accents, their superior tailoring, or what they drive. I patch them up after drunken binges and refer them to clinics for their STDs. More to the point, I give every Fresher my custom-made anti-drugs talk. It ends with graphic shots of overdosed kids."

"Ah, so you spoke to Perdita Falconer. What was she like?" Mary sat up straighter.

"Nice girl. Good manners, not like most of them. You could see that she knew better than to make cheap cracks about my background."
"She lived in London before Oxford."
"Yep, and her daddy had been around the block with drugs, so she told me. Of all the Freshers I thought she was safe. Poor girl, she assured me that she saw no glamor in chemicals. She said ... I remember because it was so unusual: 'Jamie, I've seen my dad desperate to get clean, heard his stories of rehab. I've no intention of wasting my life.'"
"Sounds ... a little unsympathetic."
"It wasn't. She was being realistic. Empathy for her dad, but well primed to avoid the temptations, or so I thought. How wrong I was."

He spoke easily, but his voice deepened and became more hesitant when describing Perdita. He's playing a part, thought Mary. Well, I don't blame him. The police must have questioned him very carefully. I hope they did it because he's the college nurse, not because of his color.

"You weren't wrong in your instincts about Perdita. At least the family doesn't think so." Jamie stiffened, so Mary continued. "Originally, the police thought suicide. Now they say death by misadventure. The family believe she was murdered."

She swallowed, noticing Jamie's intent expression. Mary's voice grew hoarse. "Someone gave her enough psilocybin to kill."

Perdita Falconer was becoming real, too real. For a moment, Mary tasted the grief of Patrick and Simon. She hurried on. "The autopsy found she consumed the drug in wine, probably port, which would disguise the flavor. Her ... fathers told me Perdita didn't like strong wine, although she would accept a glass in company. She was a polite girl." As an afterthought, Mary added, "Of course, a place like Cardinal has its own port."

Jamie nodded. "Most students keep a bottle of college port in their rooms. I've seen them pour each other glasses while lazing on the lawns." He paused for a moment. "She liked a glass of wine, she said," he muttered, not looking at Mary. Skepticism, something Mary was familiar with, hovered in Jamie's expression.

"Yes, I know what you're thinking, Jamie. I thought the same until ..." Mary paused then plunged on. "Well, you see, there may have been attempts on the lives of her father and grandfather."

Jamie sat up straight, his body alert. "That changes things. I did wonder."

He's not surprised there's more to Perdita's death, realized Mary. How interesting.

"Her father, and grandfather too? So not a killer in this college?" Jamie asked.

"Probably not."

"What happened to the father and ... grandfather, you say?"

"A shooter got the grandfather in the leg on his Devon farm. He claims it was poachers, but his son-in-law, Patrick McCarthy, links it to Perdita's father nearly getting mown down in the street."

Jamie queried with his eyebrows.

"Simon wouldn't report it, and Patrick only glimpsed the van. He'd gone to help Simon home from the pub."

"Ah, the father drinks. I see what you're getting at. Too many incidents to conclude coincidence." Jamie's eyes gleamed. "God forgive me, I want there to be a murderer after the Falconer family so we in the College feel less to blame."

"How could you be to blame?" He said nothing, so she continued. "She came again, didn't she, after the first routine visit? Why was that? Did she talk about her family? That's why you feel you could have done more." Mary felt a tug pulling her forward. She reached into the dark. *"She came shortly before she died."*

Her intuition had a knack to leading her to where she took risks. She had struck a spark in Jamie. His jaw tightened as he leaned toward her. His next words terrified her.

"Just why are *you* here today, Miss Wandwalker?"

"I'm here for my son."

As soon as the words were out, Mary pushed her chair back and leapt to her feet. Horror in her gut rose and scorched her face. Jamie rose and held out a hand. She could not bear to see his sympathy, or astonishment. Not for something she'd spent decades hiding away. All she could do was run.

She turned and ran, banging the consulting room door behind her and clattering round and round down the stone stairs. Her shoes beat a tattoo until she fell into the freezing November air. As Mary raced across the quad with her handbag flying, she smelled cooking meat and roasting potatoes. A leaf from the plane tree floated onto her chest. She thrust it away in her haste to get out of this hateful college. She would never, ever return.

CHAPTER 7
ENCOUNTER IN THE CHAPEL

An hour later, Mary made herself return. For, while her legs ran fast and faster, a small voice rose from her inner ground, *not too far, Mary Wandwalker. You have a party tonight. Simon and Patrick need your help.*

Of course, I'm going, she retorted, slowing to her brisk walk. I always turn to face the storm. I never let the interns down even when it meant hard sleuthing. It's just that, in the Archive, it was never about me. Not my deepest secrets, dug up, exposed to everyone, *like giving up my son.*

Glimpsing a wet bench close to the Thames by Cardinal, she sat, ignoring likely stains on her coat. Mary had barely caught her breath when she received a text. That ping is too loud, she thought, scrabbling in her handbag. Sounds like a triangle a child would bong. No, don't think of that. After the quickest glance, she thrust her phone back under a clean handkerchief and an Agatha Christie mystery for the train.

The message allowed her time, and so Mary Wandwalker stared at the churning river. That's me, she thought, all mud and water, no firm ground. Thin boats darted past. Drops of sweat from four or eight rowers joined the steady current. Mary dimly recalled college races at the end of term. David used to row for Cardinal. She didn't want to think about that. Nevertheless, the text could not be ignored.

> Your son, George in danger. Meet me Cardinal
> Chapel, in thirty minutes. CJ

Got to find out what is going on. After all, my son is a Falconer too. Therefore, just before the Cardinal's Tom Tower bell chimed 1p.m., Mary entered the chapel by the side door. She could pretend that it was not part of the college itself. Town worshippers frequented this entrance for centuries when they slipped in for services.

A musky smell greeted Mary. An occasional visitor to old churches, she recognized furniture polish, candle wax and smoke from the few lighted candles. With hours until Evensong, the unheated space chilled even through her gray winter coat. Where were her gloves? Mary shoved her raw hands into her pockets.

She felt obscurely comforted by the rows of Victorian pews. In her overwrought state they reminded her of the church of her childhood in a rural village in Surrey. She, an only child of older parents, accompanied her devout mother to church. She craned her neck to the vaulted ceiling, a stone sky.

Ah, so much bigger than the wooden beams of that parish church, which had been hugged by lurching gravestones. Here in the city of learning. Angels and patriarchs hung from columns that branched like pollarded trees. Grandeur, Mary thought. Was this 600-year-old chapel really all for the glory of God? Or was it designed to laud the college founder, Cardinal Wolsey? Mary Wandwalker had her suspicions.

She hoped she was alone. Despite wanting the story behind the text, she hoped that no CJ, whoever he was, would disturb the sense of ordered time in this place. She could rest, restore her defenses before the unknown trials of Falconer House. Patrick's sadness infected her, she realized. She eased into the nearest pew and prepared to wait for a decent interval, 10 minutes perhaps?

Footsteps echo extraordinarily loud on stone, Mary reflected. She tensed and turned to see a figure in a black robe crossing from behind a set of choir stalls. He turned and gave a rapid bow to the altar then disappeared into an archway. Must be a side chapel, probably a Lady chapel, Mary guessed. She could not remember being in Cardinal Chapel as a student, having dropped church attendance after the sudden deaths of both parents from influenza shortly before she entered Oxford.

"Are you Miss Wandwalker?"

Mary shot to her feet at the woman's voice. Drat, she crept up on me while I mused about the past. The woman's green eyes were huge, her curly hair a faded red. Nervous, but not in the same way I am, Mary concluded. No, she told herself, I am not scared. I'm … full of trepidation about meeting my son. But I'm not scared of a middle-aged woman carrying a few extra pounds, and in a brown gaberdine that has seen better days.

"Yes, I'm Miss Wandwalker. Did you send that note?"

"Can we sit somewhere else? These pews are hard. I know where they keep the chairs with cushions."

The woman did not wait for Mary. After a quick survey of the empty church, she led Mary toward the bookshop in the west end. Out of sight of the main body of the church a row of wooden chairs rested below a magnificent stained-glass window of the Nativity. Next to the chairs was a tower of cushions, with a handwritten notice, "for cleaning."

"Kneelers," said the woman, banging two of the cushions together to release the worst of the dust. Mary took a step back. The woman pulled out two chairs, adding the threadbare cushions. Immediately, she sat, looking expectantly at Mary.

"You're CJ?" Mary said, dragging the chair inches farther away before sitting.

The woman smiled sadly. Brown freckles moved up and down her cheeks as she did so. "I'm Caroline Jones, your son George's wife. You do know he's your son, don't you?"

"Yes."

Mary's fierce return sounded to her like a crow squawk. She stopped, astonished. She wasn't going to cry. Miss Wandwalker never cried. Yet, mention of her baby was too intimate. In the last few days strangers kept ripping off the layers of protection guarding the wound that never healed. She made herself sit still. *If I run now, that baby inside won't stop crying.*

The woman with round shoulders was trying not to stare. Mary noticed that she was too pale under the freckles.

"So sorry, Miss Wandwalker. This must be terribly hard for you." Caroline Jones clasped her hands and waited.

Mary compressed her lips. No one before now, she realized, had tried to understand how hard it was for her. Not really. Patrick showed strained concern, Perdita's father was wrapped in his own in grief, and as for Mr. Jeffreys … Mary ground her teeth.

In front of her the woman's freckles danced. This was a bigger smile, despite dark shadows under those leaf green eyes. Can someone appear fragile and strong at the same time? Mary wondered. She could not help liking this woman. If only she would shut up about George.

"We do understand, George and I, how this must hurt you."

"George," Mary croaked. She swayed. Caroline shot out a hand to Mary's forearm. Mary felt a warm current reach though her coat. George, she thought. I'm going to have to get used to that name. "The baby" won't suffice if I am going to be around these people. He must be 40 years old next month, about the age of this woman here.

"You are… his wife? He has a wife?" Mary noticed herself relaxing slightly at the thought of this woman as his wife.

"For 18 years. We've no children, and his parents, I mean adoptive parents, died two years ago within three months of each other. Cancer. It devastated George." Caroline paused and noticed Mary's expression. "Don't be scared Miss Wandwalker, he doesn't know I'm here. I wouldn't interfere between you two, it's just…"

"The note said he's in danger," Mary whispered. Be practical, focus. It was all she could do.

Caroline sighed. She looked very weary. Too weary.

"Are you ill?" said Mary, too bluntly. It was her way.

Caroline tried to smile. "I have … a condition. I guess you have a right to know. It's chronic clinical depression. The National Health Service can only offer so much. Further treatments cost a lot of money. It puts a terrible burden on George."

"Oh," Mary sat back. "You need money. I see."

"No, no. I mean, yes, we do, erm…" She took a breath. Mary saw dignity amongst the marks of suffering.

With a rueful glance, Caroline began again. "Look, Miss Wandwalker, meeting me today has nothing to do with money. That is, George did plan to ask you for a loan. However, it's not why he wants to be in touch. You must believe me."

Caroline was wringing her hands. Mary shook her head in disappointment, and relief. Requests for money she could deal with.

"How much money?" Her voice was colder than she intended.

There was a pause. Caroline gazed at Mary with reproach. She stood up. "Miss Wandwalker, I asked to see you because George is in real danger from a criminal gang. He could die."

Mary choked. "How?" She did not recognize her strangled tone, nor the stab to her heart. "Oh, sit down, Mrs. Jones. I did not mean to insult you. Nor George. What danger?"

Caroline inclined her head and sat.

"The Falconers must have told you that George is undercover?"

"Undercover?" It came out as a muffled screech. "George? My baby? He's a spy." Like his grandfather, Sir Daniel Falconer, she thought but did not say.

"No, not a spy," said Caroline. She looked confused. "George is a Detective Sergeant in Thames Valley Police. The Falconers didn't tell you? I mean Patrick McCarthy and Simon Falconer. We met them at Perdita Falconer's funeral. Oh!"

Caroline now appeared to comprehend. "I see. They didn't tell you about George being involved in the psilocybin investigation? About George going undercover at Falconer House?"

"Falconer House."

The squawk became a squeak. Mary clapped her hand over her mouth as a bald elderly gent shuffled past them to unlock the Bookstore.

He took no notice of the two seated women, the shabby one and the older one with a smart coat and well-cut grey hair.

Instinctively, Mary and Caroline huddled closer under the glowing stained glass.

"Falconer House?" repeated Mary in a whisper. "That's where I'm going tonight. 'They,' bloody Patrick McCarthy and Simon Falconer, want me to remember something from the time I went there. That was a party too — in 1978. Ridiculous idea. I'm not going. Not if George…"

A cold hand grabbed Mary's chilled one. Too tight, Mary wanted to shake herself free, but for the intensity of those green eyes. Gradually, heat from Caroline reached her finger bones. Mary met the woman's eyes, red rimmed, and yet interested — in her. Despite herself, Mary saw a determination in this sick woman that she could not help respecting.

"Miss Wandwalker, Patrick and Simon would not let you meet George unexpectedly. They've asked him to keep away from the estate tonight. Please, what do they want you to remember from 1978? It could be important."

Caroline looked down to where she gripped Mary's hand and let go. The cool air on Mary's released flesh felt kind.

"I don't see how it matters after all this time," said Mary grumpily. "Something about Perdita Falconer's suicide note." Then into Caroline's feverish energy, "Or the letter that is not a suicide note. Perdita used words that I wrote to the Falconers. Words that I overheard on my one visit."

"Gotta be about the Kestrel," said Caroline, nodding her head. "Yes, George told me about his drug inquiry. We're both living on the Falconer estate. George is posing as a gardener.

I'm the wife who helps in the kitchen. One of the Russians, or Eastern Europeans, at Falconer House ..."

"... Could be the Kestrel," Mary finished. "I didn't know about all this. No one told me that George is part of the police operation. Or that the drug dealer, this Kestrel, might be living at Falconer House."

Then louder, "The bastards did not warn me. They know I won't go if George is there." She clenched her coat with both cold hands. "I can't go. I'm telling Patrick and Simon to leave me out of it."

There it was. She couldn't go. She couldn't look George's wife in the eye, either. Dammit, thought Mary as Caroline steadied herself on the hard chair. I know that body language. I've done it myself to Mr. Jeffreys.

"You *can* go, Miss Wandwalker. I know you can. There is no danger of running into George. Sir Viktor Solokov and his evil wife don't invite gardeners to parties."

Exhaustion, sternness, and dry humor blended in Caroline's tone. Mary met her eyes reluctantly. The younger woman reached out, this time merely touching Mary's arm.

"I absolutely promise you won't see George tonight. He's staying well out of the way. Right now, he's focused on finding the Kestrel. Solokov is the rich businessman who is renting Falconer House. He's officially the chief suspect. Despite being Russian, he got a knighthood by dodgy donations to the Conservatives."

She paused and licked her lips, instantly alerting Mary. "I don't see Solokov the way George does. I think the wife, Anna, is behind the psilocybin poisoning. She may be using Solokov as a cover. She's a user — of people, drugs too, possibly. Did you know that the Eastern Europeans that Solokov is sponsoring at Oxford colleges could be doing the distribution? George is trying to check them out."

Caroline took a deep breath. "George won't leave, he says, until he knows who killed Perdita Falconer." She stopped. To

Mary's horror, tears began to gather in the too pale woman's green eyes.

"What are you not telling me," Mary rapped out. She wasn't going to have to *hug* this stranger, was she?

"You're right. Perdita Falconer is not the only reason. Not the real reason he won't leave, despite my begging him." Caroline pulled out a used tissue and tried to wipe her face.

"No, no, take this. And blow your nose."

Caroline seized the ironed handkerchief that Mary held out. She proceeded to clear her nostrils loudly and extensively.

"No, keep it, Mrs. Jones." Mary's stomach felt tight before she asked the question. She had a sensation of taking a first step on a rope bridge. "Now you are feeling better, what is George really doing?"

Caroline nodded and sniffed. "Give me a second," she whispered.

Keen to avoid more tears, Mary carried on. "The police investigated the psilocybin that killed Perdita," she said slowly. "Patrick and Simon explained that. Not that George was involved. Of course, his adoptive father was in the Metropolitan police, wasn't he? Didn't George meet Perdita Falconer?"

"We both did, once, for coffee," said Caroline, sadly. "Sweet girl. Surprisingly mature for 19. Said she quite understood family matters couldn't be rushed. She asked about you, Miss Wandwalker."

Mary winced. They were turning her insides out, putting it all on display. A whisper stopped her.

George could die. He needs you.

Had Caroline said those words? Mary directed her most regal frown at the younger woman. Another step on the rope bridge. "You'd better tell me the real problem, Mrs. Jones."

Caroline gave a tiny gasp. Then the words flooded out. "George is in danger at Falconer House not only because he's an undercover cop. You see, he's having an affair with Anna Solokov."

"*What?*" said Mary. "An affair, George?" She could barely take in that the crying baby was now an adult with a wife. Now there was someone else? That couldn't be true, could it?

"Mrs. Jones. You are telling me that *your husband George Jones, my son, is sleeping with someone who could be a drug dealer?* The drug dealer responsible for Perdita's overdose. How do you know?"

Caroline was a picture of misery. Then she put her head up. Mary saw it again, the strength. Mary heard the words. "I asked him if he was having an affair. He told me he was involved with Anna Solokov."

Stunned, Mary searched the woman in front of her for lies, deceit, even rage. None of those appeared in this troubled woman. Caroline looked down at the stone slab between them then back to Mary. Her voice penetrated to the heart.

"Miss Wandwalker, I'm not here about our marriage. That remains whatever happens." A touch of defiance came into Caroline's voice. Mary nodded so Caroline would go on. "I asked to see you, rather, about George's safety. She's so beautiful, Anna Solokov. I don't blame George. I'd fall in love with her myself given the chance."

Caroline leaned forward, her voice tense and low. "She's manipulating him, blinding him to what is going on. He'll be framed for some terrible crime. Or worse, she, or her husband, or those creepy so-called students, will kill him."

"Tell me more." Mary could not help asking.

"I'm sure Anna Solokov is behind Perdita's death. George thinks it was her husband, Viktor, and that she's terrified of him. He won't take me seriously. *You,* Miss Wandwalker, are my last hope. Your Mr. Jeffreys really impressed him. It's just possible George might listen to you. You see, he's determined to rescue Anna."

Mary was starting to see a pattern. "He couldn't save Perdita Falconer, and so ..."

"Yes, that's part of it. Perdita was family, and George has always been all about family. That's why he's stayed with a sick wife all these years."

Caroline suddenly looked older. Without thinking Mary replied.

"No, that's not why he stayed with you."

Caroline blinked. "How ... you can't ...?"

"He's my son, Mrs. Jones," said Mary, astounding herself.

CHAPTER 8
AT THE JONES COTTAGE

Thirty minutes later Caroline was driving Mary to the cottage on the Falconer estate. Mary was not quite sure how it happened. She noticed the other woman's increased strain. Mrs. Jones is a rebuke to me, she thought. If my son's wife can keep going through agonizing betrayal, fear, not to mention mental illness, then I can too.

Enjoy the irony, she told herself. You who made yourself safe by learning every twist in the labyrinthine Archives. Now you are being driven by a tortured woman you don't know to a house that you couldn't even locate on a map. Caroline noticed Mary's tension.

"I made George do it. Look for you, that is," said the other woman baldly. "I made George do the research where he found the name of his birth mother. He dug up your name and that of your boss."

"Why, why on earth would you do that?" Mary's whisper sounded like that of a scared child, she thought in disgust. "Why did you make him find me?" she said, louder.

Caroline stopped for a red SUV with an improbable number of children in it.

"Quicker once we get to the ring road," muttered Caroline. "As for looking for George's birth parents, I never thought it would lead to meeting Perdita, then her death, and straight into this nightmare with Anna Solokov. It's my fault he is in danger."

Mary knew she should reassure Caroline. How could she have known? Finding birth parents rarely meant discovering a killer targeting your whole family. She realized to her shame that she resented Caroline Jones. The woman continued to stir up her neat, safe life. Hang on, that was Mr. Jeffreys turfing her out of the Archive. Mary sighed.

"The truth, Miss Wandwalker?"

Oh no, not that, thought Mary. That's always something bad.

"I made George find you because he will never know peace otherwise."

In the pause, Mary could hear Mr. Jeffreys.

And you him; you will never know peace until you know your son, Miss Wandwalker.

*****

For a while Mary sat in silence apart from squawks from the engine every time Caroline changed gear. Not the engine's fault, Mary judged. Eventually, the car shook off the city's lights, and the country night closed in. Mary called Patrick McCarthy to update him on meeting her for the party.

"I'll wait on Mrs. Jones' doorstep, the gardener's cottage" she said into his voicemail.

As they approached the Falconer estate, Mary's stomach wobbled. She clung to Caroline's reassurance.

"Yes, I promise George won't be at the cottage," Caroline repeated. "He knows not to risk running into you. We're counting on a proper meeting when you feel ready."

Ready, I'll never be ready, Mary muttered silently. *But you will do it,* came a reply out of the black hole inside her. Mary sniffed. She had a bad feeling about the party at Falconer House. One reason she agreed to accompany Caroline home was that it ended the pretense that she had a choice about going.

No more running away, she told herself. Not with the baby, um, George Jones, and the Falconers in danger from this Kestrel and his/her toxic psilocybin. A cold claw squeezed her lungs, forcing her to take quick breaths as the car began down a narrow road. She saw she'd attracted Caroline's attention and sharply waved her attention back to the road.

"Watch for oncoming traffic, Mrs. Jones, please."

"Don't worry. Although it is single lane, there are passing places. People know to back up. I am familiar with this road."

I'm not, thought Mary, turning to the rain now silvering the passenger window. That's just the problem. I don't know where we are going. I've no idea what to expect tonight at Falconer House. This is all like stepping off a cliff. I cannot see what is at the bottom, and the fall will kill me anyway.

Mary risked a glance at Caroline's set jaw. The other woman was hunched over the steering wheel, peering into the dark, where neither trees nor hedges nor farm buildings could be identified. Mary tensed as the car splashed through deepening pools of water.

"Sorry, Miss Wandwalker, I'm not a good driver," Caroline said to Mary's frown in the mirror. "The mercy is I'm safe. I'm very careful … about everything. You don't need to worry about my depression medication affecting my driving."

Mary swallowed. Was this woman aware of David's fatal car accident? She wondered. Perhaps George had looked up the death of his father? Mary sat up, trying to glean details of this strange land. It's all I can do, she told herself grimly, keep fighting by finding out stuff. It's what I do best. The track we are on winds with the hedgerows. These fields are very old, probably over a thousand years.

She shivered: Something is slowly detonating in my chest; the thing that Mr. Jeffreys had tried to explain: The Falconers are threatened. *My son is a Falconer.* Not only a Falconer, but one having an affair with a dangerous woman, she reminded herself, looking at the hurt in Caroline's profile.

"Er, Mrs. Jones," said Mary. "We should talk some more about … you know, the situation at Falconer House with the Russian oligarch. I forgot the name you said?"

"Viktor Solokov. But the one to watch out for tonight is his wife, Anna. Like I said, she's dangerous ... and beautiful. Much younger than Solokov. He's about George's age."

A heavy gust of wind and rain drummed on the car roof, so Caroline had to shout.

"We're almost there. Call me Caroline."

The car swung around a 90-degree angle toward a patch of light. Mary could make out a building with a dripping thatched roof.

Just before the front gate, Caroline parked and switched off the engine. Mary breathed in the scent of sodden leaves that permeated the warm interior of the vehicle. She waited for her hostess to make a move. Caroline appeared puzzled.

"That's odd. I didn't leave a light on."

It took Mary a second. "What? Who? Oh, my God."

Someone in the cottage could spot the two female shapes in the car. Mary lunged for the door. "You said ... no, you *promised* me. *He* would not be here." Unable to control her movements, Mary's voice cracked. Both hands grappled with the car door.

Stumbling into pounding rain, Mary crouched in the dark. Ridiculous, she said to herself. Get up, don't be a coward. She backed into the shadows under the trees, then stood up. I'm not beaten by this, she thought. *I have a right to see George in my own way.*

She caught a wail that was neither rain nor wind. Caroline, indifferent to the weather, stared at the lighted windows.

"Miss Wandwalker," she moaned, not looking back at Mary. Caroline appeared mesmerized by the moving silhouettes inside the house. Hang on, *there are two of them*, thought Mary.

"So sorry ..." Caroline's voice dried.

Mary's feet were sinking into viscous mud. It's over my shoes. I can't move, Mary thought in panic. Is it really him?

It felt like minutes. It could have been only a few seconds. The two women watched with water dripping down their necks, as the front door began to move. There was a confusion of shadows, and a naked arm snaked out. A slender foot caught a dribble of light, revealing gold slippers.

Finally, the woman kicked the door wide to reveal herself as an alien with two heads and far too many limbs. The writhing creature was backlit from blazing lights within the cottage. Mary gagged. Soon her tired mind reorganized the picture. No alien from the stars, she was staring at two people locked in an embrace. The couple had eyes, arms, and tongues only for each other.

A goodbye scene, Mary concluded. She made herself focus on the woman. Unnecessarily prolonged, this performance, Mary realized, especially as the young woman spotted her audience with a leer at Caroline. In the dark and rain her lover failed to notice his wife, let alone the other woman. No, the man kept hands and mouth entangled in the young woman's waterfall of blue-black hair flowing over her shoulders. Her green silk dress glowed in the yellow lamplight. Gold thread glittered over the woman's curves.

With all her being, Mary wanted to keep her eyes on the dress. She could not. She had to look at him. His arms around the woman made her ache inside. George would be two decades older than the woman he held. Mary saw a 40-year-old man with threads of silver in wavy hair in need of a trim. Unlike the woman, he had on work clothes: loose jeans and baggy fawn sweater. When he moved, Mary glimpsed weariness creasing his forehead.

George is afraid, an inner voice said to Mary. Afraid of what he is doing, kissing Anna Solokov on his wife's doorstep on the estate rented by the woman's husband.

A bolt shot through Mary like lightning. *He wants Caroline to see this. He wants her to stop him.* She tried to recall Caroline in the chapel. Didn't she say that George would not give up Anna Solokov? That he refused Caroline's pleading? He's convinced Anna is in danger. Even so, she knew in her bones that her son wanted to be stopped. Even if he wouldn't let anyone stop him.

Marriages, Mary thought, I don't understand them. No way that my influence could surpass Caroline's. *This is so damn hard.* She swallowed. George Jones's short hair was lighter than her own. With a jolt she remembered that exact shade, David's dark blond. Yes, she'd trimmed David's hair with a pair of nail scissors before a Cardinal College ball.

Mary looked away. *David, you're so much younger than your son.*

She shut her eyes. The past leapt from the ground while the rain ran down her cheeks. The night had barely begun. Once I knew passion, she thought. Once I was loved. When I was the age of that girl, it was David kissing me. It was David who brought me home, to Falconer House.

CHAPTER 9
GEORGE AND ANNA

Seeing George embrace Anna Solokov made the affair into a nightmare for Caroline Jones. That's what she told Mary an hour later in the cottage. It wasn't much of a conversation. Mostly they sat in silence on each side of the hearth basking in the smoky heat. Waiting for Patrick to call for Mary, they became mesmerized by the yellow flames rising and falling. Then Caroline put a hand on her chest.

"It was a knife to my heart when I saw them kissing. Before that, well, I could pretend it wasn't serious, not real. Now I can't," she said.

Mary coughed. Caroline's admission struck her as familiar. Hadn't she too conned herself about her dismissal from the Archive? Yet Caroline clutching a blanket to herself and staring into the log fire gave Mary pause. Every few minutes Caroline rocked up and back, holding her open wound. Mary's instinct would be to pluck out the blade from her own pain and use it to stab Anna Solokov.

Of course, Anna would be back at Falconer House by now, preparing for the Solokov party. Mary recalled the girl grabbing a satin cloak and, careless of the rain destroying its expensive sheen, flinging it over her revealing attire. Shutting her eyes, Mary relived the moments she had gazed at her son, out there in the cold rain.

Anna Solokov vanished into the dark, leaving George staring after her with his back to the onlookers. Thinking back, Mary longed for him to turn around and see them both, his wife and birth mother, frozen in the rain. No, she'd die if he'd turned around. *He was turning.*

Surely, he saw her, or did his gaze simply rest on Caroline? After mere seconds, he averted his head. Pulling a long jacket from inside the cottage door, George Jones slipped around the house in the opposite direction to his lover.

Once he'd gone, Mary had, very tentatively, approached Caroline. She could not see where she was putting her feet, only that parts of the ground were stickier than others. Leaves, she'd hoped, not manure from a gardener's boots. Finally, she took the gardener's wife's cold hand. There was no life in it. Caroline had left her body. Her roots were cold.

"Caroline," whispered Mary. "Caroline, speak to me."

Dropping Mary's hand, Caroline emitted a sound like wind tearing at a tree. Then with no sign she remembered Mary's existence, she marched into the cottage, slamming the door behind her.

Mary's pent-up feelings exploded in silence. That was George Jones, who had disappeared seconds ago, her son. She'd been promised no such unplanned encounters. How could they … Patrick McCarthy, Simon Falconer, Caroline Jones — all of them — how could they do this? She was incandescent that he had appeared without warning and, yes, yes, angry that he had simply vanished. How dare he?

Mary shivered again. She stamped her foot and regretted it as water splashed her shins. You have a party to go to, she reflected. Patrick will pick me up in a couple of hours. Inclined to laugh like a maniac, her throat was too bitter. The cottage lights dimmed in front of Mary. Time to act.

Marching up to the doorstep, she was about to hammer on the door when it opened. Caroline was so pale she was bluish, her face wetter than Mary's. She did not speak.

"Let me in, Mrs. Jones. I have a party to attend this evening, and my hair is ruined."

Caroline stepped back in a daze while Mary pushed past, flopping down on a shabby sofa. Yes, it was rude, but this day was beyond enough. Caroline trailed in, not looking at Mary.

She is sick, Mary suddenly remembered; some long-term illness, didn't she say? She wouldn't be this crushed if George often had affairs. This betrayal is probably the first. That tells me about the marriage, and about George. With Caroline sitting opposite her, Mary noticed the steel in her posture and the dignity of her expression.

No heat reached Mary from the fireplace. She frowned at the mounds of white ash mixed with blackened sticks. Fire died recently, she judged. Worth a try, so she bent down to use tongs to bash lumps of charred wood that burst into a million fireflies that failed to reignite. Mary noticed a stack of dry wood in the corner. When she put on her best glare, Caroline nodded and knelt to rake out the ashes in preparation for reigniting the fire.

"George usually does the fire," muttered Caroline. "I'll try to do it the way he showed me."

Mary took stock of her surroundings, painfully aware that her son lived here. This house reeked of damp and neglect, she concluded. Its furniture must have been purchased for a grander dwelling and deposited here when worn out.

It took a while to melt Caroline to some semblance of normality, and another to warm up the cottage. Meanwhile, they consumed several pots of tea, saying little. There was nothing more to say until Mary Wandwalker could see for herself the Solokovs at Falconer house.

CHAPTER 10
PARTY GAMES

The silence between them mellowed into sleepiness in Mary, exhaustion in Caroline Jones. Mary dozed by the fire. She was kept awake only by the first pangs of hunger. When a car engine interrupted the patter of rain, Caroline revived enough to go to the window.

"He's here. Patrick McCarthy with your ride to Falconer House."

"You're sure? Do be sure."

Mary perched on the edge of the sofa. Dressing carefully half an hour before, she worried that her 1940s wine red dress would pick up the dust pervading the cottage. Plus, she noted the rain's habit of increasing in intensity then easing off. No doubt she would find herself in a deluge the moment she opened the door. For two pins she'd give up the Falconer House party and stay right here.

"Yes, it must be for you," said Caroline, sounding very weary. "It's not George's car. He sent a text. He's gone to meet his handler and won't be back until tomorrow."

She turned to Mary with a grimace. "I didn't tell him about meeting you. He could not predict I'd bring you ho… to this house. I told him I would not be back until late tonight. George didn't spot you. Did he?"

Mary decided silence was the best answer. She was certain, well almost certain, that George had sensed something. Perhaps, after all, he had glimpsed his wife and birth mother. *Brisk*, she said to herself, not for the first time that day. Brisk is how I'll get through this. She rose and picked up her coat just as the door got a thumping.

"Oh dear, Patrick will be getting soaked. I must dash. Thank you, um ... Caroline for your ... erm ... letting me wait."

At the very last moment Caroline stood up, stopping Mary with her hand on the door.

"Miss Wandwalker, thank you for being here. I know it hurt you, but you helped me."

Mary waited a microsecond before deciding she had no reply. She opened the front door to a male figure under an umbrella. In less than a minute she was in a heated vehicle, which Patrick was backing out.

"Bloody hell, it is dark down this track. No streetlights in the county, I suppose," he remarked.

"I was almost asleep. We won't stay long, will we?" Mary appealed to his damp profile. There was something different about Patrick. Had he tried to shave the goatee and given up? No, it must be the rain making it so stringy.

"Not long, no. Just enough to see if you can remember your 1970s visit. Don't forget that you're our only hope of deciphering the letter. Trap and nest, be dammed. Your letter from 40 years ago has the same words as that so-called suicide note. We've got to know why. The bloody police still think Perdy wrote it."

Maybe she did, Mary wanted to say. Suicide in a 19-year-old with a complicated family is not unknown, however loved she was. Perhaps Patrick guessed her thoughts because he burst out.

"Miss Wandwalker, you've gotta see that the killer is responsible for Perdy's note. That mention of the Kestrel is simply taunting us. After all, he, or she, the psilocybin dealer, is quite possibly based at Falconer House."

"A detail you omitted when inviting me to the Solokov reception," Mary added, tartly.

"Yes, erm well, we did not want you to get sidetracked. Tonight, I'll be the one sneaking around to spot drugs, especially in spiked wine."

"You also forgot to mention that my ... that is, George Jones is an undercover policeman on the estate." This time the resentment in Mary's tone deepened.

"Ah, about that, Mr. Jeffreys said ..."

"Not him, not now," Mary interjected. Brisk, she reminded herself. A quick wander around a crowded room, a glass of wine *not* spiked with psilocybin, a glance at the celebrated-but-not-by-the-artist's-son, portrait. Then she would insist on Patrick driving her to Oxford Station. Mary continued.

"What were you about to say about the letter that Perdita — probably — didn't write?"

"*Definitely* didn't write. Don't forget that bit about the Falconer family as a trap is straight out of your letter, Miss Wandwalker, well before Perdita was born." Patrick thumped the steering wheel. "Jeffreys said there was a Kestrel present that day too. Don't you see, it connects. Back then there was a spy known as the Kestrel, and today the Kestrel is the nom de plume of a drug dealer associated with the same place: Falconer House."

"Yes, Patrick," said Mary. "I agree it is a mystery. My overheard words that Falconers are a trap not a nest in the note found after Perdita Falconer died. Just bear in mind my memory may not hold the answers that you and Simon want."

Patrick was not having any of her caution. "There is something going on at Falconer House that links you to Perdita's death. You can lead us through the labyrinth. Mr. Jeffreys says you don't know your own remarkable powers."

Mary sniffed and smiled in the darkened car.

"No, don't be a skeptic. The police can't see it. I believe you can. Perdita was *happy*. Not like her father, struggling with addictions, or even her mad political mother, Belinda Bishop, M. P. Don't blame Richard for walking out on her at last."

Mary flinched at the name Bishop. Patrick did not seem to notice.

"Everyone adored Perdita, and she loved us back," said Patrick, banging the steering wheel. "She was overjoyed to meet her cousin, George Jones, and his wife. Wanted us to invite them to London."

Mary gulped. "All right, Mr. McCarthy. I will try to see if the house jogs my memory. In 1978, I overheard those words. Unfortunately, I don't recall anything about a Kestrel. That was Mr. Jeffreys. By the way, speaking of Perdita's mother, do you think Belinda Bishop and ... her husband, um Richard, will be at the party?"

"With Solokov slipping money to the Conservative Party, I wouldn't bet against it. Si says since Perdy's death, Belinda's done nothing but hobnobbing with the rich and powerful. Ambition gone mad, I call it."

I'd call it something else, thought Mary.

At last, the car rolled onto a smooth driveway. Light bloomed ahead of them through the trees. They must be close to Falconer House. Mary gripped her handbag even tighter.

"The party started an hour ago?" she queried.

"Too right," said Patrick. "Apologies for cutting it fine. I can never make myself allow enough time when my father's involved."

"I see."

There it was, their destination. Falconer House rose above invisible gardens like a liner on the ocean of Oxfordshire. It must have looked very different in June sunshine, Mary thought. I have no image of it from 1978. Her mouth dried. All that weeping, the pregnancy, sickness, soreness, a baby crying as they took him away. That golden summer day is buried under all that.

"Falconer House," said Patrick unnecessarily. "Missed the portrait unveiling. It was set for half an hour ago. Good."

"It might have been interesting to see what Viktor Solokov has to say for himself," Mary pointed out. "And your father, Mike McCarthy."

"Oh, my father's old news," sighed Patrick. "Right now, I'm just terrified that someone's out to get Simon, perhaps all the Falconers." Patrick braked the car. Mary wondered if it had to do with the complications of finding a parking space in the row of cars. She was wrong.

"Miss Wandwalker," he said. "I should tell you about this morning. Simon nearly broke his neck on the Barbican steps, you see." He fixed haunted eyes on Mary.

"Broke his neck?"

"Nearly. And what gets me is that he won't take it seriously. He says it was tourists being careless, where I see a fiendishly clever murder attempt."

"Mr. McCarthy, you'd better explain."

"Patrick, please. You'll be tempted to laugh. It was a banana skin. Left on the steps closest to our apartment at the time Si likes to get a coffee in the Barbican café."

"A banana skin?"

"Yes, I know it sounds like ... like nothing. It's not. Before Si would have stepped on it, something hit him on the back of his neck. Fortunately, he was ... well not feeling too good, and so he had both hands on the rail. His foot slipped, but he didn't fall."

Still hung over, interpreted Mary. "What hit him?"

"I went out to search and found small stones on several of the brick stairs. They cover the flower beds. Squirrels dig in the beds, the stones fly onto the paths, get stuck in shoe treads then come out all over the place."

"So, it really could be another coincidence."

"Except Si has a red mark on his neck that Belinda began cooing over. She arrived unannounced, like she always does."

"You don't seem to like Belinda."

Patrick put his head in his hands. Then he noticed that figures with umbrellas were approaching.

"Let's talk inside. Or, if not, on the way to the station. These people are here to escort you inside. I will park the car then join you."

Minutes later, Mary Wandwalker was ushered into the main hall of Falconer House. So many people together produced an aroma of wet skin, dry cleaning chemicals, and the successive punches of different perfumes. Mary found herself in a dance of arms holding up slender glasses with gold and pink liquids. Ingress was complicated by waiters walking in and out with food.

Mary found she rather liked the appreciative glances from men, some of them rather younger than herself. She also received tiny nods of approval from both sexes for her dark red gown with its flattering full skirt and shapely shoulders. However, the crowd in the marble lobby was excessive. Always careful of personal space, she became aware of fingers made sticky by oysters, drips from strawberries dipped in chocolate, and eruptions of crumbs from tiny squares of toast with either caviar or smoked salmon.

"Have you seen my portrait?"

A short white-haired red-faced man in a black bow tie stepped in front of Mary, determined for her attention.

"Er no. Are you Sir Viktor Solokov?"

"Mike McCarthy at your service."

He gave an elaborate bow that narrowly missed a large lady's behind in blue satin and a young waiter balancing a tray of champagne about his head. "A beautiful lady like you should see my painting. Your dress compliments my color scheme. This portrait is my best yet." His red face was sweating.

"First, I want a drink. We've not been introduced. I'm Mary Wandwalker, and I'm here with your son." McCarthy's smile froze.

"Then you really do need to see some decent art."

Without waiting for permission, he grabbed Mary's elbow and marched her to the other side of the room. There, under the largest glittering chandelier Mary had ever seen, a life-size painting was displayed on an easel. Mary had the impression of brilliant colors she could not focus on immediately. The fever in the painter's eye forced her to take a second look.

The portrait was of a man standing in riding breeches, his dark hair contrasting with a pure white horse behind him that in turn led to a diminutive Falconer house over his muscular left shoulder. With tiny flecks of violet in his blue eyes, the painted Viktor Solokov appeared to be scanning the crowded party.

McCarthy's painted a pastiche of Gainsborough, Mary thought. Yet the concentration of those eyes is unusual. How odd. I suppose the familiarity of the style and composition is the reason it reminds me of something.

"Father, you've stolen my guest." Patrick's tone was acid. "Miss Wandwalker, do have this glass of champagne and come away from that gruesome painting."

Mary gulped the sparkling wine and took the plate of hors oeuvres Patrick offered.

"My son, you have no conception of portraiture," said Mike McCarthy. "And even less of an artistic career. I despair of you."

Mary chewed her second piece of smoked salmon, avoiding looking at the older artist. Mike McCarthy's knuckles on his glass were white, as was Patrick's mouth as he glared at his father.

"Perhaps not the time to discuss art," she suggested diplomatically.

"It never is," snapped Patrick.

"It's never about art," replied his father tartly.

"Heaven forbid," grunted Patrick, and disappeared into the crowd. Mary remained looking thoughtfully after Patrick. Another fraught family, she noted. Is the hostility between these two part of the Falconers' problem?

CHAPTER 11
MARY'S QUEST

Deserted in the marble lobby of Falconer House, Mary was not alone. Brewed long like fine tea, Viktor Solokov's party reached optimum energy. Mature bodies in expensive evening dress huddled together. Their perspiration gave a sour undertone to the sickly spices of perfumes.

An avoider of empty occasions with too much alcohol, Mary instinctively backed into a pillar, then discovered it to be a marble statue of a barely draped female. Naturally she'd given some thought to the request of Patrick and Simon Falconer to remember that summer garden party in 1978. After decades of trying to blank out everything about the Falconers, she had merely the faintest recollection of this grand lobby.

Remember, you are here for the death of Perdita Falconer, she told herself. How sad was that Barbican apartment with Patrick and Simon. What a contrast to this elegant 18th-century hall with its elegant 18th-century-style flattery in the new portrait. People were starting to move away, looking for more seats. They perilously balanced plates of food and overfull glasses.

Suddenly, Mary realized that the portrait on the easel was not alone. As the suits and designer dresses funneled toward inner rooms, she discovered more Falconers on the wall. Mary edged closer.

Were these family portraits here before? Not all, that one looks more recent. Abandoning her empty plate on the staircase, holding her empty glass, Mary squeezed around a large man talking too loudly. Yes, another, much earlier Mike McCarthy painting. Curious, thought Mary. Not the same style as the over-the-top tribute to Viktor Solokov as the modern lord of the manor. In fact, she liked it.

The much simpler painting depicted a woman in her 50s seated under a winter tree. She wore a black dress. A white streak adorned her otherwise brown hair done up in an old-fashioned bun. She stared straight at the viewer as if she had a question to ask. It was very direct, quite arresting, Mary decided.

That firm jaw reminded her of the man in the other portrait, Viktor Solokov, no relation, of course. The woman looked sad, so did the tree. Then she read the label, Lady Margaret Falconer, nee Fisher, as a widow in 1980. *The woman who told me to leave the Falconer family alone.*

It must be before Mike McCarthy got so mannered in painting the rich. Then she stared again.

Something was wrong. It was to do with her visit long ago.

"That's not the hostess I met here," Mary said aloud.

"No, it's not," came a voice she knew too well. "Well done, Miss Wandwalker. You've remembered Rosalind Forrest, Sir Daniel's mistress."

Mary turned to see Mr. Jeffreys offering to take her empty glass. He handed it to a passing waiter.

"Sir Daniel's…? What did you say?"

"Did I hear you mention my mother?"

It was the man from the new portrait. Mary gasped. For surely, he had just stepped out of the painting, his cheeks, his perfect shiny black hair glistening as if painted. Mary swayed. How many glasses of champagne had she had?

Mr. Jeffreys took her arm. Of course, the man facing her was not painted but rather glowed with the sheen of money. His exquisitely cut dark blue suit made his white shirt shimmer. He wore no tie, which drew attention to the highlights gleaming through waves of burnished hair. The man stood in front of Mary, his thin mouth a line, waiting.

"Did you say, mother? I don't understand," she stammered.

"I'm Viktor Solokov," he said. His Russian accent disconcerted Mary. Solokov nodded. "I believe you, too, Miss Wandwalker, met my mother when she visited Falconer House in the '70s. It was where she met my father, Kyrill Solokov."

Anna's husband knew her name. Mary Wandwalker took note. Mr. Jeffreys appeared disconcerted by Solokov's remark about his mother. Or perhaps his mouth tightened at the name, Kyrill. Either way, he soon acquired an expression of polite interest and shook his host's hand. Mary could not read the Russian's expression, unusual for her. His blue eyes flickered over her like an intrusive patting-down by airport security, Mary thought.

By contrast, Viktor Solokov returned Mr. Jeffreys urbanity in tones that cut like a sword.

"My mother, you will remember, Jeffreys. She was the actress, Rosalind Forrest, from Los Angeles. She and my father, Kyrill, became friends of Sir Daniel. On occasions Rosalind acted as hostess when Lady Margaret visited their Devon estate."

"Ah, yes, of course," murmured Mr. Jeffreys. "Solokov, I don't think you've actually met..."

"Miss Wandwalker, *ex* Chief Archivist at your little collection of dirty secrets," said Solokov. He's needling Mr. Jeffreys, thought Mary. Not many would dare do that. She met Solokov's curious glance with a double take. That's a tiny scar on his left cheekbone. The expensive hair is meant to draw attention away from it, I bet. He checked me out with that gratuitous "ex" archivist. Solokov finds your pain threshold.

Still scrutinizing Mary, Solokov clicked his fingers to summon a beauty in sky blue, the complement to his attire.

"My wife, Lady Anna."

As Anna bent toward her for an air kiss, Mary involuntarily stepped back. Reading calculated triumph in the young woman, Mary guessed that Anna had indeed glimpsed her at the cottage.

She had to know Mary's connection to George Jones. Neither defiance nor fear challenged from her black eyes, only recognition. Mary stiffened. Her appraisal of Anna considered her lipstick a little darker than necessary for the strapless dress. She had time to change after her tryst with George.

"Hello, Lady Anna," said Mary with all the dignity she possessed. *Show no fear.*

Anna put her hand on Solokov's arm. "So, you are Miss Wandwalker. I have heard so much of your ... talents."

Good God, was she really going to mention George? *Here? In front of such a husband?* Mary held her breath. Anna gave a sly smile. "You should see our gardens while you are here," she said with a slight accent Mary could not place. "Don't Englishwomen of your age like gardens?"

"Hardly tonight, I think," said Viktor Solokov, before Mary could reply. "The gardens do well in moonlight, but England is living up to its damp reputation. Feel free to explore the house instead, Miss Wandwalker. In fact, as an alum of the venerable university, I'd like you to meet some of our Eastern European students. Anna, introduce them, will you."

He vanished into the throng as silently as he'd arrived, leaving a tension between Anna and Mary that Mr. Jeffreys pretended not to notice.

What about the atmosphere created by Viktor Solokov? Mary wondered. Mr. Jeffreys was never ruffled, but there was a silent exchange between him and Solokov that bothered her. Left behind, Anna rubbed her jeweled hands together. They had been fists while her husband spoke.

"Viktor is correct," she said, the light in her face dimmed. "We want old-timers like you two to talk to our students. They are from countries like Hungary and Poland. Viktor cannot bring Russians because his country is not in the European Union. Come." She flounced off.

Mr. Jeffreys raised his eyebrows at Mary. She was glad to see his equanimity restored. "Shall we?" he said. "What was that about gardens?"

He remembered who the gardener really was, she could tell. *No more of George tonight.* Especially, resolved Mary, I want to avoid the topic of George and Anna, let alone my meeting with

George's wife, Caroline. Mary groaned inwardly. Mr. Jeffreys had his ways of digging up what she tried to hide.

She pointed to an open door with chairs beyond. "Let's sit down. I've seen the Falconer House gardens," said Mary. "That day you, Patrick, and Simon want me to remember. In June 1978, the lawn shone like green silk. You could smell roses in full bloom. They served strawberries and cream outside. That was the day I came to Falconer House with David."

CHAPTER 12
A SUMMER GARDEN IN 1978

Mary led the way to wing chairs in what proved to be a corner of the Falconer House library.

"Go on, Mary. You, both of you, came to a garden party?" prompted Mr. Jeffreys.

Mary stuck out her hand to a passing waiter and grabbed a tiny square of toast with a black disc. Finding herself chewing an undercooked mushroom, Mary had a moment of panic. She waved at Mr. Jeffreys to wait, while she turned away and spat the black remains into her white handkerchief and returned it to her handbag at her feet. Mr. Jeffreys grinned.

"Hardly likely to serve those kinds of mushrooms tonight, Miss Wandwalker," he observed. "Nevertheless, I applaud your discretion."

You're laughing at me, thought Mary.

"Tell me about that afternoon at Falconer house," said Mr. Jeffreys. Mary could see the effort he put into restraining his urgency. "Go on, Miss Wandwalker."

"Give me a moment," she said. "This house, it's strange and not strange. Like my shoes on the marble floor in the lobby. The tapping brought back seeing tables there with flowers. No, I know that's not what you want. That afternoon is hard to reconstruct. It gets blurred with ... what happened later."

Mary grimaced. She had to detach her impressions of the Falconer family from her only other glimpse of them, at David's funeral. Slowed by the raging nausea that she did not realize was early pregnancy, Mary had tiptoed, unnoticed, into the back of the parish church.

Forty years later, remembering that day, Mary Wandwalker's stomach churned again. This is no good. David's niece is newly dead. If only for her, I must get back to that day in the garden. I promised Patrick and Perdita's grieving father. God, I hope Simon stops self-medicating with alcohol.

Knowing Mr. Jeffreys's limited patience, Mary took another sweep of the library busy with partygoers. Hadn't she taken a peek that day of the garden party, when David went off to phone his mother? That's right, she had. For a terrible second the house screamed at her. Perhaps it was seeing her son, George, earlier that evening. Mary felt a door opening deep inside.

She would have to meet her son, someday. It was inevitable now, like the change of the seasons. When it happened, George would want her memories. More immediately, Patrick McCarthy would grill her on the drive back to London.

"Miss Wandwalker."

He spoke her name with the quiet authority of those long years at the Archive.

"All right, Mr. Jeffreys," she said in a low tone. "I'm doing my best. I did write that letter to Lady Margaret about someone describing the family as a trap and not a nest. I did hear those words that afternoon in the garden. Here is what I remember right now." She swallowed then let the vision of June sunshine dazzle her dry eyes.

"David phoned his mother in Devon while I explored the house. I joined him in the garden." Mary's speech slowed. "I remember cool, damp shade and warm sun on bare legs of the women in those '70s floral dresses." She sniffed.

"You would not believe how nervous I was to meet the Falconer family. David had parked his sports car illegally outside my college, and I ran out just as a bobby began writing a ticket. We drove the back lanes with hedges sprouting new growth in all directions. He coughed with hay fever because of

A SUMMER GARDEN IN 1978

the hawthorn blossom. It bubbled up with a pinkish tinge and thick perfume."

Mary glanced toward the framed watercolor landscapes above her head. She didn't need to look at Mr. Jeffreys. From old earth would emerge seeds lost underground.

"After getting out of the car, the first thing I noticed was scent so sweet I could taste it. David explained that Sir Daniel had rose bushes planted for David's mother. He said ... I think he said. ... Yes, there it was, that warm grasp of her hand and the young man's barely suppressed excitement at bringing his girl home.

"Look, look at the roses. ... Drives the gardeners nutty because they can't keep the deer away. My mother loves them. Pa likes to give these summer parties and have guests wander among roses where he can keep an eye on them. Very strategic is my Pa."

Mary drew a shuddering sigh: "He kissed me there and then. I went weak at the knees and had to grab his arm. I said...

"Sir Daniel I know from Oxford. What about your mother, Lady Margaret? And your brother?"

"Told you my Ma's checking on her horses in Devon, darling. Don't know about Arthur. Pa always asks him. Arthur prefers to work on the farm with Ma at this time of year. He's become a real stick in the mud after leaving Oxford. No, my father's friend Rosalind Forrest will be hostess today. Come on, darling. I know we said we'd wait to announce the engagement, but this is going to be our home. I want you to see everything."

Had Mary imagined the tiny hesitation before "friend"? Certainly, Rosalind Forrest had appeared very comfortable in greeting Sir Daniel's guests.

"Don't be nervous," said David. "Pa is the same here as in his history tutorials at Oxford. You were the shy girl with the sharpest mind, he told me."

"His eyes are the same as yours," said Mary, smiling at Daniel's son. "Sort of a fierce blue, mesmerizing."

"*My father really thinks he is a falcon,*" David had said. "*He's a trained falcon, devoted to seizing prey for Queen and country.*"

"As a history tutor?"

"*My darling innocent. Everyone knows my Pa is more than a history tutor. He's been a spy forever, another goddam family tradition I don't want. These days it is the Russians. You remember the family motto: Service through Family. He's the falcon in service while Arthur and I are the family: the heir and the spare: it's positively medieval.*"

David had kissed her hand in a mock courtly gesture then took her to greet his parent and Miss Forrest.

****

Mary's reverie got interrupted. She had not noticed the arrival of Patrick. Now he was balancing foot to foot. He wanted to be part of the conversation.

"What did you make of Rosalind? She was hugely famous, then sort of faded away."

The spell broken, Mr. Jeffreys frowned. Patrick, chastened, threw himself into a chair in what Mary realized was a characteristic gesture.

"So sorry. I'm an idiot to interrupt your train of thought. Miss Wandwalker, please ignore me. Can you go back and…"

Mr. Jeffreys broke in. "I will leave you two. Too many of us chatting in corners will attract suspicion."

"Sorry," said Patrick again. "Can I ask you a favor, Mr. J.? Could you look out for Simon's ex, Belinda? You know her husband, the saintly Richard Bishop, has moved out? I promised Simon I'd watch for her. She's in hot pursuit of Richard, you see. He's here somewhere."

Instinctively, Mary ducked lower to become invisible in the high-backed chair. Patrick did not seem to notice. He continued, "Last time I saw Richard he'd dodged behind Apollo in the lobby. He knows how to avoid his wife."

"Belinda Choudhry MP and I are not on familiar terms," said Mr. Jeffreys, repressively. "However, I would like a word with Dr. Bishop."

Jeffreys did his trick of vanishing and leaving the crowd undisturbed. One person noticed him go, the lady of the house. She darted from the crowd.

"Where's that man going? In olden days, he'd be a servant in a house like this."

Anna's racism slapped Mary in the face. She turned scarlet. Patrick too gaped at Anna.

Anna suddenly paled.

She's been acting, Mary realized. She's muffed her lines. Just who is this young woman? And who is Viktor Solokov to have a wife drilled in some charade?

"English is not your first language, is it, Lady Anna? You have a slight accent. Mr. Jeffreys is a high-ranking member of the Civil Service. Don't insult him."

"No, I say, rather not," added Patrick. "Jeffreys would be outraged. They say the Government can't do without him."

"Never speak like that again," said Mary, glaring at Anna Solokov.

Anna's black eyes gave nothing away as she tossed her perfectly groomed head.

"Viktor wants you to meet some of the students. They are in the second drawing room," she announced. "Come when you've finished your private talk. Anna added a sly smile at "private talk."

She indicated a corridor, then minced away in the direction of the stairs.

"Quite a little madam," remarked Mary.

"I don't trust her," returned Patrick. "She's got those bright eyes that suggest coke. Simon used to ... never mind." He took Mary's arm. "Miss Wandwalker, even from across the room I saw how you came alive when you talked about 1978." He gave a crooked smile. Mary swallowed.

"I saw in you that girl of 40 years ago. The Falconers put a spell on people. I know, believe me, I know. Please, please tell me more. I know it is your story, and you don't want to go there. But you hearing words used by Perdita in her cursed note, that's *our* story."

Sorrow seeped from Patrick. Mary bowed her head. "I'm trying, Patrick. Right now, it's starting to come back. Okay, let's return to the lobby, the part of the house I remember best."

Patrick got up with alacrity. The lobby was no longer so crowded. Recalling the flowers in cut glass vases in 1978, Mary's nose bathed in those long-ago scents of freesias, roses, and white lilac. Then the scents of sweat, grassy champagne and warring aftershave flooded back. She turned to face Patrick.

"David and I ignored the food so we could hold hands. I dragged him to the roses, orange, red, pink, and golden." She turned to Patrick. "Tonight, when we arrived, the lights on the terrace caught the first part of the lawn. No roses."

"I believe Lady Margaret had them moved after Sir Daniel died. There's a rose garden in the back beyond the kitchen herbs. Both have a hawthorn hedge to deter the deer. But please continue."

"Sir Daniel tutored me for a term," Mary said. "So, I could tell he was distracted when David brought me to say hello."

"Distracted, how?"

"He …" Mary knocked her hand in frustration against a golden pillar. "These pillars, they didn't used to be gold, did they?"

"No, Miss Wandwalker. Viktor Solokov upped the gilding when he took over the lease. Between you and me, Si refused to come tonight because he can't stand what the Solokov's done with the place. 'Bloody hotel,' he calls it. 'Too much flash and an empty heart.'"

"I see what he means. So back at the garden party, I'd just been making polite conversation about the roses. Sir Daniel smiled and said his wife loved them. He was about to say more when a waiter came and whispered in his ear. Sir Daniel's mood changed. He called to a woman who had her back to us. "'Rosalind,'" he said. "'He's here, Rosalind. In the garden.' He sounded worried and she ... yes, she looked frightened. She ignored David and me and ran off. Away from the gardens and into the house, I think."

"You met the famous Rosalind Forrest?"

"Yes, Sir Daniel mentioned her name. 'The great actress from Los Angeles,' he said. Then he strode off into the garden. After the man he mentioned, David and I supposed."

"About Rosalind Forrest ..." Patrick leaned toward Mary as if he wanted to swallow every inflection. "You heard what Jeffreys said earlier. Were she and Sir Daniel lovers?"

"Definitely." Mary's response had been unthinking. "You know I wasn't sure then, but I am now. Even then, I knew not to ask questions of David."

"Can you recall any more? Anything said between them?"

"No, David pulled me away. And before you ask, that comment about the Falconer family being a trap not a nest, that wasn't Sir Daniel or Rosalind."

"Who did say it? Miss Wandwalker, it means everything to Si."

"You too, Patrick," said Mary in her shrewd way. "You loved Perdita as much as her birth father."

In fact, she said to herself. It's Patrick who is desperate to know, Simon is simply devastated.

A group of partygoers next to them moved off, revealing several empty chairs. Mary took one, and Patrick followed her, as if in a cloud. Then he nodded. "Not loved. I love her," he said. "Our little Perdy; I don't believe love ends. If only you could remember ..."

Mary patted his hand. "I wish I could. I was so stupidly happy. No attention to anything, anyone, but David."

"Did he ...?"

"No, I know it wasn't David. The voice I heard saying the Falconer family was a trap not a nest sounded older, heavier, darker. She gasped. *In the garden. He stood behind me in the garden as I was looking back at the house*, waiting for David. I turned around, and he'd gone."

"A man's voice?" Patrick's free hand tugged the hair over his forehead. "A man? Please say you know it was a man."

"Yes, it was a man." Mary spoke wonderingly. "How strange, I can hear it now. Something odd about the voice. Definitely a man, though. David wasn't with me. There were long shadows everywhere, and I was sitting at the table with a plate of cakes. And then ..."

"Yes, yes, yes." Leaning closer to Mary, Patrick's elbow knocked a wine glass from a side table. Dregs of sticky champagne wet Mary's ankles.

"Oh, I'm so sorry. Si says I'm too clumsy for a painter. I can hold my brush in place for hours while knocking over every cup or glass in the room." He knelt and picked up the bigger pieces.

"Don't worry, sir, I'll get someone with gloves to sort it." The waitress was a plain girl with scraped-back hair and a few extra pounds.

"Thank you," muttered Patrick. He stepped back and shot an anguished glance at Mary, first her face and then her feet picking delicately around the scattering of shards.

"No harm done," she said, as she pulled her chair away from the debris.

"But you were going to tell me who it was." Again, he leaned in.

"No, I really wasn't." Mary was tart because suddenly felt very tired. Going back to that garden party had been like digging a tunnel into another world. With her bare hands. "A whole crowd descended at that moment on the way to the car park. The man, whoever it was, vanished before I could identify him. How much longer do we have to stay?"

Patrick sighed. "I want to get going, too. Before we do, I need to check with Jeffreys if he's seen Belinda. Si's worried about how she is taking Perdita's death, especially now that she's lost her anchor in Richard. Belinda gets on my ... never mind. Si reminds me she's Perdy's mother. If she's not coping, he feels it." He paused to take up a more humorous tone.

"Plus, we should check for drugs, especially of the shroom variety. Guests here are far older than the gilded youth at Oxford. It would say something if they're using, too." He got up, stretched, and turned back apologetically. "Look Miss W, hang on for a few more minutes. I'll be right back."

Mary's stomach groaned in tune with her mood. No, don't be silly, she told herself sternly. I'll get some of that posh buffet food. With something inside me, I can convince Patrick to get out of here. The Falconers are crazy. Hard to narrow down who sees them as a target.

It was when she had filled a plate with chicken salad and maneuvered her chair to a discreet corner that she was interrupted.

"Mary Wandwalker, what a wonderful surprise. I've been trying to get your phone number from the Archives. Why did you leave?"

His hair more grizzled, the man with the smile she could never resist had secured a tray for his plate of food. Placing it on a miraculously empty side table, he deftly removed Mary's plate from her lap, put it next to his, and brought the table to her chair. Then he darted around couples struggling with finger food to a waiter with a red stripe in his ponytail. From him, he procured two slender glasses of seemingly endless champagne. This attentive man with a natty brown jacket brought the drinks to Mary. He seated himself before she could object.

"Richard Bishop," she said, wondering what to say to Perdita's stepfather, one of her ex-lovers, and she remembered with a sinking heart, the estranged husband of jealous, bereaved Belinda. "Hello, Richard. I didn't expect to see you."

"Oh, Mary, come now. We are virtually in Oxford. These days, I'm living in College. Come to dinner with me at High Table. We may be one of the poorer colleges, but we can still manage five courses." He saw her looking skeptical and became somber. "My life has changed since ... the death." The charm glimmered no more. A trickle of something dark shaded his amiable features.

"Yes, I heard about Perdita. Richard, I'm so sorry."

He put down his glass. His hand shook as if it had been struck.

"She was ... lovely. The best stepdaughter a man could wish for." To which Mary nodded.

"I can't remember which college ..." she began.

"Sumer. Sumer College is where I'm based, almost in Summertown, north Oxford. Should appeal to you because it was founded by a woman who wanted to name it Inanna after the Sumerian goddess. Back then, the powers that be couldn't stomach a pagan temple of learning in Christian Oxford."

Mary forced a smile. "Now, I remember Sumer. I went to a garden production there that nearly got rained off. We stuck it out through drizzle with the real downpour when they took their bows. Shakespeare, probably. All I recall is sitting outside and getting wetter and wetter. I did that sort of thing as a student."

"I'm surprised they bothered with acting on our tiny lawn. Nothing like the multiple quads of Cardinal where I used to meet our girl."

There was a pause. Then Richard pulled his chair closer. "I'm so glad I found you, Mary. You see, I know about your connection to Perdita. You'll understand when I say that I came tonight to scout out Anna Solokov."

Mary pushed the plate of food away and edged her chair back, hitting the wall.

"Connection?" Her voice cracked.

"He came to see me, your boy. I've been planning to get in touch to tell you. It was the day before Perdita ... Well, it was the day before. He said she was getting involved with a crowd of psilocybin takers. You know about the toxicity of distilled psilocybin?"

Mary froze. What do you mean by "your boy"? she wanted to ask. Even though she knew. Better let Richard rattle on.

"I couldn't believe what he said about Perdita. Not after Simon took her to all those NA meetings in London. Back then, I thought he was overdoing it, frightening a young girl. But when George said that he was a cop and mentioned Anna Solokov I began to wonder. I'd run into her coming away from Perdita's rooms in Cardinal. She's not like anyone else."

Richard had been speaking quickly. Suddenly, he leapt up, grabbed another glass of champagne from a passing waiter and downed in one gulp. He returned to Mary, who maintained a stare at his shoes. Expensive and poorly kept, was her verdict.

Richard had not finished. "I should have talked to her at once. God knows, the rumors about harmful psilocybin even reached Sumer. Most of our students can't afford exclusive drugs, they tell me. That day when he left, I made up my mind to have it out with Perdy about her new friends, especially Anna Solokov. It was too late."

Richard's voice had got lower as his chair moved closer. His knee was now touching Mary's.

"Please look at me."

Mary raised her head to the wreck of his face.

"Who went to see you?" she said. She knew it was stupid to ask.

"George Jones, the undercover cop. He came to see me at Sumer. Told me he'd just discovered Perdita was his cousin. And now he was worried. George Jones, your…"

Mary kissed him. Afterward, she could not decide if it was to stop him saying the word "son" or because she had no words for his grief. He responded to the kiss with the same enthusiasm as years ago. What started in desperation stirred the roots of their passion. She tasted tears on his lips before she pulled away.

"Richard! How could you! Kissing that old woman in public!" Belinda Choudhry was loud enough to draw eyes from across the room. Mary was to realize that she rarely let go of her public speaking voice. This time Mary rose to her feet to confront Perdita's mother and the estranged wife of the man wiping her own lipstick from his mouth.

"Ms. Choudhry, I presume."

Slightly too plump for her beauty, Belinda exuded Indian princess with glorious black tresses coiled around her head and large sapphire earrings bouncing each side of a pout.

I should be noticing the sadness around her eyes, thought Mary. Instead, she was entranced by the pink satin evening dress that was slightly too tight and definitely too pale for her generous figure.

Mary found tart expressions about pink mermaids on her lips. They died at the frown of Patrick McCarthy arriving beside the angry woman. He and Belinda looked for all the world like parents catching naughty teenagers at a party. Too ridiculous, thought Mary, determined to retrieve her dignity.

"High Table dinner, you said, Richard," she said. "Why certainly. I'll call you at Sumer. Right now, it is getting late. Mr. McCarthy is going to drive me home."

Stepping away from the stares of the Oxfordshire great and good, she seized Patrick by the arm and marched him to the front door.

"Miss Wandwalker, don't you think we should …?" said Patrick.

"We're leaving. I've had enough."

"Er, yes, ma'am."

The endless discordance of this night had one more note. Patrick was unlocking the car when Mary heard the crunch of footsteps.

"Listen."

"I can't hear anything. It's so dark."

"There, by those trees." A figure swam toward them wrapped in a dark hooded cloak. Mary shrank back.

"Miss Wandwalker. Wait, please." It was Anna Solokov. Even her "please" was imperious, thought Mary.

"Mary Wandwalker, I must talk to you. Meet me in London, Monday. Here is the time and address." After pushing a lump of wet paper into Mary's hand, Anna was gone in a waft of smoky

A SUMMER GARDEN IN 1978

perfume over perspiration and rain. So, George's lover wanted to talk to the mother he had never met? Mary's head ached.

"London? I was going to drive you to Oxford station, but London's no problem. Gotta get back to Si tonight. To tell him the memory experiment failed," Patrick added sadly.

"It did not fail," said Mary through her teeth. "There's more I can dig up, I know it."

She snapped on her seat belt as if it held ammunition. Her eyes glittered at Patrick. "And if it is the last thing I do on this earth, I am going get the truth out of Anna Solokov — about drugs and what she wants with my son. Take me back to London. I have an appointment to keep."

CHAPTER 13
NOT ACCIDENT PRONE?

Perhaps it was the determination to get the truth from Anna Solokov that precipitated Mary's extreme exhaustion on the drive back to London. Arriving at her Greenwich apartment after midnight, Mary crawled into bed. She woke in the dark, her old-fashioned alarm clock showing it was 6. Too early, so she rolled over and slept again.

The next time she opened her eyes it was 8 o'clock, and a weak winter sun was sliding through the gap in her curtains. Saturday, she thought as she switched on her bedside radio, kept permanently on BBC Radio 4. Church music flooded her bedroom. Mary sat up.

"What? Oh no, it can't be."

For it was not Saturday but Sunday, at least according to the BBC. Her iPhone agreed, the numerals glowing with righteous indifference to Mary's consternation. Yes, she had slept through an entire day and a night. Dimly she recalled stumbling to the bathroom a few times. Somehow the rest of her body remained buried in sleep for a whole day. It was a mystery, especially since she did not feel at all refreshed. Jagged images from her Friday trip to Oxford hurt her insides.

The pallor of Caroline Jones's sadness morphed into the serpentine body of Anna wrapped around Caroline's husband, Mary's long-lost son. She searched for any part of the trip that did not make her brain ache. Ah, Richard's lips, his arms around her, interrupted by braying Belinda. Too soon, Belinda became Viktor Solokov, and. ... Enough. No more.

Having survived the last 36 hours without food, Mary felt no hunger. Coffee was another matter. She took her earthy brew back to bed. Eventually, her insides started crying out for food. She returned to her kitchen for toast and soup from a tin. Pulling out the tin of mushroom soup first, she gagged, then returned it to the very back of her cupboard. She would never eat mushrooms again. Finally, she switched on London's early evening news.

"An ambulance has been called to a Soho pub, several people have collapsed in mysterious circumstances at The Dragon and the Raven. We go over now to our correspondent on the scene, Thandiwe Parker." The camera shifted to a young woman whose brown skin glowed in the streetlight above her cream fitted coat. She held a microphone and gestured to the brick and windows visible behind her. On the very edge of the shot was a painted sign with a green winged creature breathing fire at a big black bird. The young woman spoke more softly than was ideal for broadcasting, but Mary could follow her story.

"I'm here in Soho after five customers of the popular and historic The Dragon and the Raven have been collected into two ambulances and taken to Charing Cross Hospital. Something they ingested in the crowded pub has made them dangerously ill. For the moment the unknown toxin has not proved fatal, but police and ambulance crews are taking no chances. Among the victims was the peer's son, Simon Falconer ..."

"What?" yelled Mary. "Simon? Poisoned?"

"With the hospital on fast-track to find the correct antidote, the police are starting to question bartenders and customers who were in the pub when the first victims fell ill. They would also like to speak to anyone who was in the pub earlier and who left before the police arrived. They know that a group of students, possibly of Eastern European origin, were drinking there earlier tonight. Now back to the studio ..."

"Eastern European? With a Russian man, perhaps?" Mary sat back stunned. Dazed, she went in search of her phone. There were seven messages from Patrick asking her to call. Mary's hand shook as she pressed the reply button.

"Patrick, it's me, Mary Wandwalker. How is Simon?" She was hoarse.

"They're sending him home after pumping his stomach," was the blunt reply. "No prizes for guessing the poison: It was psilocybin. 'Dangerously concentrated,' and I quote. Swallowing it with whisky saved lives. He's over the worst, they say. Doctors prescribed bed rest for a couple of days."

Patrick paused. She could hear him breathing too fast. "God, Miss Wandwalker, I'm terrified. This Falconer thing is out of control."

"You were in the pub with him? I thought …"

"You thought right. I was not in the pub. Rather, I went to collect him as soon as I realized he'd come off the wagon. My fault, I should have stayed home. Sunday is never easy. Yet what with everything, Perdita. … Well, I'm behind with a couple of commissions, and we need the money. I popped out to my studio for a couple of hours. When I returned to an empty flat, I knew. My beloved always goes to the same pub to start a bender. Some kind of ritual."

"He gives you a chance to find him."

"I suppose that's what a shrink would say. To be honest, I don't know anymore. I'm exhausted with it all. Grief is bad enough. Now Si is unraveling. Anyhow, you don't need to hear all our troubles. When I got to the pub, the first victim was frothing at the mouth. Simon was kneeling beside him when he keeled over. Banged his head on the floor and some sort of slime. … The medics collected it in one of their bags. I told them to test for psilocybin. After confirming the toxin, they treated Simon right away."

"He will be okay, won't he?" Mary thought she heard a groan. It was hard to tell with the street noises and sirens lamenting into the night.

"This time." Patrick appeared to be trying to clear his throat. "This time, the doc says. But what next? Where will this end, Miss Wandwalker?"

"I'll talk to Mr. Jeffreys," said Mary. It was the most comforting thing she could think of.

"Would you? That would be a big relief. Look Mary, Simon will be out any second and I have the meter running. Can I talk to you tomorrow, after you've met with Anna Solokov? Come to the apartment. This can't go on."

After agreeing, Mary meant to call Mr. Jeffreys right away. Somehow her body felt too stiff to move. Then her phone rang, and she knew without looking who it was.

"This can't go on," Mr. Jeffreys said, even before she identified herself.

"Of course not." This time her automatic reply worked like a wet towel on her face. It was indeed time to get serious. "So, you know about the poisoning in the pub?"

"Of course, I know," he muttered. "The poisoning in the pub after the overdose of a student who was, more than most students, anti-drugs. Psilocybin, possibly from Falconer House in both cases. Perdita Falconer's so-called overdose is looking less and less accidental, even to the police."

"I asked Patrick if Simon is going to be okay. What do you think?"

"Miss Wandwalker, my omniscience, like my medical skills, is exaggerated. I am neither a doctor nor Sherlock Holmes."

Mr. Jeffreys is testy. That means he's worried, she thought.

He grunted. "Whatever way you look at it, the Falconers are too accident prone to leave their future to the mysterious ways of the universe. Of course, it doesn't help that Simon Falconer is a recovering alcoholic. If it were not for the three other victims in the pub, the police would put Simon's mystery illness down to excess."

"He is lucky to have Patrick."

"Indeed," said Mr. Jeffreys. "Do I gather you have a date with the enigmatic Lady Anna? Is that meeting tomorrow the sole fruit of your trip to Falconer House?"

Mary bit back intemperate words. Friday felt like the longest day of her not exactly short life.

"Quite a lot happened in Oxford, Mr. Jeffreys," she said, trying for restraint. "What with the nurse at Cardinal College, then Caroline Jones telling things *you* had kept back, going to the cottage she shares with George. Did you know that he …"? Her voice wobbled. "That we saw him kissing Anna Solokov? Worst of all," she whispered, "I think he sensed *me*."

She tried for dignity. "You see, Mr. Jeffreys, I am still processing my impressions of Falconer House."

Mr. Jeffreys let out a sound between a grunt and a growl. "I am disappointed that you did not meet Viktor Solokov's student proteges. Any of his Eastern Europeans could be distributing psilocybin. Anna Solokov isn't working alone."

"Eastern European students," shouted Mary in frustration. "Have you told your cop friends that the students who left the pub tonight could be Solokov's?"

"What students? I was only told about Simon Falconer in the hospital."

"On the news, Mr. Jeffreys. Students, probably from Eastern Europe, left the bar right before the first person became ill."

"Most interesting." Mr. Jeffreys paused. Mary could hear his mind sparking like an engine. "That report will be followed up. I'll make sure of it. If these students are part of Solokov's group, then it fits the pattern. Don't ask, Mary. You see what I see. Someone is targeting the Falconer family from present-day Falconer House."

"You mean it's not over?" said Mary in a small voice.

"Not likely," came Mr. Jeffreys's hardheaded assessment. He added: "Your meeting with Lady Anna is now crucial."

"You are suspicious of her." Mary had her own reasons for envisioning Anna Solokov in jail. She wanted Mr. Jeffreys's.

"Try this, Miss Wandwalker. I'm having a hard time believing that a man as ambitious as Viktor Solokov would bother peddling psilocybin to a few rich students. Such clients are guaranteed to attract the attention of the same authorities he's keen to impress. On the other hand, if his wife is a user, she could have contacts in the drug trade in Eastern Europe."

"I'm not sure I agree with you," responded Mary. "Going back to the party, Anna Solokov seemed to be controlled by Viktor." Mary reflected. "Or, at least, that's the impression she gave me when he was around."

"All right, Mary. All I'm saying is to be careful with that woman. Whatever she is, she's wily, capable of manipulating the men she seduces."

An image of George Jones looking over Anna's head seared into Mary. She swallowed. "I intend to keep an open mind.," she lied.

"Naturally," came the dry reply. "My contacts in Interpol are digging. Check your email before you leave tomorrow. And Mary …"

"Yes?"

"Watch your back."

CHAPTER 14
THE MYSTERIES OF ANNA SOLOKOV

To Mary's surprise, Anna's note named a cafe in Greenwich southeast London, close to Mary's own apartment. It gave her the uneasy feeling that the Solokovs might know more about her than she would like. So reflected Mary ensconced at a window table in the tiny coffeeshop attached to the Cutty Sark Bookstore.

She could glimpse the ship itself by twisting her neck in the direction of the Thames. Powered by wind in sails big as thunder clouds, the tea clipper Cutty Sark plowed the ocean between London and China. A couple of years ago, there was a terrible fire, recalled Mary. I saw a red glow from my apartment, she recalled. The sirens went on for hours. A glass coffin now encased the lower half of the ship. She did not want to see it.

I remember thinking it's a ship half out of the bottle, thought Mary. Even in November, tourists make the pilgrimage to see what the fire left uneaten. The Cutty Sark means adventure, with its smells of cured tea and salt. It stands for travel without carbon pollution. She gave a wry smile, wondering if the wounded ship spoke to the future as well as the past.

With a future as unpredictable as the wild woods around Falconer House, Mary picked up the tiny spoon next to her coffee cup and banged it. The ting sound felt somehow intimate. I'm waiting for my lost son's mistress, she reminded herself. I'm meeting Anna Solokov, like I met George's wife, before meeting *him*. Going to need more coffee, she muttered, switching on her phone to scroll through the overnight emails.

A thief, a high-class escort, and a suspected computer hacker. These were the (unproven) allegations against Anna Solokov that greeted Mary from her inbox. Mr. Jeffreys had summarized his telephone calls to European colleagues, including extracts from Interpol's Organized and Serious Crime database. Mary read through everything twice, her eyebrows climbing into her fringe. If Anna Solokov was going to keep her waiting, then Mary had suitably sensational reading.

Anna Solokov, formerly Anna Vronsky (name thought to have been taken from Russian mafia boss whose lover she had been), birth name and date: unknown. First arrests came from thefts of politicians' houses where she had been entertaining as an escort. Later suspected of stealing financial records in Berlin. As well as being a member of a high-end burglary ring in Strasbourg, she was linked a drug cartel in Spain, and a sex trafficking gang in Romania. Documents proving marriage to Viktor Solokov eighteen months ago yet to be authenticated.

Viktor Solokov (see Anna Solokov), born 1979 Petrograd (now St. Petersburg. Father: Kyrill Solokov, Russian businessman; mother: Rosalind Solokov nee Forrest, film actress residing in Los Angeles. Viktor grew up a dual citizen of both Russia and the United States. Mother died 1990 from cocaine overdose while shooting a TV episode in New York. Father died 2011 in St. Petersburg.

Viktor Solokov has no police record. Nor can his businesses be traced before 2011 (think about that, Mary Wandwalker, Jeffreys had emphasized). Marriage to Anna Vronsky may have taken place at about the time that Viktor's financial firm made large investments in the UK. Donations to the conservative party followed from 2017, Solokov rewarded with a knighthood for "services to business and cultural development."

I suspect, noted Mr. Jeffreys, that the sponsorship of Eastern European (European Union) students attending Oxford was a belated diversification into cultural value. When questions got asked by the peerages committee, he had powerful advocates from the University.

So intent was Mary on her phone that she let the remains of her coffee get cold. Viktor Solokov's mother died of drugs when he was 11, Mary thought. Of *drugs*: Wouldn't that made him less, not more likely, to take up selling magic mushrooms to Oxford students? Perhaps people are not that rational, mused Mary, recalling a few surprises among her staff. These included crimes she'd solved herself.

Back to Solokov, whose mother was American. *That's right, I met her,* recalled Mary. Mr. Jeffreys said she had an affair with Sir Daniel. Maybe she had a predilection for 'shrooms and passed it on to Solokov senior? On the other hand, (a phrase Mary really liked), Anna's criminal career might include drug manufacture. Her background could easily include the ability to distill psilocybin.

Could Anna be the brains behind what happened to Perdita, as Mr. Jeffreys suspects? Her criminal record would suggest it. There is something not right about this situation. Something I am not seeing.

"The Falconers are not accident prone."

The young female voice startled Mary, who dropped the teaspoon she had been using to scrape coffee froth from the bottom of her cup. Anna Solokov glowed fierce and splendid in a scarlet coat, rain dripping off the hair that flowed over her shoulders. She took the seat opposite Mary and held out a Harrods carrier bag. "You're to have this. George says."

Mary took the bag in silence. A young man seemingly flushed by proximity to Anna arrived with her cappuccino and a croissant. He bowed. She nodded graciously. Then she attacked the croissant with her teeth and both hands. It was gone before Mary could glance into the plastic bag, purple with the silver logo of London's most expensive department store.

Ostentatious, Mary said to herself as she saw what looked like folded silk in a range of crimson leaf shapes on gray. Her mouth opened yet no words came out.

"I'm getting another coffee," Mary said finally, rising to wave her cup at the Barista. He waved and nodded with enthusiasm. Before another cappuccino could materialize, Mary stuck her hand in the bag, not taking her eyes off Anna. Just what is this woman doing?

"Don't look now. Put it on the floor," hissed Anna. "George said get you a scarf. He said they made acceptable presents for old women."

"Old ...?" Mary felt absurd. Why should that hurt?

Anna sniffed, "He said women of your age. That's old, right?"

The smile playing about her lips seemed both cruel and humorous. Quick as a flash, Anna shot out a hand that glittered with rings, curled her fingers around Mary's, let go, and thrust her hand back inside her coat. Mary was reminded of a gun returning to a holster.

Confusing, Mary thought. She's trying to confuse me. Her coffee arrived. Mary's hand shook as she held the chocolate sprinkled froth to her lips. Too hot. She blew a hole and tried again. The coffee tasted more bitter this time. "Why the scarf?" she managed.

"It's not the wrong color," Anna pronounced. "I chose the color myself. It will work with your skin and eyes. And is bigger than usual. Wear it as a shawl." Anna banged her empty cup down. She was gazing at the wall behind Mary, where a mirror hung.

"We came to that big boat out there called the Cutty Sark. Stupid to name it after a sailor shirt. This hour the students tour the boat with Viktor." She forced her inscrutable black eyes to Mary. "We don't have much time."

Mary remembered the mirror. Had Anna seen someone approaching? "Time for what?" she said.

Anna drummed her fingers on the table.

"The scarf is ..." she began very quietly.

"A bribe, that's right, isn't it Anna."

Anna tensed. Viktor Solokov loomed over her shoulders like a bear peering around a tree. Something about his Russian accent was vaguely familiar, thought Mary. She met Viktor's cold blue eyes. Just how long had he been lurking behind that bookshelf. What else had he heard? Surely not Anna's reference to George?

"A bribe, yes, I suppose," Anna echoed.

While Viktor squeezed into the last seat at the tiny table, Anna jerked her chin toward Mary. For a second, she conveyed pure anguish. Even Anna's rouged cheeks sank. The glance hit Mary like a disintegrating clod of earth.

Then the bleakness was gone, replaced with a mechanical smile. Mary's face ached from Anna's emotions. Whatever they meant, she questioned what she saw. Don't forget that list of crimes attributed to her, Mary told herself. The Anna before her now had metamorphosed into Viktor's consort. In that role, she could be deadly, deadly to George.

Anna shook her shining hair. "Darling," she said to Viktor, putting her fingers on his arm. "Bribe is your little joke. You didn't give me a chance to invite Miss Wandwalker. I'm the hostess, after all. Get yourself a coffee while I explain." Viktor bowed ironically.

"Don't be too long about it, Anna. We are expected at the Tower of London."

It was too few steps to the counter with the shining expresso machine and stand of pastries. There was no way Anna and Mary could be private. Anna kicked the bag with the scarf further under Mary's chair.

"My husband wants to invite you to our 'tea party' on Thursday." She said "tea party" as if these words were unfamiliar. Anna gave a twisted smile. "Viktor wants to invite back some guests from his portrait party on Friday night, those who did not get to meet our students."

Those students are likely candidates for distributing the psilocybin. Mary could hear Mr. Jeffreys's dry voice. She might add that the same students could have spiked Simon Falconer's whisky in the London pub.

"I don't know if I have anything to offer your students," Mary replied politely to Anna. While the idea of returning to Falconer House repelled her, it would give her an opportunity to pry Anna Solokov away from George. She did not need to see Anna's scarlet false nails to understand the depth of her claws. "It was 40 years ago that I was a student. Nothing about Oxford University is the same."

For some reason, Anna Solokov appeared as keen to get Mary to Falconer House as she could possibly be to go. A flash of consternation gave way to another whisper: "Please come."

Mary shivered as Viktor Solokov slid into his chair.

"Oh Miss Wandwalker, you are 'having us on,' as you English say." There was something disconcerting in Viktor's chortle. "Oxford never changes," he said, revealing too many teeth. "A discussion of long ago will be illuminating, I'm sure. Your friend Mr. Jeffreys is coming. I will ask him about his experiences as the first African student in your college."

"Black."

"I beg your pardon."

"Black. Mr. Jeffreys prefers to be called Black. He is Black British. His parents were from Kenya. He is British."

"Of course," said Viktor, grinning. He knows, thought Mary. He knows Mr. Jeffreys hates mention of racism during his time in Oxford. Why is this man trying to stir up trouble? Mary's foot struck the carrier bag with the scarf that Anna had forced under her chair. She felt with her other foot. Yes, there was something un-scarf-like at the bottom of the bag.

"Thank you." Mary spoke loudly and before she could change her mind. "For the lovely scarf, Lady Anna. As it happens, I am already going to Oxford on Thursday to meet a friend for dinner. A tea party beforehand would be delightful. What time should I arrive?" She stood up.

"Three p.m.," said Anna and Viktor together. "Must you go now, Miss Wandwalker?" That was Viktor, holding Anna's arm rather tightly. Mary caught the sound of Anna's hasty breathing.

"Yes, I'm about to visit a sick friend. Won't your students be looking for you on the Cutty Sark?" Mary's knuckles whitened on the carrier bag as she extricated herself from the corner.

"So looking forward to the tea party on Thursday," she gushed as she practically ran out of the Bookshop. You don't need to be scared, she tried telling herself. It was no good. Mary Wandwalker darted into the Cutty Sark Docklands Light Railway station and practically flung herself down the long escalator into the dark. Underground feels safe, she told herself, even though the Archive is no longer my home.

Bloody Falconers, she thought as she waited for the Dockland Light Railway train to take her under the Thames to the glass towers of the financial district. The excuse to Viktor about a sick friend had been that, an excuse. Yet, she found herself heading for the Barbican Center and the far-from-healthy Simon Falconer. Yes, Patrick and Simon should know about the Solokovs, Mr. Jeffreys too.

Mary sent her ex-boss a text then shut her eyes. She knew the route by heart. The train rattled between gray fingers of water from the old docks. It shot across steel bridges tempered like blades and sliced through transparent offices silvered with rain. *Is Anna Solokov afraid of her husband? Or is she a superb actor manipulating him as well as George?*

The Solokovs pulled Mary toward the past she was running from. Or running to, she thought as she changed trains at Bank Station for the Barbican. Better concentrate on this morning and Anna, she told herself with typical determination. I dislike her. I distrust her, yet there was that squeeze of the hand. It's as if she's a battleground between a scared young woman and a formidably skilled criminal.

Just before the darkness gave way to the fluorescence and concrete of Barbican Station, came the jolt of realization. It fired Mary like lightning.

Unbelievable and true. Anna Solokov is neither a frightened girl nor a criminal spider in the center of a huge web of drugs and God knows. No, that dangerous young woman could easily do both at different times and to different people. No doubt that is part of George's attraction to her. She is victim. Yet when necessary, or when it suits her, she is victimizer. *Does he imagine he is battling for her soul?*

There is no safe ground with Anna Solokov. Mary's knees weakened at the image of her son, George, wrestling a dark figure on Falconer house lawn. *George could die,* came the horrifying unbidden thought.

Caroline is right, thought Mary, as she joined the other passengers snaking toward the tall escalators. Never had Mary felt so much one of the living body of unpredictable, indecipherable humanity. Caroline is right that George is in a danger and that the police don't understand. I've got to help him.

CHAPTER 15
TRAP, NOT A NEST

Hours later, sitting in the Barbican apartment, Mary's haunches protested. Surely her backside had fused with the most uncomfortable seat in London, if not the entire British Isles. Glum, frightened, and weary, no one wanted to embark on yet another round of fruitless speculation. The Solokovs could have poisoned Simon in the pub. One or both could be the Kestrel who supplied Perdita with the fatal overdose. There was no proof to take to the police. There was only an invitation to tea at Falconer House.

Mary did not know whether to laugh or cry. Her companions, somber Mr. Jeffreys, overwrought Patrick McCarthy, and the poisoning victim himself, Simon in post-bender defiance — none of them were particularly concerned by George's affair with a suspect. Mary realized that this peril would be left to herself, the mother he'd never met, and Caroline, the sick wife he was hurtling so badly.

We're in trouble, thought Mary wearily. Neither Mr. Jeffreys, nor driven Patrick, nor queasy, red-faced Simon Falconer could agree who should go to the tea party. They argued. Ridiculous, thought Mary. She did not say so, having sympathy for Patrick's hair as he tugged on it when trying to persuade Simon to take precautions. The Falconer heir had a new attitude.

Gone was Simon's morose hiding in addictions. He now wanted to take the fight to the enemy. That is, he insisted on going to the tea party. Mary's lips could not help twitching. After acrimonious debate, one pot of coffee, two of tea, a delivery of fish and chips, which Simon refused to eat, Patrick was rubbing the condensation fogging the apartment's windows.

"I can't make any of sense of what the Solokovs are up to," he announced. "All I know is Simon's not going to that bloody tea party. It's got to be a trap."

"Trap," said Mary. She leapt to her feet knocking over her empty mug. "Trap, not a nest," she repeated.

"Yes, Miss Wandwalker," said Mr. Jeffreys, testily. "Those are the words from 1978 and today. What of it?" He brushed an invisible scrap of lint from another formidably expensive suit, this one-off had an orange thread. Mary ignored him.

"One golden day you will see the Falconer family is a trap, not a nest." It was a vision. She could take one step and go back 40 years. "I've got it. I know what was bothering me about that male voice. It was Viktor Solokov."

"Nonsense," shouted Patrick. "Nonsense, Miss Wandwalker. Viktor wasn't even born in 1978. I noticed the date in The Guardian when there was a fuss about his knighthood."

"Buying a knighthood," muttered Simon.

The sunlight faded in Mary's memory. "You misunderstand me," she said. "Of course, it wasn't Viktor in 1978," said Mary, sitting back down. She was composed. "But today he provided the clue I needed. Meeting him with Anna this morning, I wasn't distracted by all the noise at the Falconer house party."

"Miss Wandwalker, what clue?" Patrick sounded distraught.

She paused. "All right, then. Pay attention. The man I heard saying those words about trap and nest in 1978 had a Russian accent."

"Ah," said Mr. Jeffreys, folding his hands. "That confirms my suspicions. Well done, Miss Wandwalker. Undoubtedly you heard Kyrill Solokov, father to our Viktor."

"What?" shouted Patrick. "You *knew,* Jeffreys. Why didn't you say before?"

"Knew what?" That was Simon. He looked confused. Mary did not blame him. Two Kestrels, 40 years apart, how could they be connected? And yet they had to be. Now they could be father and son. Mary's head swam.

Mr. Jeffreys started rubbing his hands.

"I didn't 'know,' as you so baldly put it, Patrick. Miss Wandwalker's recollections merely confirm a hypothesis."

Simon had had enough.

"Shut up, both of you. You can tough it out on the way to Falconer House. I am coming with you to that damn tea party."

There was sudden silence. Patrick shut his eyes, his jaw clenched. Mary noticed that his blue shirt looked soiled. Simon, by contrast, had a scarlet kimono from which laundry-smelling orange striped pajamas peeked. His bare feet wiggled at her. Wanting to laugh, Mary glanced at Patrick and decided not to risk it. His face made a pattern of misery.

Mr. Jeffreys's chair creaked.

Ignoring his husband, Simon chewed dry toast as if grinding Patrick's objections to powder. Mr. Jeffreys grinned at Mary. She searched for inspiration.

"All right, it's time to decide. The Solokovs invited us to tea 'to meet the students.' Maybe it is what it sounds. They want to help their East Europeans integrate into Oxford. Patrick, we know how you feel. Yet, to me, the event is too ... too obvious to be an attempt on Simon's life."

"You'd think that of a London pub," retorted Patrick. "Too much risk to try to murder someone with tourists everywhere. But they did. Si could have died. Don't forget that Jeffreys here got confirmation. What Simon ingested was the same psilocybin that killed darling Perdy."

This silence Mary felt she could not break. She'd never met Perdita Falconer. *George did,* came that voice again from her own earth. *George, your son who is having an affair with* ... Thinking about leaving, her eyes strayed to her handbag. Sticking out was a plastic item in familiar colors.

"The bag from Anna Solokov," expostulated Mary, startling herself. "I forgot all about it. She gave me something in secret. Said it was from George."

MURDER ON FAMILY GROUNDS

"A message?" Mr. Jeffreys looked hopeful.

"No, it's a tin, an old tobacco tin. I peeked on the way over." Everyone leaned forward, as Mary reached into the bottom of the carrier bag, pushing the scarf aside. "Someone stuck a label on. ... Oh."

"What?" cried Patrick and Simon together.

"Give me that scarf." Using it to cover his fingers, Mr. Jeffreys took the tin from Mary. "Faded biro. Yes, I can just make out 'David'. I believe this is Sir Daniel's writing. It's a very long time since I saw it."

"Not David's," said Mary in a voice she did not recognize. "It's not David's writing. I have the letters he sent me. I know them by heart."

Simon and Patrick averted their eyes. Mr. Jeffreys opened the tin with a penknife from his pocket. Despite his care, when the lid came off, his hand jerked. Brownish granules spilled on the glass coffee table. More grains lingered inside.

"Do you think it used to be full?" enquired Patrick. He took out a pair of spectacles and used them to peer at the uneven lumps. Simon knelt down, pushed Patrick out of the way, then bent over for a huge sniff.

"Ground up magic mushrooms," he announced. "Probably still volatile. I could ..."

No, exclaimed Patrick, Mr. Jeffreys and Mary.

Simon shot a mischievous grin at Patrick and raised his eyebrows at Mary. *You too,* he seemed to be saying. *You are treating me like family now?*

Mr. Jeffreys cleared his throat. "Don't anyone else touch the tin. There could be fingerprints that are not Anna Solokov's or Miss Wandwalker's. I will get the contents analyzed as well and compared to recent compounds. That Detective Sergeant Jones sent this to us via Lady Anna and Miss Wandwalker is ... rather interesting."

"He trusts her. I don't," Mary fired back. "And, by the way, David did not do drugs. Even psilocybin, or magic mushrooms. I'd know it."

110

This time the pause was tight for a different reason.

"Look," said Mary. "I know it was 40 years ago. So, let's stick to Perdita and attempts on Simon. Not David. His death was a car accident."

Mr. Jeffreys spoke gently to the open tin. "Have you ever wondered why such a skilled driver crashed his vehicle in broad daylight?"

This time the silence held knives, all for Mary. She swallowed.

"David? That crash wasn't an accident. What do you know?" She suddenly found she couldn't speak.

"Nothing for certain," said Mr. Jeffreys, continuing to stare at the mushroom crumbs. "However, I did hear that an autopsy was done on David's body." He glanced at Simon. "Apparently Sir Daniel ordered the investigation shut down. He had a lot of influence. After all these years ..." He shrugged his shoulders. "I suspect Sir Daniel hid documents about the car crash in his private papers."

"Exhumation?" queried Patrick, quietly.

"No one is digging up my uncle." Simon sounded outraged. He struggled into a sitting position and put a hand on Mary's arm.

"All right then," broke in Patrick. "If we don't trouble the dead of 40 years ago, how can we protect Simon and any other Falconer from this ... this campaign of poisoning?"

"Any other Falconer?" whispered Mary.

"George," said Patrick. "And don't forget Simon's troubled father. Arthur got shot in the leg, remember."

"No one remembers Arthur," said Simon, almost savagely. "Least of all me. George might be in danger," he added doubtfully. "This affair with Anna Solokov could mean that his Falconer connection is known to whoever murdered Perdy.

"Not necessarily," snapped Mr. Jeffreys. "Like I said earlier, speculation is not evidence. Probability is not evidence. Face it, you two, the police will do nothing against the Solokovs without something more than an old tin.

"So, we get evidence," said Mary with all the firmness she could muster. "You have this stuff with David's name on it tested, and we go to this infernal tea party. We snoop."

"Who is *we*?" Patrick would not relent. "Simon stays safe right here."

"Patrick, darling. This time you can't stop me," said Simon. He sounded tired yet resolved to Mary. "The Kestrel remains free after killing our Perdita. For her sake, I'm not running anymore." He brushed his too long hair out of his eyes. Mary looked. David did that exact same gesture. It bit her like a snake.

"I won't let ..."

"Pat, take it on the chin. I hid away and nearly got pushed down the steps right here in the Barbican. I ran away into a bender, and they got me with psilocybin. We gotta fight this."

"Even if you are bait?" Patrick appeared close to tears.

"I'm going to be in danger until we find out exactly who's got it in for the Falconers and why." Simon caught Mary's expression and continued. "Who has *always* had it in for the Falconers. Go on Jeffreys, spill. What do you know about Mary's Russian voice in 1978?"

Mr. Jeffreys took a deep breath. When no one spoke, he surveyed the company.

"Very well. The Kestrel in 1978 was indeed a Russian, Kyrill Solokov. We always knew that Kyrill, a Russian agent, took the nom de plume of 'the Kestrel' when working with Sir Daniel. A compliment to the name, Falconer, or so we thought." Jeffreys paused, frowned at Simon, then turned to Mary. "Thanks to Miss Wandwalker here we know that it was Kyrill, aka the Kestrel, she overheard. No other Russians visited Falconer House in that year. Don't forget, it was the Cold War. Russians did not easily travel in the West."

"Are you implying a threat to the Falconers in 1978?" That was Patrick.

"Two Falconers died before their time in that same year," said Mary slowly. "David's death was devastating. I never asked how Sir Daniel died. Something happened in France, didn't it?"

Mr. Jeffreys looked enigmatic.

"Don't go all Secret Service on us," said Simon, rudely. "I overheard Pa talking at his mother's funeral in 2015. A young Black guy brought the news of my grandfather's death. Everyone knew Sir Daniel spied for Queen and Country."

Mr. Jeffreys watched Simon, who leaned forward. "Yeah, Pa admitted to my mother that Sir Daniel hosted a defector from the Russian Security Services. You've just confirmed that the Russian's code name as the Kestrel. That young guy had to be you, Jeffreys."

"If the Kestrel in 1978 said 'trap and nest,'" said Patrick slowly, "then today's Kestrel said them to Perdy. ... Oh, it's too, too confusing."

Mr. Jeffreys's pained expression met Mary's pale strain. He finally nodded.

Simon wasn't letting it go. "Well, was my grandfather murdered? And was it the Kestrel?"

"Yes," said Mr. Jeffreys. "The Kestrel, Kyrill Solokov, shot and killed Sir Daniel Falconer. Sir Daniel took Kyrill to France to be debriefed by the Americans in Paris. That was where Solokov had chosen to live afterwards."

Mr. Jeffreys's voice darkened. "Or so the Kestrel said. Neither man arrived. Sir Daniel's body washed up on a beach in Brittany. Only then did we in the Service discover that the Kestrel was a double agent, not a real defector. A cable intercept to Moscow proved to be Kyrill Solokov. He confirmed executing Sir Daniel on the orders of his Russian masters."

"You locked the bastard in the darkest dungeon under the Tower of London? You tortured him on the rack. You cut off his head."

Mary winced at the sarcasm in Simon's tone.

Mr. Jeffreys licked his lips. "No. My superiors decided against revealing what we now knew. They wanted to keep using the Kestrel."

"What?" Patrick went to put an arm around Simon. Sir Daniel's grandson spluttered.

"You have to understand," began Mr. Jeffreys, not looking at either man. "If a double agent does not know he is exposed, he will go on to offer valuable intelligence to maintain his cover. Therefore, since there was nothing that would stand up in a criminal court ..."

"You let him go?" Mary was incredulous. "Kyrill Solokov, Sir Daniel's murderer? I suppose he went on to become rich and powerful after the Berlin Wall came down."

Mr. Jeffreys nodded. "His son is now good friends with our prime minister," he remarked.

"Words fail me," said Mary, looking grim.

CHAPTER 16
THE KESTREL THEN AND NOW

After the revelation that the Kestrel in 1978 murdered Sir Daniel Falconer, Simon did not hold back. His bitterness cut like acid, Mary thought. Even weakened from the psilocybin, he refused Patrick's attempts to calm him down.

Almost in tears, Simon said, "Dammit, Jeffreys. What's the use of you creeps in dark corners? Wouldn't anyone avenge my grandfather?"

Mr. Jeffreys refused to be drawn. Simon's hands began to shake. He angrily threw off Patrick's attempts to calm him down. Eventually, Mary went into their kitchen. She returned with a glass of water, making Simon drink it. He lay back gasping and scowling on the couch. He wasn't finished, Mary guessed. Neither was Mr. Jeffreys.

After Mr. Jeffreys repeated that the authorities' had no proof that Kyrill Solokov had killed Sir Daniel, he added that the double agent's value protected British spies who were still alive. He did not say that it was time Simon grew up. Rather, Mary could see the words quivering on his lips. Patrick nodded at Mr. Jeffreys, appearing to comprehend. Simon closed his mouth, only to open it again, this time to demand the instant arrest of Viktor Solokov.

Mr. Jeffreys banged his left fist in his right palm.

"To be the son of Kyrill, aka the Kestrel, is not a criminal offence," he retorted. "Kyrill died in 2011 in Moscow of natural causes. I'm sorry, Simon. Right now, there is nothing concrete against Viktor. Mere suspicion and his parent killing a man I ... deeply respected. No, it's not enough."

"But ... but..."

"Why?" said Mary. Her reasonable tone cut through Simon's near tantrum as she intended it to. She waited until all three men were listening. Only the sound of a humming fridge disturbed the room. Barbican insulation doubled as soundproofing, she recalled.

"Why, *Why* the Kestrel now?" she began. "Why would a drug dealer in the 21st century take the non de plume of a killer from 40 years ago? Even if they are father and son, calling oneself the Kestrel today, as we know the psilocybin supplier does, is asking to get caught. So why? There's got to be more to it."

"Which brings us to Lady Anna," said Mr. Jeffreys, sagely. "She could be today's Kestrel. Taking the alias of Viktor's father is a shrewd move. She's setting her husband up. He gets caught while she flees."

Mr. Jeffreys really did not like Anna Solokov, Mary reflected. He saw her as a spider weaving a dark web. Mary wanted to say that Anna Solokov had to be more complex. After all, George loves her, doesn't he?

"All right," broke in Patrick. "If not Victor, and Miss Wandwalker looks unconvinced about the Lady Anna, what about other suspects? Anyone with historical knowledge could use the name of Kestrel to deflect attention."

They all looked at him. Mr. Jeffreys scratched his chin, Mary leaned back in her chair, Simon chewed his cheek.

"Well, you know," continued Patrick, undaunted. "I've been wondering about Richard Bishop."

"Richard Bishop?" Mary almost fell off her chair.

"Belinda's husband?" Simon turned redder than Mary would have believed possible. "If that bastard gave psilocybin to Perdy I'll ... I'll ..."

"No, no, Si. I don't mean that," Patrick said hastily. "Richard cared for Perdita all right. He'd never hurt her. If he was the Kestrel, and I admit it's a long shot, then Perdita got the psilocybin in error. Listen, it's not so far-fetched."

Mary wanted to protest. She opened her mouth. The words would not come. Patrick looked grateful. He then plunged in.

"Richard would be in it for the money. He's always been envious, jealous or whatever, of Belinda coming from huge wealth. You know her father's Raymond Choudhry of the Choudhry Corporation in India, Miss Wandwalker. Jeffreys, don't look like that. I know for a fact that Bishop came across chatter about the 1970s Kestrel. Don't forget, he includes the history of the Security Services in his research. Hell, it's even on his webpage at Sumer College."

Turning to Simon, Patrick appealed, "Si, you were there. Remember that time Richard and Belinda brought Perdy to the Falconer estate to meet us? She must have been about 12. Your father scared Perdy with that doom-laden warning about strong psilocybin mushrooms."

"I can't see Richard …" began Mary. Her desire to defend her ex-lover foundered. She recalled how their breakup kicked dust into an old wound. Then she noticed Mr. Jeffreys stopping an outburst from Simon by lifting an eyebrow.

"I, too, wonder about Richard Bishop. A man like that, overlooked in a complicated family; he might well harbor resentment." Mr. Jeffreys began thoughtfully. "Bishop's breakthrough research changed how we see espionage and the British state. Mary found the documents that made his success possible."

Mr. Jeffreys paused to see that he had the attention of the room. He did. "Although his monograph officially ends with the Second World War, Sir Daniel's time, I know that Bishop interviewed retired agents for that epilogue on the late 20th century. Some of those men and women were familiar with the Kestrel case. It was a scandal, you know, that Sir Daniel was so exposed. Heads rolled."

"Literally, I hope," muttered Simon.

Mr. Jeffreys ignored him. "If Bishop knew about the Kestrel of 1978, then it's a small step to using the alias. With today's drug scene in Oxford, his regular contact with students is an opportunity."

"A side business in drugs," Simon crowed. "The admirable Dick! Bel will be cross."

"Wait a minute, Si, Mr. J. We're leaving out Richard Bishop's real connection to the Solokovs," insisted Patrick. He flourished both hands. "Bishop's involved with Viktor Solokov's Eastern European students. Several take courses with him at Sumer. He's very popular, I hear."

"Ah," said Mr. Jeffreys. "Miss Wandwalker...?"

"Yes, I told you I've accepted dinner with him on Thursday, the day of the tea party."

Mr. Jeffreys gave his trademark half grin. "Splendid. You can snoop around his rooms at Sumer."

Simon frowned. "Belinda really won't like it. I don't think she's given up on the marriage. It took her long enough to let go of *me*."

"A good thing it is High Table," said Mr. Jeffreys with a frown. "Bishop is not my top suspect. Even so, dinner with the dons means everyone eats from the same pot. Be careful if he offers Port afterwards."

"No one is trying to kill me," said Mary with dignity. "Of course, I'll be careful. It's hard to think of Richard Bishop as a drug dealer, but Patrick has a point about the Solokov students. I'll be your sleuth at Sumer, as well as going to the Solokov tea party beforehand."

"There is another thing you can do, Miss Wandwalker," said Mr. Jeffreys. "You, that is, rather than any of us."

"What do you mean?" chimed in Simon and Patrick.

Mr. Jeffreys sighed. "Sir Daniel died unexpectedly. Although I was tasked with removing his security material, and did so after I talked to the family, I always thought there were more documents hidden away in Falconer House. His personal papers got mixed up with intelligence material."

Mary felt her heart beat faster. "You mean there could be something about David's death? From the police investigation that Sir Daniel stopped?"

"That, and Sir Daniel's relations with Kyrill Solokov, aka the Kestrel." Mr. Jeffreys sighed. "After the funeral Lady Margaret could not banish me fast enough. When she died and your father rented out Falconer House, Simon, every scrap of paper got boxed and sealed. I suspect the Falconer relics are in the attic."

Mr. Jeffreys spread out his hands. "My guess is that the Solokovs would not bother with old papers. It would be perfectly reasonable ..." Mr. Jeffreys paused for a sly grin at Mary — "for a Falconer like Simon, who has recently encountered a renowned archivist, to ask Mary to examine the Falconer papers."

Mary gulped. The bastard, she thought, sneaking me into archival work when he just fired me. Mr. Jeffreys kept talking.

"As I said before, Miss Wandwalker, your unique skills are a kind of detection. There could be evidence in Sir Daniel's papers."

"You mean about Kyrill Solokov? What good would that do?" Patrick demanded. "We know he was a double agent. You said he killed Sir Daniel."

Simon leaned toward Mary "Please, Miss Wandwalker."

"Any information, actual evidence, on Solokov senior could encourage Viktor to talk," insisted Mr. Jeffreys. "Haven't you noticed how sensitive he is about his family?"

Patrick's eyes shone. "Miss Wandwalker...?

"All right," Mary said, quickly. "Enough. I'll go through Sir Daniel's papers for you. If Viktor and Anna Solokov let me."

Her throat felt like parchment. Checking her watch, she saw that it was past time for her to leave.

"I'll be going," she said. "We will meet at Falconer House, something I never thought to say. However, Patrick, you do realize what this means? Simon *must* go to the tea party on Thursday. Solokov is more likely to be persuaded in person. We know he wants Simon at Falconer House."

Patrick groaned. "I'm not giving up yet. When it comes to Falconers, there's an ace up my sleeve. I think he is about to arrive."

There was a sharp rap on the front door. Mr. Jeffreys stood up and beckoned Mary.

"Patrick's reinforcements. Miss Wandwalker, I will leave you to your family reunion."

Mary's whole body jerked. She dropped her handbag with a bang and almost fell with it. *It couldn't be. Not here. Not now.* Trying to steady herself, her hand thrashed until it was caught in a large male grasp.

"Mary, I've got you. Sit up. Don't panic. It isn't him. It isn't George. Patrick told me who he invited. Forgive me." Mr. Jeffreys was gentle. Mary shrugged off his arm. Patrick was opening the door.

It was worse than her fear. It was an old ghost in horrible angry tweed. "David," she gasped. "David, my god it can't be."

The old man with the stick glared. "My brother David died 40 years ago. I'm Arthur Falconer. Who the hell are you?"

CHAPTER 17
THREE FALCONERS

While Patrick settled Arthur Falconer, he introduced Mary without mentioning her role in the family, while Simon sulked. Mr. Jeffreys took a phone call outside the apartment. After a couple of minutes, he returned, saying, with a grave glance at Mary, that he had to miss the Solokov tea party. The Ministry demanded his presence on Thursday.

"Watch the Falconers," he said to Mary, as he left. "Simon will go to the tea. Don't forget there will be *three* Falconers at Falconer House."

That would be Simon, his father Arthur, and ... Mary grabbed her handbag from the floor. *George is a Falconer, too.* Would the Solokovs include their gardener at the tea party? She thought not. Although that Lady Anna is capable of anything, she reflected grimly.

After the introduction to Mary, the old man grumbled about his unhealed leg. No, he did not want to discuss his shooting as part of some anti-Falconer plot. Mary surreptitiously recovered her coat from the back of the sofa. Arthur's facial bone structure made her ache all over. He was the ghost of her dead lover, a ghost she could not reach for.

She saw David trapped in the body of a man old before his time. Sixty-five-year-old Arthur's hair had faded. Unlike his son, discontent melted his flesh. The old green tweed suit now flapped over a sunken chest. He could not help scowling at Simon.

Yet it was Arthur Falconer who made the decisive move. Shaking his stick at Patrick, he announced that, dammit all, he would grace the Solokov tea party with his presence, "to see what that damn shark has done to my house." He didn't see what all the fuss was about.

Patrick threw up his hands. "I surrender."

Simon, triumphant, would accompany his father, Patrick, and Mary to Falconer House. In fact, after more sniping between father and son, Patrick turned to Mary at the apartment door.

"*Not* what I hoped when I asked Arthur to speak to Simon. He does not seem to care about the danger to the Falconers. Miss Wandwalker, I beg you. Come in the car with us. I can't stand hours of those two bickering."

Patrick and Mary agreed on a rendezvous close to Paddington Station at noon on the day of the tea party. Afterward, they would drop Mary at Sumer College for her dinner date with Richard Bishop.

*****

Later, when Mary recalled the journey from London to Oxfordshire, it was with the knowledge that, yet again, crucial details had been kept from her. In fact, she'd been roped into a charade, even though it was to get her into Falconer House as a spy.

Simon fidgeted most of the way. His father muttered curses at the gunshot wound in his leg — too painful in this suburban car, he'd jibed; while Patrick, driving through mist and drizzle, remained tight-lipped. Mary sat in the back with Simon, to give Arthur more leg space, she'd said. Meeting Patrick's eyes she saw relief that father and son would not sit together.

Tired of trying to decide between Viktor and Anna Solokov as the brains behind the lethal psilocybin, Mary tugged at her seat belt until she could rest her head. Instead of worrying about what was to come, she would summon her ideal afternoon tea.

Therefore, she banished the aftershaves of her companions and imagined the sweet-sharp tang of strawberries. A cool stickiness met the finger she jabbed into nonexistent jam in chilled silver dishes. Was that a strawberry seed in her fingernail?

Next, Mary conjured up bowls of yellow clotted cream. On warm sweet scones, the thick cream acted like butter, melting at the edges. Spoonfuls of jelly intoxicated with sweetness. On her tongue the tartness of fruit pierced the sugar and cool buttery cream to provide a melody of flavors. Jam on her tongue blended with the floury, melt-in-the-mouth dough of scones. That china pot of tea prevented unalloyed gluttony, a deadly sin. She would reach out to pour the amber brew. Small jugs of milk for the tea turned the meal into a ritual.

Cream teas are sublime, Mary thought, with her own sense of humor. When was the last time? Wait, didn't she and Richard Bishop indulge that afternoon they went to Kenwood House on Hampstead Heath? Yes, she'd initiated him into cream on scones. Piling it recklessly high, he'd dropped a great dollop on his tie. That was when he made his big confession. Worried about the stain, he'd admitted that he had not *quite* left his wife.

That was over a decade ago. Mary left him over that lie. She refused to be anyone's dirty secret. Now, after the death of Perdita, Richard Bishop had finally separated from Belinda Choudhury, M.P. Why exactly had Mary agreed to dine with him this evening? Yes, she'd agreed to snoop, but that had not been why she'd said yes. He'd held her hand as they said goodbye at the Falconer portrait party. Some old feelings no longer felt so old.

First things first, she told herself, as Patrick swung into the driveway of Falconer House. George, my son. I am not ready for this. Caroline said he was away from the estate today. Despite what happened at the cottage, I trust her. She was straight with me *and* cared about my feelings. More than the bloody Falconers.

Mary swallowed as the vehicle crunched to a halt. She blanked out Arthur's grumbling, Patrick's sighs, and Simon slamming the car door. First, the Solokovs in their chosen setting, she thought, then Perdita's stepfather, Richard Bishop. I will find out what he means to me.

CHAPTER 18
AFTERNOON TEA AT FALCONER HOUSE

As a social gathering this tea party is distinctly odd, Mary reflected. After a half hour and one cup of murky liquid her head throbbed. Fortunately, she carried a supply of aspirin. Managing to gulp tablets with the muddy dregs in her mug, she pondered clues to the real purposes of the Solokovs. Why introduce their Eastern European students, who knew so little of Falconer House, to the family who knew so much?

Even the food is a jumble, thought Mary, gazing at the huge oval table with its drying sandwiches and big multicolored cakes, none of which had been sliced. Anna Solokov glowered behind four teapots, one with a Chinese bamboo handle, the other painted with mountains, and the final two, red and black art deco. She pouted when anyone approached for liquid refreshment.

The pots were hemmed in by cups and saucers from unmatched sets. Mary could see no milk, and so requested China tea. After Anna handed over a dark green cupful with a glare, Mary decided not to risk asking for cake, although she was partial to fruitcake. Those big beasts were all armored with icing. That huge one that resembles a slice from a marble pillar looked like it could stop a grenade.

"Sandwich, Miss Wandwalker? These are cheese. I made them myself." The young man wore his mousy hair in a ponytail with a lock of crimson on the left side. Mary checked twice to see he was male, since an almost identical figure sported a blue stripe in her even paler ponytail. There was something familiar about these, too. Ah, yes, they served the champagne the last time she had been in this gilded lobby.

"I like cheese," said Mary. She picked a crustless four-inch square with a block of orange cheddar thicker than the bread. She took a tiny bite and winced.

"Take several then," said the young man, leaning too close. "I'm Johann. Over there is my sister, Helga. We're twins. This fall we started chemistry at Sumer. Hungary needs lots of chemists."

"Chemistry," murmured Mary, letting Johann guide her to a grouping of soft chairs. She could see Arthur Falconer on the other side of the room jabbing his stick at the tea pots. He'd wrinkled his nose at the gold-painted pillars on arrival. A few of the students' jaws dropped at his suit, which today mixed purple with brown. Mary suppressed a grin. Another young person in a woolly hat seemed to be taking Arthur's food order. He scowled at the golden pillars yet made no comment. Helga leaned earnestly toward Simon, who held a teacup as if he did not know what to do with it.

Chemistry, how very interesting, thought Mary. Chemistry between people can be so revealing. More to the point, chemistry can make drugs like psilocybin distilled into a lethal potion. She wondered how she could get Johann to open up. Perhaps his experiments included mushrooms.

"Tell me," said Johann, still holding the sandwiches. "Were you one of the first ladies to get a degree?"

Mary choked on her chunk of cheese. She grabbed her teacup and swallowed half the liquid. Ugh. Far too strong.

"Hardly," she said. "I was accepted by St. Julian's College in the 1970s. Women were first awarded degrees in 1920."

She drew back from his open mouth and took another sip of tea. Oh well, it had caffeine, all right. "Johann, tell me about studying chemistry at Sumer. Is it true that all kinds of household products, even food, have toxic chemicals? Mushrooms, for example?"

Johann sat back licked his red lips. He had furry eyebrows that almost met in the middle.

"Has Miss Wandwalker stumped you?"

The voice from behind Mary was suave and deep. A pulse of tension ran over Johann from the furry eyebrows down through the prominent jaw and unshaven chin. Without looking, Mary knew her host had arrived.

"She was asking about ... erm, mushrooms." Johann said. He did not look up at Viktor Solokov.

"Chemistry," corrected Mary. She liked to be brisk where young people were concerned. "I was wondering if chemistry was responsible for your extraordinary array of cakes. Tell me, might I have some fruitcake." Mary guided the gaze of Johann and Viktor to the loaded table. Each cake appeared as formidable as a plinth.

"Anna, the fruitcake. Which is it?" Viktor's arrogant voice brought Anna to her feet.

"They forgot the labels," Anna muttered. "I can't find them in the boxes. She took a regular tea knife and stabbed the nearest cake. Since the implement was designed for spreading jam, she had to give it a whack as if spearing a fish.

Her reaction to Viktor is off, thought Mary. Too immediate, too trained, too resentful. I wish Mr. Jeffreys was here. He would not think that Anna was controlling Viktor right now.

Yes, she's an accomplished actress, echoed in her mind. It was familiar. Mary recalled that voice incandescent against Anna. Caroline, the betrayed wife, would insist that Anna cannot be trusted. She of all people would not be surprised at the dirt Mr. Jeffreys had found. Anna had seduced her beloved George. Mary did not want to think about George today. Soon, soon, she would arrange a meeting.

Meanwhile, how interesting that watching Anna brought Caroline back into her consciousness. Plunging her blunt knife into cakes, Anna appeared oblivious to everything except her husband's command. Her loose hair flapped about her face like a veil. She's hiding, thought Mary, or she wants to.

Anna came to the cake with marblelike frosting. So hard was the carapace that she had to bang on the handle of her knife. The snowy surface chipped before yielding a big crack that could be heard across the room. Everyone seemed to be watching Anna as she stared nonplussed at the nearly black residue on the blade. She looked up. Mary glimpsed defiance before Anna held the knife up to her nose, shot out a red tongue and licked the blade clean.

"English fruitcake," she announced. "Next time we make our own labels. Helga, you cut and serve it. Go to the kitchen for the chopping knife. That Jones woman knows where to find it."

Anna sat down, ignoring Mary, as if her request for cake was an affront. Viktor hovered near Mary. She caught Simon looking at her and intercepted a nod. It wasn't just her imagination that this was a very peculiar setup.

Helga left the room in a streak of blue and brown. To avoid talking to Viktor, Mary let her gaze wander. Perhaps close to the house there was a disused stable where mushroom poison brewed, dark and intoxicating. Was it only designed for unwary Falconers? Mary remembered that psilocybin dealing at the university remained small scale.

Waiting for the cake gave her a chance to look over the Solokov students. Besides Johann and Helga, the woolly hatted boy with almost colorless curls leaned on Arthur's chair. The old man flushed and winced in a way that suggested his leg was bothering him. Simon watched his father while pretending to listen to an overweight girl in pigtails. She also animated the young man sitting beside her with a shaved head and tattoos covering his neck. Both Simon's attendants had their backs to Mary. She regretted being too far away to read the tattoos.

"You drive today?" said Johann. He was trying to keep Mary's attention, she realized, especially with Viktor standing nearby with folded arms, his cold blue eyes shifting between guests. Anna was pouring tea no one had asked for.

"No, I came with Sir Arthur and Simon Falconer, driven by …" Hang on a moment. Where was Patrick? She'd not seen him since entering Falconer House. "Erm. Perhaps I should go and look for my friend. He may have gotten lost."

"No, no, you have to stay." Johann grasped Mary's right arm with a grip of steel, as she tried to rise. "Please," he added.

Mary locked her gray eyes on his too bright ones. She noted the pulse in his temple. Putting her hand on Johann's rough one made his fingers relax. She shook off his hold and sat back. Patrick must be taking a break from the tension between Simon and Arthur, she reflected.

Johann coughed. His husky tone was apologetic. "Here, Miss Wandwalker, here is the woman to cut your cake."

Mary swiveled to see Caroline, of all people, carrying a huge knife that glittered when the chandelier caught it. It was far too late on a November afternoon for daylight. Behind her came Helga, looking smug.

Thank goodness, Mary thought, it's a chef's knife. It can cut through anything, even frosting that appears to be welded on. Mary knew the sickle design on the wooden handle. A long-ago lover, claiming to be a kitchen genius, had sourced the most expensive chef knives. That had been before Mary got tired of his foodie dramas. Pulling her gaze from the wicked blade, Mary met Caroline's nod.

"Left behind by a caterer," she muttered waving the daggerlike implement.

"Caterer?" Arthur queried, irritably, rubbing his leg. "Must be from my son's failed attempt to rent out Falconer House for weddings."

"Years ago," retorted Simon. "And I almost made a profit."

Arthur harrumphed. Mary saw Patrick reappear from a door she remembered. Almost concealed by blending into the cream paint, it opened to the passage that ended at the Library. When Patrick bent and whispered in Simon's ear, she guessed he'd taken the opportunity to search for Sir Daniel's missing papers. No good, she assumed from Simon slumping in his chair. Nevertheless, he rallied enough to glare at his father. In turn, Arthur tried to turn his back on his son. He did not quite manage it, judging from the yelp of pain from his wounded leg.

Meanwhile, Caroline stalked the fruitcake with her flashing blade, Mary thought, trying not to grin. That marble circle might open of its own accord, swallow the knife, and suck down Caroline's arm.

"Would you like some help?" called Mary. Caroline shook her head, took the knife in both hands, and began sawing.

Crack. The white surface splintered like an ice flow on a summer's day. Caroline dragged the knife down through the dark interior. The serrated edge reluctantly dug in. Soon crumbling slices, dark as black bog, emitted a fragrance of spices and sugar. The company began to sniff. Several guests looked appreciatively toward the table.

If Caroline helps in the kitchens, thought Mary, she must be able to cook. Perhaps she baked for this extraordinary tea party. "No," Anna had said, "labels." They bought everything in Oxford. In fact, Mary was wrong about this one cake.

"Somebody wanted fruitcake," said Caroline. She tried to smile. It made Mary sad seeing the strain around her mouth. Caroline put a big slice on a small plate. "It's turned out quite moist, the only cake we made here."

Mary raised her hand. Too late, she put it down.

Made here? By whom, she wondered, wishing it did not look so ... earthy. The smell reminded her of leaf mold in Falcon Wood, where magic mushrooms sprouted, reaching up for human fingers.

"Your cake, Miss Wandwalker."

Caroline sounded unnaturally bright. She handed Mary a porcelain plate too delicate for the almost black cake with great lumps of icing flaking off. Bright and desperate, thought Mary looking at Caroline.

"Do you know what's in the cake?" Mary enquired, trying not to sound alarmed. She poked at what could have been blackberries.

"We used molasses," broke in Helga. "Lady Anna decided we should cook for the tea, at least one item. Then we discovered we'd run out of brown sugar."

"Ah," said Mary. "Molasses, that would account for the color."

"Raw cane sugar," said Patrick loudly. "That's right, isn't it Miss Wandwalker? Molasses is the black syrup straight from the cane. In the olden days, Falconer House would have imported it from its slave plantations in Antigua."

The silence lasted painful seconds. A stick clattered to the stone floor beside Arthur.

"My family never owned slaves," he shouted. "That's a base lie. The Falconers were abolitionists."

Viktor's blue eyes gleamed. His lips seemed redder than ever. He's a vampire, Mary thought. And he smells blood.

"Well, actually, Pa ..." Simon held out a hand and Patrick went to take it. "Actually, that's not quite true. We've been doing a bit of digging at the London Library. It started out as one of Patrick's portrait projects."

Patrick took up the tale. "I've been wanting to paint alternative ancestral portraits for yonks," he said, quickly.

Arthur was turning purple. Mary was fascinated. She hadn't missed the significant look from Patrick. Something was going on, and she was to be a part of it. Painful family history dug up for a reason. Why now?

Patrick continued speaking to the Solokovs.

"My *Anne of Cleves* won an award you know. The National Portrait Gallery bought it."

"Although they haven't hung it yet," muttered Simon.

"My father's on the Board," returned Patrick through his teeth.

"So, sugar ...? Slaves and family portraits?" Caroline sounded hoarse. Viktor and Anna glared at her. "Sorry, Sir Viktor ... I was just going."

"Stay," Anna commanded. Caroline dropped into a chair. Mary could see that Viktor wanted to object. She decided to intervene.

"How very kind of Mrs. Jones to help serve tea," interrupted Mary. "You were saying, Patrick. You found something in the London Library about slaves and the Falconers?"

All heads swiveled back to Patrick. Mary noticed that the students, including Johann and Helga, were riveted by the drama. Family disunion among the Falconers reassured them. Mary raised her eyebrows. Patrick hesitated. Sitting on the arm of Simon's chair, he poked his husband with his elbow.

"Well, Pa, it's like this." Simon shifted. There was a wild energy about him, Mary decided. What dirty secrets did he have to horrify Arthur? Simon was about to let it all out.

"Those Falconer abolitionists you spoke of in the late 18th century, Sir Robert and Lady Elizabeth, they're not mentioned anywhere in the anti-slavery history. No protests in Parliament, no subscriptions to abolitionist newsletters, not a single petition, nada. Family fiction, Papa."

He leaned back, hands curled into fists. Arthur might have been a target on a shooting range.

Sir Arthur opened his mouth, then closed it.

"Also," began Patrick. "There is the matter of the Lucy Estate Trust."

Arthur's hand on the teacup trembled.

"And that is?" queried Mary. She sensed that her role was to keep the conversation going. Or at least not let it collapse into a shouting match between father and son. Why hadn't Simon and Patrick confided their plan to her? There was something about this terrible history that they wanted out in the open, or at least before the Solokovs and the students.

"We found a consortium," replied Patrick. "Happened a lot in the West Indies when families wanted to conceal ownership of slave plantations. The Lucy Estate was owned by six families in the 18th century. James and Robert Falconer signed the tax deeds. At its height it had 350 adult slaves, of whom 127 were women. Thirty-seven babies were born in one year; 19 survived into the next."

Mary's molasses cake sat on the coffee table in front of her. She pushed it away.

"I suppose you will include the slaves in the portraits, Patrick? That would be quite something."

To her surprise, Anna appeared utterly absorbed. Caroline stole glances at her set profile.

Patrick sighed. "My portraits will be different. I don't do realistic heads like everyone expects. Nor did those 18th-century artists." He waved in the direction of the older paintings in the lobby. "Portrait painters then did what my father does, more flattery than realism."

Patrick carefully faced away from Mike McCarthy's new painting of Viktor Solokov.

"You see, Miss Wandwalker, I want to find a way of doing portraits to uncover what has been hidden away. Just think, those Falconer men visited the West Indies. They probably had more children than they realized. I want to paint the lost Falconers."

Mary blinked. Simon looked shocked. Clearly the thought that slave owners fathered sons and daughters had not come home. Home to Simon meant Falconer House, where plantation slaves, Falconers or not, never set foot.

Mary dared not look at Arthur. The electricity in the room shifted. Viktor Solokov sweated and moved closer to his wife. Anna dodged away from him. She grabbed a seat next to Helga, keeping her head down. Caroline followed Anna with her eyes. Perhaps it was time to end this tea party, or whatever it is, thought Mary. As she was about to suggest leaving, Arthur stopped her.

"No, no, no," he shouted. "Wait a moment." Arthur staggered to his feet. He pointed at his stick, which had fallen onto the carpet. Johann, who had taken over the teapots, now dived for the stick. He handed it to Arthur in return for the patrician's nod.

"I do *not* believe this so-called research," Arthur bellowed at Simon and Patrick. "My family will not be betrayed." He struck the carpet with his stick. A tiny thump was all it managed. "If there is any truth in these scurrilous rumors," he shouted, "it will be in the family papers."

"And where are they?" asked Patrick. Mary suddenly saw what was happening. She stood up. For two pins, she'd walk out.

"Right here at Falconer House," said Arthur. "We need someone who is not a Falconer to research them. Someone with expertise in old documents."

"Allow me to volunteer." The words fell out of Mary's mouth like a rejected piece of cake. Drat, Mary. What are you doing?

"Most kind," said Arthur with a bow. Caroline and Anna turned to her with identical expressions, noted Mary, fascinated. They both wanted to say that she is a member of the Falconer family. Caroline was too sensitive of her feelings. Anna had her own reasons for her tight lips.

"I can have the files sent to you." Viktor's offer was too smooth.

"Not good enough," snapped Arthur. "I want to go home, boy. My leg's hurting something terrible."

Simon nodded and pulled himself upright. Patrick went over to the side table to retrieve their coats.

Arthur gave a theatrical sigh, then addressed Viktor Solokov. Mary could see them outside, squaring up, knight to knight, ancient Baron to dodgy political donor. Arthur's determination increased as his pain worsened. Mary guessed the agony in his leg provided energy, at least right now.

"No, can do Sir Viktor," gasped Arthur. "The Falconer family papers have been in a muddle for over a century. There could be crucial letters anywhere in this house. Miss Wandwalker will have to move in for a few days."

Mary gulped. She had not agreed to that. Nevertheless, she admired Arthur's technique.

"Naturally, it would be our pleasure to have Miss Wandwalker as our guest." Viktor's tone conveyed no pleasure at all. On the other hand, Mary could see no anger. He was simply calculating, she judged. Anna, on the other hand, had plenty of feelings.

"Another guest? Oh Viktor, as if I did not have enough to do," she stormed off.

"My wife is secretly delighted," said Viktor without expression.

"I can see it," retorted Mary. "Well, tonight I have a dinner engagement in Oxford. Perhaps I could join your party tomorrow, Sir Viktor, and see what I can achieve in a weekend?"

Viktor inclined his head. "Take one of my cards from the hall table as you leave," he instructed. "No need for you to make a trip back to London. My wife and the girls can supply you with what you require for your stay. Let us know what time you would like to arrive, and Johann will collect you in the limousine."

"We Falconers appreciate your hospitality," said Simon, with only a touch of irony. "Miss Wandwalker, we're eternally grateful. Moreover, you will be contributing to a major development in portrait art. Patrick's project is more than an act of reparation for us Falconers. It's of national importance in exposing a shameful history."

Mary saw Patrick flush. It's the first time I've seen him be grateful rather than the other way around, she noted.

Simon caught her eye and grinned. "Yes, Miss Wandwalker, time to get you into Oxford for your date with my ex-wife's husband, our Dr. Richard Bishop."

Mary caught an eyebrow twitch from Viktor at the name. The students were openly astonished that she had a date, except for Helga shooting her a knowing smile. Helga is Johann's twin, Mary recalled. They are both doing chemistry at the same college as Richard.

Hmm. I must ask him tonight about the Solokov protegees.

CHAPTER 19
FROM FALCONER HOUSE TO OXFORD

After formal goodbyes, Sir Viktor and Lady Anna Solokov began to withdraw.

"Tomorrow," mouthed Anna, maliciously, Mary thought. With Caroline hovering at the rear, the students escorted the visitors to Patrick's mud-stained vehicle.

Raining again, lamented Mary, as the car turned from the Falconer graveled drive to the road leading to Oxford. Headlights grazed bare hedgerows. I'll get soaked running into Sumer College. At this rate, I'm never going to look smart in front of Richard. Never mind, don't get distracted. It was time to speak her mind.

"Gentlemen, I want a word. You set me up. I knew nothing about the Falconers and slavery. You planned it all. Why didn't you tell me?"

"Miss Wandwalker, I'm shocked, shocked, you can think such a thing." Simon grinned at her. Patrick gave Mary a worried side glance in the mirror above the driver's seat.

"Mr. Jeffreys thought it better not to tell you. He said that someone like Anna, I say, Viktor, too, is always looking for collusion. Much better if you looked taken by surprise. He did not want you to appear as part of a gang."

Mary sniffed. She did not like to be underestimated. She leaned forward to address Sir Arthur.

"Are you feeling better, Sir Arthur? I have some aspirin."

"Ha, fooled you, did I, Miss Wandwalker? Leg's a lot better than I said. Can scarcely feel a thing." He gave a short bark of real laughter. "I'm not quite the old boot I pretended to be in there, you know. I may be the last closeted gay in England, but at school I wowed them in amateur dramatics. My Juliet won a prize."

"So, you don't resent Patrick's work including the Falconers and slaves?" Mary was genuinely curious.

"My dear, he and I cooked up the project last night. We wanted to make sure that unpleasant Viktor couldn't refuse. That's right, isn't it, Patrick?"

After getting a grunt in reply, Arthur continued. "You and Simon told Miss Wandwalker I was a dinosaur who did not know I was extinct. I've been playing that role for years. Keep my old tweed for the purpose. Just ask my poor wife."

He stopped. His voice changed. "Then my granddaughter, Perdita, died. Some things you can't hide from." He pulled out a handkerchief and blew his nose loudly. Silence pervaded the car until they joined the main road and the traffic entering Oxford.

Patrick coughed. "You know, Miss Wandwalker, staying at Falconer House gives you a wonderful opportunity to meet George on your own terms. You can both go for a walk on the grounds. Get together somewhere private."

"He's desperate to set something up," added Simon. He was scrolling on his phone and missed Mary's look of panic.

"Ah, yes, of course. I do want to meet him."

And it was true, to her inner delight. She longed to meet her son, despite the pain that surrounded any attempt to picture the idea. Maybe not on the estate where she had once planned to live with his father. Above the black splayed trees on either side of the road she could just make out the orange-colored horizon that was Oxford. Even in the dark and the rain, the shining city beckoned. There in Oxford, she would arrange to see George. A new beginning for herself and her son was over there. It existed. Events were driving her toward him.

Her mind went back to that evening at the cottage with Caroline Jones. Until Mary made her light the fire, the betrayed wife sat alone in the gloom. *Mrs. Jones is the only person who really respects my feelings*, Mary realized. She's not hidden things from me nor manipulated me to get what she wants. There was something comforting in that. Mary rested her head on the back of the seat. For the moment it was enough to observe this family she was, and was not, a part of.

Arthur started again. "You know, Patrick, I've decided. No trick this time. I really want you to do that portrait of slave-owning Falconers. Paint the slaves and add those incriminating documents, whatever you want."

Patrick froze and almost missed the turn to the highway. Simon leaned forward and clapped him on the shoulder. Arthur continued. "I know we thought it up as a ruse, but it feels right, somehow. What with getting shot, and … and all that's been happening to you, Simon, it is time the Falconers faced their past."

He had been going to mention Perdita. Sitting behind him, Mary felt a tickle at the back of her head as her hair lifted. Arthur cleared his throat. "I'm a selfish old beast, spent my life is various sorts of hiding. None of that matters beside Perdita. I see her everywhere. Such a taking little thing. She loved visiting the Devon farm. I sat her on a tractor when she was 3 years old."

"That's enough, Pa," said Simon quietly. "Or we'll be a sideshow of weeping queens. Saving Miss Wandwalker, of course."

The car was too quiet. "Perdita sounds … nice," ventured Mary.

"Ha." Simon gave a bitter shout. "Nice? Nice? Perdita's wasn't nice. She was stroppy and funny, silent when we wanted her to talk, wouldn't stop chatting when it was time for bed. She was shy in company, watched out of those big violet eyes. She used to steal pages from Patrick's sketch pads instead of using her own…"

"She'd snaffle my brushes when I brought them back to wash," mused Patrick. "She was enchanting."

"She also wrote beautiful thank-you letters," said Arthur. "Only thing negative she ever said about her life was that she didn't like her mother's political ... what do ye call 'em, soirees, that's it. Hated having to be polite to a bunch of MPs and businessmen. It was always men with Belinda bloody Choudhry. Don't blame Perdita for trying to bunk off."

"Yeah, she refused to wear a sari and appear as the dutiful daughter," agreed Simon. "I backed her up, of course."

"She was in that beautiful purple sari the last time I saw her," said Arthur.

"That was for you, Pa," said Simon, gently. "She wore it for your birthday because you said purple was your favorite color for her. Darling Perdy spent the money you sent on that shimmering silk."

There was a choking sound from Arthur.

"You all miss her," said Mary. Simon opened his mouth. He's going to say "unbearably," thought Mary. He didn't. Mary had a stab of old pain, pain about David. She closed her lips tight. Would she ever feel this way about George? Did she? No, she did not know him, another pain altogether.

"You didn't used to be this, um, enlightened, Dad. I remember ..." Simon tailed off then shook his head. Guess he doesn't want to spoil this good moment, thought Mary.

"Didn't have a grandchild killed before. End of the line. All that's left is how the Falconers will be remembered. I can see how that's going. At least let's go down in a blaze of honesty."

Mary watched from her front-seat mirror as Arthur frowned from under his bushy eyebrows. He spoke again.

"What I mean to say is that I won't let this family be buried under the weight of the past. For Perdita." He coughed, although Mary stayed silent. "That's right, Miss Wandwalker, for David, too."

"You're an inspiration, Arthur," said Patrick.

"I agree," said Mary. She caught a nod from the old man. Simon removed his hand from Patrick's shoulder to glance at his father. His expression was curious, Mary thought. That's a start, isn't it? She wondered.

CHAPTER 20
DINNER IN SUMER COLLEGE

Two hours later Mary joined the faculty of Sumer College as they discarded sherry glasses and formed a line. She took the arm of Richard Bishop, splendid in his voluminous gown. As an Oxford graduate, she was obliged to wear one as well, and not just any gown. It had to be the correct signifier of her terminal degree. Luckily, Richard had a spare MA gown, complete with scarlet hood, in his rooms.

The centuries-old formality of processing from the Senior Common Room through the quad exposed the faculty, or Fellows, to more rain than their undergraduates. These junior members, as they were known, ran for it. Some of them pulled arms through their scrappy gowns on the hall's steps. Laughing and chatting, they rushed ahead of the stately procession to be on their benches before the clock finished striking 7 p.m.

"Yes, these traditions are rather silly, Miss Wandwalker."

"I said nothing."

"You were thinking it," returned Richard grinning as they reached the raised platform where the Fellows dined. He helped her pull out a huge chair of carved oak. No cushions; tradition, not comfort, was what Oxford did, she reflected. A newer college like Sumer simply purchased antique furniture to hide their status as upstarts from the 19th century.

In rows below her, the undergraduates were flapping their short gowns, resembling starlings on a line, thought Mary. They twittered on their phones and to each other, sexes indistinguishable.

"How are you, Richard?" said Mary. There was a warmth in her voice that she would rather not examine. Surely, he could not be involved with the psilocybin ring.

"Inconsolable."

Mary stared at him. He explained.

"You see, Mary, Perdita was only 8 months old when Belinda and I married. The three of us were a family."

Startled by his rapid switch into deep emotion, she touched his arm, about to speak when they heard a banging. Everyone got to their feet. The wooden mallet ceased. Silence descended. A student with cornrow braids popped her head over the lectern to read the Latin grace. Before she had finished, college servants approached with the meal, and faculty gossip flowed. Talking privately had to wait.

After a meal of smoked salmon, cassoulet, and strawberry mousse, there was the return slow march to the Senior Common Room, in colder rain. The students had long since departed. Their repast of packet soup, tough chicken and raspberry jelly did not encourage lingering. It brought back memories, thought Mary, spying on the nearest table of huge young men, the College rowing crew, no doubt.

Richard whispered into Mary's ear as they left the Hall. She nodded, and they ducked through a doorway into the next quad and Dr. Richard Bishop's rooms. These consisted of a study where he could teach small groups of students and a bedroom beyond. Mary looked away from the bedroom door. Several suitcases near it confirmed his status as "separated" from Belinda Choudhry.

Without speaking, Richard produced an excellent college Port. Mary felt dangerously comfortable after all that food. "What the hell.?" she thought, accepting a glass. I *like* Port, unlike poor Perdita. Mary continued to ponder Richard's earlier reaction. Claiming to be "inconsolable" was drawing a line in the sand. Was she supposed to console him, or did it amount to a command to "keep away" from his intimate concerns?

DINNER IN SUMER COLLEGE

Making small talk in the dining hall had been easier than she'd feared. She'd forgotten what a charming host Richard could be. Such was the clamor in the dining hall that she'd even managed a "research" question or two. Richard agreed to check through his records for older contacts in the security services. This was Oxford, for God's sake. As in Sir Daniel's 1970s, you could not cross a quad at night without seeing multiple lighted windows. Most faculty spied on their peers. A few would be spying for their country.

Rain streamed on aging windows as Richard turned down the mock flames of his gas heater. These added a hint of the elemental to a room overlooking the Victorian brick quad. Not for Sumer the carved stone of older and wealthier colleges. Their original endowments advertised powerful patrons in church and state. No, founded for poor men to serve the Anglican Church in the mid-19th century, Sumer lacked the historical flowering in stone of Cardinal College. Even Mary's own institution began as a medieval residence hall.

Sharp as a diamond, Mary experienced a moment as her young self, waiting for David Falconer by the fishpond in Cardinal's first quad. So dazzling was the lawn that it took time to identify the young man walking toward her. There was his confident smile and the way he pulled at the tuft of his hair low on his forehead.

She swallowed and turned from the window with a smile. This would never do, here in the room of an ex-lover who kept glancing at her with those sad brown eyes.

Had Richard envied Perdita her berth in Cardinal College? Had he itched at her access to endowed cellars and superior, even luxurious, rooms? And yet, thought Mary, noting her surroundings with polite interest, Sumer's modest study suited him. He had the typical fellow's books piled on every wall, coffee table, and desk. Most provided wall décor in dull red or mint green. These were minus their dust jackets. The coffee table groaned under new volumes of history, probably review copies. A torn wrapper featured a dramatic photograph of men in top hats squaring up for a fight in what looked like the Houses of Parliament.

"Which one is your book?" she asked. Despite the enormous quantities of rich food compared to her usual diet, she merely felt mellow.

"Mary, I'm hurt you should ask that. One book, indeed." She looked up to his smiling eyes. The pain was elsewhere.

"Joking, Mary. I forget you're not one of us, despite a lifetime in that old Archive. No, don't look at me like that. Us academics publish or ... get asked politely to leave, the Oxford way. As well as this one where you helped," he indicated the torn cover. "My three others poke out from that shelf by my teaching chair. I might need to check a reference to impress a student."

Most probably a beautiful female with amazing hair, Mary thought, but did not say.

"Sorry," she muttered. "I did know publish or perish. Must be getting sleepy. I should head over to the college guest room." There was a tiny pause.

"No, you shouldn't. You should come to bed with me. For old times' sake, if you like."

Mary blinked. This was unexpected. Oh, all right, she said to her sterner self. I did wonder; maybe I even hoped. It has been a long time. The pause was getting longer. I won't be rushed, she told herself, swilling the remains of her Port around the glass. It is red as blood, she mused. It even has that purplish tinge that blood gets, or so I read in the Archives. Another painful subject. She touched the glass to her lips and swallowed the liquid that tasted of the sun shining on faraway hillsides in happier days. Richard's gaze began to heat up her face.

"I... Oh Mary, don't let's be alone tonight."

She could not turn to him, not see the raw need, not yet.

"Inconsolable," he'd said. Dead stepdaughter, Perdita, had grown up in Richard's house with Richard's nurturing. So, she'd been his baby, too, Mary belatedly realized. He was inconsolable. All evening that word weighed on her, leaden, tugging her back to the Falconer family. Neither the chattering of undergraduates, nor the fine wines and gourmet repast, could wipe away the inconsolability of Richard, or of herself.

He's asked her to go to bed with him. He deserved a reply. She was searching for a way to decline without closing the door on the future, when he stood up, holding out his hand. His expression hopeful, and yet she saw ruin in his face.

"I can't talk about her, you know."

"Belinda? Your wife?" Of course, it wasn't Belinda.

"Perdita. My little bird, I called her when she was a baby. When Belinda and I first got married. I can't be in the same room as Belinda now."

"I'm not Belinda."

Mary rose and put her hand in his. His lips were warm. Soon his kisses made her whole body sing. She felt his heat inside her belly, yearned for him. He pulled her up to his chest. So long, it had been so long since she responded to a man's desire. They laced fingers and ran to the bedroom like teenagers. He nuzzled her neck, while unzipping her dress. Mary's back warmed to his touch despite the chill in the tiny room.

When he tossed her last garments to the floor, she pulled him down on top of her. He wasn't David, no one could be. Yet it came back, firing her thighs, how good she and Richard were together. Too long, those years apart, she knew now.

Her hands knew how to caress in that special way he liked. Her aloneness burned into smoke that dissipated in his scent, his touch. His lips and teeth made a map of her navel, her entrances. It was as if they had been practicing. Or waiting, she thought. As if my body has been waiting for him. For the inconsolable one.

CHAPTER 21
AFTER LOVE

At the sound of knocking Mary opened her eyes to diffuse daylight shining through too thin curtains. She closed them again. Must be dreaming. This was not her bedroom. It was too cramped, and the sheets she was wrapped in were old: She could smell the too hot iron. At least the banging was not close. Could be the door to the next room. Dreams are peculiar.

The knocking stopped. Mary sat up. *Owww*! She put her throbbing head back on the pillow, very slowly. Last night began to intrude with the daylight. Too much wine, too much food. Too much ... Richard. Mary's eyelids had weights on them. She forced her eyes open on the name: Richard, lovemaking, last night. The tiny bedroom was barely larger than the single bed. She was alone in it. He's gone. Thank goodness, Mary thought. Now to get out of here.

Discovering her clothes scrunched up and dusty under the bed, she shook them and sneezed. Dressing in a hurry, she was searching for her second shoe when she heard a rattling from the next room. After footsteps came a tapping. A dark head with cold-flushed cheeks appeared around the door.

"Good, you're awake," said Richard, not looking directly at her. "Earlier I couldn't rouse you. That's when I went out to get croissants and coffee for you. Just going to put the kettle on for my tea."

He disappeared. Oh dear, thought Mary. He's awkward about last night. I'm too old for this. She grabbed the shoe from behind her handbag and checked her hair in the tiny mirror. Fortunately, her gray bob achieved neatness with a few firm finger combs. She'd never wanted a cut that required a fuss each morning. Now to deal with the man.

"Richard," she said to his back, as he bashed his teabag with a spoon. "Richard, don't worry. Last night was just ... nice. I know you're still married. Why don't I take this coffee and leave you to begin your day." It wasn't a question. It was an exit line.

"No. Don't go. Please. I want to talk. About us."

Richard's voice was too loud, his words too urgent. Mary could feel his tension snaking across the faded carpet to wrap around her feet. To hold her in place. Sitting down with a bump, she reached for her coffee, took off the plastic lid and blew on it. *Coffee please now*, she thought. *Go to drinking temperature — fast.* A carton appeared on the table in front of her knees.

"Milk. To cool your coffee."

"Th ...thanks." She sloshed in the milk, then hunched over the coffee.

"About my marriage," he began.

"You don't have to explain anything to me."

"I want to. You see, I don't want last night to be the end. I want it to be a fresh start."

Mary's hand wobbled dangerously. Coffee dripped onto her fingers, and a few drops found her skirt. She tutted. Coffee stains, she knew. After a sustaining gulp, she returned the paper cup to the table and reached for the warm croissant. Richard had found a tea plate and balanced it on a pile of books. Mary did not actually like croissants, preferring the yeastiness of real bread. Playing for time, she picked up the pastry and began to nibble.

"I am sorry this is so ...confusing," Richard continued. "I actually ran into Belinda at that Falconer House party. She'd heard about you being there. Of course, she remembered you. I tried not revealing your name when I told her about our ...

relationship, years ago. But, well, you don't know how insistent she can be."

Richard eased himself into the only space on the sofa that had neither papers nor books. He picked up the paper bag with the remaining croissant. Without looking up, Mary knew he was trying to get her to meet his eyes. However, his conversational gambit did not reassure.

"Belinda's been giving me a hard time. She even said she wants to talk to you. Every day she phones to berate me about something. You're just her latest excuse."

"Grief?" suggested Mary. "She must be devastated about Perdita." Belinda Choudhry MP's strident Conservative politics repelled Mary. Nevertheless, the image of a brilliant sari topped by a ravaged face was beginning to haunt her. At that Falconer House party Mary had ducked into the restroom rather than meet those tormented eyes.

"Oh yes, we are both … you see, Mary, we cannot talk to each other about our darling girl. Too terrified of blaming each other, I suppose."

He fiddled with the paper bag, leading up to something, Mary felt.

"About Belinda, you should know that grief, any kind of hurt really, with my … wife it goes to rage. Doesn't matter who is nearby. She lashes out. I feel sorry for her constituency workers. You know her father's that obscenely rich Raymond Choudhry. Lavished his attention on the crown prince, Belinda's little brother, Rajiv. Their mother died shortly after giving birth to her."

Richard sighed, then pulled out the pastry and munched absently. Crumbs fell from his fingers. He stared gloomily into space. Mary wanted to raise the subject of her leaving again. Too late, he was talking …

"You see, right from the start, Belinda tried to impress her dad. No go. He trained her to be a princess who would marry another fortune to feed Choudhry Enterprises. Raymond never forgave her for marrying Simon, a useless aristo who turned out to be gay. Worse still, she hooked me, a scholar with no money. Back then I wanted to give her the attention she craved. It worked for a while, at least until we lost Perdy."

He gave Mary a crooked smile. "I've always believed that her father's indifference explains why Belinda's so possessive."

My cue, thought Mary. "I suppose she's never felt secure, despite her family wealth."

She was intrigued, despite herself. She didn't want to talk about Belinda Choudhry-Bishop. Especially not this morning of all mornings. Yet she brought an ache Mary was honest enough to recognize. Loss is an odor that never entirely goes away.

Mary shook herself. Asking about money was a shortcut to family dynamics.

"Did Belinda's father disinherit her because of her marriages?"

Richard groaned. "Worse," he said with a small smile. "No, she is still in the will. What he did was halve the portion she would have on his death and convert the rest into an allowance to alleviate the dire poverty Belinda married into."

"Poverty, what poverty? She married Simon first," Mary exclaimed. "He's the heir …"

"To Falconer House, that's right, as well as the farm in Devon. Even though the Falconers are too strapped for cash to live in their grand old house, it's still worth a few million. Too bad there's no question of selling. Did you know the estate has a fiendish entail on heirs of the body? It means that Falconer House is a money pit. Counts as perpetual destitution to someone like Raymond Choudhry."

Richard's mouth twisted. "I think Belinda married me to stick it to her Dad after her divorce from Simon. My background is lower middle class. Age 14, I got one of those rare scholarships to a posh fee-paying school. That's where I met Simon and Belinda. Patrick too. Even then she was besotted with Simon."

"I never knew that about you." Mary was carefully neutral. There had been bitterness in his tones over Belinda and Simon that was troubling.

Richard ran his hands through his hair. "Dear Mary. Reliable, kind Miss Wandwalker, I promise you it's all over with me and Belinda. I've had enough of being the carer-spouse."

Mary could feel skepticism cooling her desire to take Richard's words at face value. He noticed. She saw strain lines deepen around his jaw.

"I adored Perdita," he said. "When she was little, I loved taking her to kindergarten and making her tea. My Oxford hours were more flexible than Bel's at the House of Commons."

Mary shivered. Even in the armchair in a warm study, it was as if he was speaking to a ghost child rising above a grave. A chill kissed the back of her neck.

Mary had only visited David Falconer's grave once. Every second in that churchyard now rushed back to Mary. Her nostrils burned with the scent of decaying flowers and cut grass. Of course, Perdita would have been buried in the family plot. In her mind she stood next to Richard facing two graves. David's would be overgrown, next to one freshly dug. Mary swallowed hard.

"Richard," she said.

He neither saw nor heard her. He was holding a dead girl and showing her to Mary.

"If only you and she had met. Perdy had Belinda's deep midnight hair, Simon's pale skin and those Falconer blue eyes. She was the happiest, most loving ..." Richard's voice dried. Mary waited.

At last Richard blinked several times. He brushed his eyes with one hand. Mary leaned forward as he lifted his forefinger to his neck, found the spot and scratched. Some old itch, probably. She glimpsed a scar. There must have been a scab, and before that, blood.

"Did you hurt yourself there on your neck?"

"Oh, it's nothing; an accident. I, er ... cut myself shaving. Well, to tell you the truth, it was when I heard about Perdy's death." He brought his eyes to meet Mary's.

"As I was saying, Perdy's death ended Belinda and me. She'll accept it eventually. You and me, we can, well, you know. Start afresh."

"Hm. Ah."

Mary was skeptical about Belinda ever letting Richard go. She did not intend to deliver her own opinion of the MP for Northwest Kensington to her husband, however estranged. There were already too many complicated feelings for one college room. Neither Richard nor she was ready for a relationship, Mary reflected. She took the last of the croissant and tore it in half. Frowning, she began to reduce the pastry to bullets.

Richard gave one of his sad smiles. "You and I ... well, it is not up to Belinda. We could be a family, you know."

At that remark, Mary stopped creating ammunition, and brushed her fingers clean. Drat, the coffee was finished. A family, he'd said. It was what she would have had with David. After losing him she'd made the Archive her home, a home characterized by very few people to please. Most of her family there took orders. She could even dismiss them. Mary believed herself a considerate boss. That was as good a family as any, surely?

Now she was ... no, she did not know what she was without the Archive. She had a vision of a man in a cottage doorway. George Jones is family, isn't he? No, I gave him up. She tried tasting those words in her mouth: George, family. Very strange, kind of bitter.

Richard was staring at her. Richard Bishop was the estranged husband of the mother of David's great-niece. Mary heard a thud and looked at her feet. One was kicking the wooden leg of the glass table. I've got to get out of here. Richard spoke to forestall her.

"I'm sorry, Mary. I see this is too fast for you. Last night was. ... Well, it was the first time I have been at peace for ... you won't believe how long."

"I might."

Her throat was dry. The warmth of a man on a cold night, it had been a long time since such comfort. Lovemaking had released her, however temporarily from fears, heavy-heartedness, and loss. For him, too, she realized. Don't throw this away like you usually do, Mary, she admonished herself.

It's not the same loss, a dissenting voice spoke inside. He's not the same as years ago. He has lost a child. You have a chance to get yours back. Mary was practiced at ignoring dissent, even the internal variety.

"Richard." She was full of purpose, even though she had no idea what to say, or what she wanted. "Richard, let's just … we can agree to…"

Bang, bang, bang. Knocking on the door again. Far too loud. Mary tensed.

CHAPTER 22
THOSE DAMN STUDENTS

Richard muttered an apology at Mary and got to his feet. "It'll be my Scout. He gives a quiet knock as he goes up the stairs to the top floor, then a loud one when he needs to get in to clean. Don't worry. He's used to me having company."

This early? Mary's eyebrows rose. What variety of company ate breakfast with a college tutor? Hadn't Simon, or Patrick, let something slip about graduate students? She and Richard would have to have a talk if they were to consider a real relationship. Right now, it was too soon. This morning she had to get to Falconer House to look for details about the 1970s Kestrel left by Sir Daniel. If there were any. She started a mental list of places where the family might have stored, or stuffed, documents.

"So, I'll, um, be going ..." she began through the hammering on the door. Richard turned to fling a confident smile just before pulling the door open. What was there made them both pause. Mary sat up ramrod straight. Richard grew an instant frown.

"Oh, Richard, brilliant. I've caught you before lectures," came a female breathy voice with a European accent. This was no college servant. Plus, Richard had said "he."

Oh, and weren't those tones rather familiar? This young woman came from Falconer House.

"Can't talk now, Helga. I'm rather busy," said Richard. Too late, he blocked Mary's view with his body. With his hands he tried to shut the door on the caller. To his evident dismay, a head with a blue stripe in her hair peeped under his arm. Forced to step aside, Richard allowed the girl to squeeze past and confront Mary. Helga wore ochre trousers. Her short duffle coat looked as if it came from a Thrift Store, it being too big for her and worn at the cuffs.

"Miss Wandwalker! So glad to meet you again. Darling Richard promised me a book after his espionage history lecture yesterday." She turned to the growling don. "*Spies and Poisons*, wasn't it?"

"Helga," said Mary, expressionlessly. "Good morning. I was not aware that you and Dr. Bishop were acquainted."

Richard distorted his face to signal to Mary. She gave him nothing in return. Crestfallen, he began running his hands over a bookcase, pulling out a few volumes. Mary might have laughed at the farcical situation had she not been, well, disappointed. It's nothing, she told herself as Helga put a hand on Richard's shoulder while he bent down to the bottom shelf. Too intimate for this to be mere student and teacher helpfulness, Mary concluded. How would Helga handle it?

"Oh, Richard and I go way back. He rather, how do you English say, 'took me under his wing,' when I first arrived six months ago."

"How very nice," said Mary. Her smile would curdle the carton of milk left out for Richard's tea.

Richard cleared his throat. "Helga is taking my special topics class on 'Scientific Innovations and Political History,'" he said. Now he held himself stiff. Clasped to his chest was a new hardback. Mary strained to decipher the title since the black lettering faded next to the glaring ruby berries, toadstools, and a purple veined tombstone. Hang on, surely, she spotted magic mushrooms?

Richard's grin was sickly as he held the book out to Helga. "Here it is, *Spies Become Scientists: Poisons and Revenge 1890-1990*, as in my lecture. You can return it to my mailbox with your paper."

The look he gave the young woman was toxic, thought Mary. Taking the book, Helga made no move. She continued to gaze at him, expectantly.

"Time to leave, Helga. Miss Wandwalker and I were in the middle of something."

Mary stood up with a residue of sardonic humor. Too ridiculous, she thought — until she remembered the poisons book in Helga's hands.

Helga refused to give ground. She had an ace to play.

"Oh no, Richard. Miss Wandwalker's coming with me. I've had a text from my brother. Johann's waiting with the limo at the College lodge. Miss Wandwalker's doing a project on the Falconers. Sir Viktor wants her to start this morning."

At the name Falconers, Richard Bishop's head jerked to Mary, eyes alight.

"A project? You didn't tell me." His tone was reproachful.

"A quick look for additions to Falconer history, not your sort," Mary replied. Not true, she reflected, given that Sir Daniel had been a spy. However, she no longer felt so trusting of Richard.

"Perhaps I could help? We could fix a time …"

"The Solokov limousine is parked on the 'no waiting' line. It will get a ticket if you …" Helga grabbed Mary by the wrist … "don't come at once."

Mary detached her wrist from Helga's too bony grip. "A ticket?" she said. She would play along because she no longer wanted to talk to Richard.

"Yeah, another parking ticket. Sir Viktor hates having to ring up the leader of the council to get the fines canceled. Come on, Miss Wandwalker. In 40 minutes, Sir Viktor needs the car to go to London. He's got a lunch at your Parliament."

Mary rose. She gave the room and the man a last flash of her gray eyes. "Another time, Dr. Bishop. Do hand me my things."

Defeated, Richard held out her bag. Noticing his sulking, Mary took her property with a grave expression. She stuck out an arm for her coat. It hung from the same door hook as

Richard's gown and took some disentangling. About to leave, there was a clang and a slosh. The opening door pushed Mary backward, so she bumped into Helga.

"*Oww*," they both exclaimed.

Mary stepped smartly aside for a stooped man with a long gray beard. He had eyes only for Richard.

"Do your room now, sir?"

"Oh, come in, one and all," snapped Richard. His bedroom door gave an unnecessary thud with him on the other side of it. The man turned to Mary, grinning broadly.

"You'll be wanting that coat out there, Ma'am. Cold and crisp it is. The best we can hope for in November. He gestured at the bedroom from which sounds of bedmaking could be heard.

"Appreciate Dr. Bishop making his own bed. A proper gentleman, he is. Not usually so ... well, never mind. It's not my place." He bent to the wastepaper basket.

Brittle, thought Mary. Richard never used to be brittle. She and Helga exchanged the briefest of glances before Viktor's protégé and Richard's led the way down to the quad.

CHAPTER 23
MARY AT FALCONER HOUSE

On the drive to Falconer House with Johann at the wheel and Helga beside her in the back, Mary inquired further about Viktor's sponsorship of students. Despite building work after Mary's time, she was aware, from appeals to alumni, that many Oxford students lodged outside their colleges. Rents in Oxford were notoriously steep. Combined with high fees, they hit applicants hard, particularly those from low-income families.

Russian oligarch Sir Viktor earned his knighthood from a grateful nation for assisting students from the poorer European Union countries students who otherwise could not afford Oxford. Mary suspected that his honor derived from an obscenely large donation to the Conservative Party. Nevertheless, Viktor paid fees, provided free board at Falconer house, and transport to and from Oxford City Center.

As the limo picked its way through growling Oxford traffic, Mary reflected that Viktor's setup was ideal for infiltrating drugs into the hands of richer undergraduates.

Neither breakfast nor lunch was formally served for the students at Falconer House, explained Helga with Johann nodding. He handled the vehicle like a maestro. The limo rapidly shook off Oxford traffic and purred into full power, like a lion after prey.

Meanwhile, Helga described how the students got a basic breakfast at Falconer House. Then a minivan took them into Oxford for the whole day. In the colleges they could find chocolate and toast in the Butteries, or informal kitchens. If flush with cash, Viktor's students would hit the assorted vegan sandwich shops or spicey cuisines of the cheaper Indian or Chinese restaurants. Cash, thought Mary, from what? Do they deal psilocybin for pocket money after handing over the real proceeds to the Kestrel?

Dinner, said Helga, was another matter. Mary sat up at her change in tone, almost reverence. For Viktor and Lady Anna embraced country house rituals neither had been born to. They insisted the students return by 6, dress smartly and gather in the marble lobby for drinks. Only the Solokovs sipped the fine wines aging in the cellar, Mary noted. The students got sodas in their glasses. Together they streamed into the formal dining room for at least three courses made — on good days, by cooks brought in from the village who sweated in the old kitchen. Would that include Caroline, Mary wondered? She and I need to talk.

On less fortunate days, Helga grouched, Anna pointed at a couple of the students at the minibus and announced they were to shop in Oxford. That evening they would cook and serve. Typically, gloomed Helga, her fellow students boiled the soup for hours, charred or undercooked a dead bird or four-legged animal. This flesh arrived with soggy lettuce, to be followed with aged ice cream chiseled from frosted blocks discovered in the freezer.

Helga went on to explain that over the long meal, Sir Viktor and Lady Anna would question, instruct, and learn about the students' Oxford education. They were keen to know who was who in the colleges and what went on in lecture halls and labs.

"Sounds like an interrogation," Mary risked.

"Oh no," said Helga.

"Oh yes," said her brother. "Sir Viktor has business in Oxford. We help."

The hairs on Mary's arms became needles that pricked. Was this it?

"Johann, don't," hissed Helga.

"Don't what," said Mary, trying to sound unconcerned.

"Nothing," returned Helga. "Just deliveries we do for Sir Viktor at the university. Saves on postage. He prefers we don't talk about it."

I'll bet, thought Mary. Could be Johann and Helga are the ones peddling 'shrooms and psilocybin to students. Perdita didn't do drugs, so why use psilocybin on her?

Johann pressed his lips together. He gave his twin a fierce glance. Johann and I are going to get friendly, Mary vowed.

Afterward, Mary referred to that the first evening at Falconer House as the lull before the storm. With Sir Viktor away in London, Anna appeared distracted. It was a lucky night, Helga whispered. Chicken casserole arrived spiced the French way, with wine and herbs. Before came the starter so old-fashioned it was positively a relic: avocado prawns. Instantly, Mary was transported back to her own student days when tiny shrimp, gray at the edges, swam in pink salad cream plonked in hard green fruit. Today, ripe avocados melted on the tongue, the prawns luscious with juice and flavor.

When a lemon pudding was announced, Mary leaned back to compliment the woman handing out the dessert in glass chalices. It was Caroline. She ignored Mary's attempt to catch her eye. Anna watched Caroline's movements like a cat about to pounce. Something's going on with those two, thought Mary, not for the first time. Something is going on *tonight*.

"Did you want to begin your research after dinner, Miss Wandwalker?" It was Helga. It occurred to Mary that this young woman had hung around her all day. Was Helga spying on her?

"Making a start would be an excellent idea," said Mary, fighting inertia from the rich food. Her mission was to find something on the 1970s Kestrel. Get it, then get out of here, she hoped. Then I will have space to meet George. *That* subject is not for the table, she told herself sternly. Not with George's wife and mistress glowering at each other.

It would be a better idea to claim some territory. "Perhaps I could begin with Sir Daniel's old study. If it is not being used, of course."

"You may begin tonight," intervened Anna. Her gracious permission had a sting in its tail. "Fortunately, you won't need to search the house, Miss Wandwalker. As soon as Sir Viktor took on the tenancy, the students gathered the remaining Falconer family papers and put them in boxes. These are stored in the attic."

Mary's jaw dropped. Anna leaned forward, breathing garlic with pure malice, Mary decided.

"Far too dangerous for you, at your age, to crawl all over the attics. What with the stepladder cracked on two treads and the floorboards loose. Viktor had the boys bring everything down and placed in the bedroom next to yours. You won't bother him or the students while you are here." She smirked.

No wandering about, no chats in corridors with these strange young people, Mary realized. She ground her teeth. "How, how ... thoughtful of Sir Viktor. Of course, I do not want to interfere with anyone's studies. However, I would get on faster — and thereby leave sooner — if one of you young people could assist. Johann, perhaps?"

"Out of the question. Sir Viktor has forbidden us to get involved with anything to do with the Falconer family."

Mary was fascinated that the emphatic refusal came from Helga and not Anna, who was shooting daggers at the young woman. Was Helga more of a confidante to Viktor? Was she watching his wife for him? It struck her that there were so many relationships that suggested a past, a twisted past. Could Helga and Viktor know about George?

"How very curious, Helga" she observed. "That Sir Viktor has issued orders about you students keeping away from the Falconers with regards to my invitation. After all, I am merely seeking old letters and pamphlets from centuries ago. Why such sensitivity about the slave trade?"

There was a clatter from the sideboard where Caroline and another woman were piling plates and scraping uneaten food into a dish. Caroline knelt to recover a handful of dirty knives she had dropped. Mary half rose to help, then noticed the blank faces at the table. She sat back down. Tension soaked into her neck. She could not find the source.

Anna scowled at her plate. Helga and Johann sat very tall, lifting food to their mouths almost in tandem. The other students bent over their pudding, shoveling it in with speed and lack of delicacy absent for the earlier courses.

Was it something I said? Mary wanted to drop in innocently. She decided to keep quiet. Yes, there really is something very odd here. She suspected that, whatever the sensitivities of the Solokov household, it concerned the Falconers. Back to Perdita's death, Mary thought, deciding not to finish the very solid pudding. I wonder if Perdita ever met Anna. That's a subject I can try with the lady of the house, if I can get her alone.

So thick was the table's silence that Mary heard Caroline piling dirty dishes on a sideboard near the door. Mary risked a glance across the room. Caroline had been waiting for it, because the flash of her green eyes was like a tiny explosion. The door swung behind the woman disappearing with her load.

Ah, Caroline wanted to talk, did she? It would have to wait. Mary would not follow her to the kitchen tonight. Her son could be there. George might be waiting for Anna or trying to square things with his wife. Caroline's marital problems could wait. In a day or two, Mary promised, she'd see her son.

Later, Mary tried to forget ignoring Caroline's mute appeal. She tried to expunge Caroline's urgency from her memory's archives. She wanted to lock it in the darkness of her inner tunnels, with their uncatalogued boxes of lost chances. May the gods of her ancient name let her forget that she, Mary Wandwalker, concluded on the evening of November 13th, 2018, that the problem of George Jones could wait.

*****

After that uncongenial dinner, Mary took her troubled digestion to her bedroom on the third floor. She received one of the gracious bedrooms before the servants' quarters on the story above, presently occupied by the students. True to Viktor's instructions, in the identical room next door she found six dusty boxes, the sort used to transport crockery between houses. These sat on two trunks. Somewhat dismayingly, there was also an open wooden crate and an old cardboard box containing files with faded writing in several colors. Someone had been going through the Falconer material.

Mary sighed at the prior searching. Interesting that there's no attempt to hide it, she thought. It ties in with what I've been feeling — that sense of oddness. Not enough about these crimes is *being concealed.* Too many signals about Falconer House, surely. Wish I could talk to Mr. Jeffreys right now. Yet I know he'd just say that feelings are not evidence, as he did before. Evidence, if there is any, is in that mound of boxes.

She turned to the blatant attempt to drown her search in the minutiae of several centuries. I do hope, she thought, that once upon a time a lonely Falconer spinster did service to future researchers by weeding out grocery bills, lists of payments to servants long deceased, old menus, and suchlike.

It took the firing of muscles she did not know she had to pull apart each box. Two she tipped over onto the aged carpet. Dust bunnies leaped up. Mary Wandwalker sneezed. After using it on her nose, she rubbed her handkerchief on the offending boxes. She nearly choked. There, in faint pencil, appeared to be a rough estimate of the contents.

If Sir Viktor or his unfriendly wife had peeked around the door at that moment, they would have been startled at the grin spreading over Miss Wandwalker, down to her twitching toes and pushed up jumper sleeves. She could feel her archivist self-materializing in the thickening night. Darting next door for an extra sweater and her nail scissors, Mary blocked out uncanny echoes of dinner below.

Ascertaining the box most likely to date from Sir Daniel's time, she dug the scissors into the parcel tape and ripped it open. With growing excitement, she smelled mold and faint odors of ink. She, Mary Wandwalker, was going to find the truth about the Kestrel and the death of Perdita Falconer. Maybe she would even learn what really happened to David. If the link between the Kestrel of 1978 and the Kestrel who sold psilocybin in Oxford today could be found, she would find it.

Mary Wandwalker removed thin cardboard folders and scanned for dates. She began making neat piles, discounting the cold that began to squeeze her feet through her slippers. I'm an archivist in service of the dead, she said to herself. Here in Falconer House, I have my world back.

CHAPTER 24
IN SERVICE OF THE LIVING AND THE DEAD

That night Mary worked into the silent dark hours and slept late. No one woke her for breakfast. As on every weekday since the university term began in October, the students departed in their minibus to find sustenance as well as lectures and tutorials in the city. Anna disappeared into her own mysterious affairs.

When Mary woke, the huge house was silent. Among the gilded columns in the lobby, and the sardonic marble gods, Viktor's new portrait winked magisterially. Mary darted under its gaze to find the remains of a do-it-yourself breakfast in the big kitchen.

Although she had planned to return to the boxes with a second cup of coffee, Mary was drawn back into the hall and the portraits, struck by the contrast between the recently painted and extremely old. Darker than originally, the most historic paintings stank of ingrained grime. The Falconers had long economized on caring for their ancestors, she decided.

Only the new portrait of Viktor Solokov gleamed as if every brushstroke had received individual polish. Its odor of oil paint warred with wax furniture polish on the wooden side tables. Concluding that no clues resided on the walls, even to the bogus project of slaveholding Falconers, Mary started up the grand staircase. Sliding her hand along the wooden banister, in her other hand she balanced her mug, now half full.

She heard rain begin before the screaming started.

Coffee splashed down Mary's skirt. The cracking sound of a cup smashing came from below her slippered feet. At the same moment a gust of wind heavy with water hammered on the front door. The screaming, too, came from outside, Mary realized. Then, as suddenly as it had begun, it stopped.

Later, much later, Mary decided that time froze while her body forgot to function. Silence spread everywhere. It wrapped the drumming rain in a parcel. It made another for the drumming blood in Mary's head. She frowned. For some reason, she was going to go out in the rain. She noticed her indoor clothes. Where were her coat and shoes?

My outdoor shoes are where I kicked them off last night. I leapt into bed to escape the chill. The bedroom is up two floors and down one long corridor. Well, at least the screaming stopped.

About to climb, she was prevented by another sound from outside. Not screaming, she reflected. Rather someone is yelling. A woman outside is shouting and yelling. In this rain?

Mary stepped down to the lobby floor. She could see a trickle of water seeping under the front door onto the polished floor. This time the noise pierced her sense of urgency. It changed back to screaming. No, she thought, that's more like howling.

Mary found herself at the door tugging at the iron bolts. Slipping through, she gasped when a handful of cold water slapped her face from another onslaught of wind. Mary pulled wet hair from her eyes and glimpsed two figures in the middle distance. Her face froze to match her sodden clothes. Under a bare tree some distance from the house one person lay horizontal on the ground.

Mary ran. Icy November rain veered wildly with the wind. She should have found her shoes. She should have stopped for a coat, anyone's coat. At least her slippers had rubber soles. At least her wool sweater *real wool*, she thought, gave her a film of protection. Unfortunately, it also held water. Mary began to stumble, her legs feeling as if encased in lead.

Halfway across the lawn, she trod in a pool of muddy water. Her feet slid forward while the rest of her tumbled backward. Sprawled in the mud, no time for the pain in her rump to come and go. Nor would she sacrifice seconds calling for help. Behind her, the house was empty. It contained only generations of ghosts. Mary clawed herself upright and with precarious balance limped onward.

Long afterward she described for the police how scrambling toward his body seemed to last for hours. How she could barely see her destination because the standing figure kept moving. Or were there two of them? Or were they trees? The wind blew rain against her eyes. She heard it battering the house. Armored by her wool sweater, Mary ploughed on.

The screams drove her forward. Three people now. The two women remained upright, she realized. One in a long gray coat kept to the left of the tree and the figure beneath it. For the first time this morning she remembered that she did not carry her phone. One of the women must have one. If that man lying on the ground is hurt, she will have called for help. Mary shook as another wave of wind and rain hit her.

I will not fall over again, she said to herself. Now she saw the blood. The man lying on the ground had a pool of blood seeping from his chest. Mary dashed the rain from her eyes with a frozen hand. Was that a knife buried in the man's chest with the blood seeping up around it? Doesn't that mean he's alive? Although with the blade at that angle, it can't be for long.

Colors swam in the water coating Mary's vision. She rubbed her face, and with every shuttering breath, even before she could see his features, she knew her son, George, the son she had never met, was dead.

I never saw David in death. *This morning I kneel beside our dead son.* The blood that had gushed when the big knife had pierced his heart is mixed with rainwater. A pool of red water surrounds the beige jacket of the gardener, the undercover cop. He would have grown up here, Mary thought. *He would have been a son of the house, not some disguised odd-job man.*

She was aware of movement, of the other women close by. In black leggings and tight leather, Anna stopped screaming as soon as she recognized Mary. Now she darted to the woman in the gray coat and clawed at her like a mad crow. Both seemed to be yelling from behind a glass wall, because Mary could not hear anything. She had no intention of stopping the fight, but then Anna broke away, having found Caroline's phone. Something popped in Mary's ears because now she could follow the call.

"Where's the ambulance? We called 10 minutes ago. A stabbing at Falconer House. Yes, he's still breathing."

"What?"

Caroline dropped down near George's feet and felt his ankles by pulling down his socks. At the same time, Mary knelt and lifted his nearest arm, heavy as wet plaster. She touched his hand. Blue veins stood against white like the marble of his father's house. So cold. Was he really breathing?

"A pulse. He has a pulse," Caroline shouted. "George, darling. George, *stay with me.*"

On her knees she crawled around George until she faced Mary across his mutilated chest. Blood dribbled from where the blade disappeared into his jacket. Caroline reached for it. Instinctively Mary shot out her arm. She clamped her viselike hand on Caroline's wrist, stopping her exerting pressure on the knife. Anna yelled at Caroline.

"No, no. Leave it in. You'll kill him if you pull it out." She threw herself down behind Caroline and tugged at the belt of her coat. For a couple of seconds all three of them were locked around the stake driven in the dying man's chest. At last Mary made her voice cut through the sound of the rain.

"Let go, Anna. I've got her. Caroline, take your hand off the knife. Now. *Do as I say.*"

Mary's commands blazed. Anna and Caroline let go. Caroline sat back and looked at the blood on her hands. Drops of rain hardly penetrated the sticky residue, as if she had been mixing oil paint with her fingers. Anna scrambled to her feet. Mary noticed her long hair had soaked into clumps like rags.

She tossed the dark strands off her face.

"Ambulance coming. If you pull out the knife, he will bleed to death. Quick, tell me before the police come. Why did you do it, Caroline?"

Caroline did not move. "No, no," she murmured. She was curled beside George's middle, below the knife, not quite touching him. Mary could not peel her eyes from the knife. There was something about its wooden hilt. She had seen it before.

"It's the chef's knife," she said. "The one used to cut the cake at the tea party."

Stupid woman, she raged to herself. Who cares about where the knife comes from? I've never been so close to my son, and he is dying.

"Correct, Miss Wandwalker," came Anna's cruel clear voice. "It is the big chef's knife that Caroline brought in. None of us have seen it since that afternoon. I came out to meet George. We were going to run away together. *She* stabbed him. Caroline did this."

"George, George darling." Caroline stroked his cheek. Anna might have been the rain on the branches above. Mary raised her head to command Anna to give Caroline and George space. Anna ignored her. Caroline should be allowed these last moments, Mary thought. For surely his life was seeping away as the blood drained into the mud. *His life, my life* draining away. Even George's clothes, the patched jacket and mud-stained trousers, even they were sinking into the earth. Mary realized she was seeing her son for the first and last time.

"How long since you called the ambulance?" Mary fixed fierce gray eyes on Anna, now cupping her hands round the phone to keep off the rain. "It'll take 30 minutes from Oxford. Call them again. Call the police, the fire brigade. Call your bloody husband. Get someone here *now*." Mary was on fire. Anger charred her throat.

Without acknowledging either woman, Anna moved farther under the tree to make another call. Only then did she look over to Mary. "Twelve minutes," she said.

I'm going to scream, Mary said to herself. She wanted to shake the young woman in perfect health who was indifferent to the cold water pelting them. She staggered to her feet. No, too unsteady. Her slippers had no grip in the liquifying mud. Taking them off, her bare feet sank up to her ankles.

There was a thump and a squelch. Putting her hands out at the last moment, Mary landed inches from George's head. His plastered hair had almost melted, Mary thought.

His eyes opened. They were Mary's exact shade of gleaming gray.

CHAPTER 25
GEORGE AND MARY

A rook cawed in the skeletal tree above them.

"Hello, Mother," George said.

It was Anna, to Mary's surprise, who had helped her back down to a kneeling position so she could hear his last words. Blood trickled from the corner of his mouth. First, Mary heard the voice of another woman.

"George, there's an ambulance coming. Hold on, darling." That was Caroline. His lips flickered.

"Too late," he breathed. Pain whitened his face, his ghost forming. To Mary the sodden daylight darkened. Rain sounded louder on the branches overhead.

"No," she said. Was that to be her first word to her son? "No, George. You must wait. You must live. Who did this to you?"

He looked at her. "One golden day…" he began with enormous effort. No, no, said Mary silently. Don't say it. "Falconers … a trap, not a nest."

There was a long shuddering breath. Rain splashed on his cracked lips. His eyes, the mirror of Mary's own, remained on her.

"*Caroline,*" he said. And then, "*Anna.*"

And he was gone. Mary knew it. Her cold bones froze as his bloodless cheeks thinned to translucence. George's eyes remained open, but they were only bits of rain clouds. His body belonged to the earth.

Caroline's wail was primal, a crow before a storm.

"George, no, George. Come back, my love."

Mary was aware of Anna sitting down under the tree. A bleak current flowed from her to the lifeless body.

They stayed: three women surrounding a dead man.

Mary lost all sense of time. It could have been hours or minutes before she heard vehicles, sirens, shouts. Anna stood up and beckoned. Without moving, Mary glimpsed figures as tiny as mice begin to run. They grew into giants standing over them.

The next thing she knew she was swaying, rising above the bloodstained ground. They were lifting her. She smelled aftershave as they carried her through the rain, her toes occasionally hitting a protruding tree root.

"Sorry, Ma'am," came an anonymous mutter.

Why were they saying sorry to her. *George is dead. I didn't save him*, she wanted to howl, yet no sound emerged.

"Put her inside the ambulance. Another one's coming for the body."

A rough blanket prickled Mary's cold neck. A paramedic, a woman all in navy blue, began questioning her. Mary could not hear anything now. She had stepped outside her body. There it was sitting on the bed, streaked in mud, feet bleeding. The mouth moved; the uniformed woman nodded. How very strange.

The other woman replaced the wool blanket with a silver thermal one. Then she knelt to wipe the blood and earth from Mary's feet. With a jolt Mary Wandwalker sat up straighter. She was back in her body. Her feet hurt. She bent automatically to help ease the proffered soft booties over her frozen toes.

Warming was agony all over. When it reached deeper. ... No, she could not, *would not* remember his face. In the distance, harsh sounds cut into the rain until she recognized them as voices getting closer and closer.

"Must interview witnesses ... right now. Essential that ..."

"In shock, all three of them. Could be dangerous ..."

"Police surgeon on his way to examine the body ..."

"Hospital treatment. ... Not fit for questions today ..."

"Impeding a murder investigation. ...My authority ..."

"Sir Viktor insists his wife stays here at Falconer House. He will hire a nurse …"

"All three of them: hot baths and bed with a sedative. Nurse will be in situ before the surgeon leaves."

"Oh, very well. If you're calling the Chief Constable …"

*****

After being put into bed in her room in Falconer House, Mary slept for over 12 hours. She awoke at midnight. The sparsely furnished room blew cold on her head, dead cold. Without stopping, without a plan, Mary seized her heavy coat and darted next door to where the Falconer papers seemed to be waiting for her. For the next two hours she delved into box after box of files and scanned old letters for any trace of the Kestrel.

Never once did she pause to ask why finding the Kestrel would soften the stone in her chest. The discipline of years did not desert her. Meticulously, she gathered letters and diaries from the 1970s, making neat piles, then tearing into the material with a ferocious hunger that she had rarely experienced in the Archives.

After a while her eyes began to tire. Somewhere in the house a clock chimed twice. Frowning, Mary shut Lady Margaret's diary for 1977. There was something about David's mother's writing that bothered her. No Kestrel, though. With a grunt, she shook the spine. Nothing fell out. Still dissatisfied, Mary took the diary back to her bed. She fell asleep before she could open it again.

In the gray morning the police were everywhere.

CHAPTER 26
THE ACCUSED

The young man, whose stiff uniform had to be new, would not meet Mary's eyes. He clicked shut the library door that cut her off from the rest of Falconer House. Everyone was taking these formal interviews too seriously, Mary thought. She was ready to sign whatever they put before her. With her son dead, nothing else mattered.

There were three of them but only one in plain clothes.

"Chief Inspector Bert Reynolds, and I've heard all the jokes," announced the bald man. Not a tall man, his too white shirt strained to stay buttoned. Muscles rather than fat, perhaps an ex-boxer, Mary noted automatically.

Indicating a chair for Mary, a uniformed woman took her own chair while wiping her face free of expression. Her boss introduced her as "my Sergeant, er, Summers." In her 40s, Mary judged, the woman had strands of fading hair tucked behind ears and wore no makeup. Reynolds appeared to forget the name of young constable whom he waved to a seat in the corner "to take notes." Mary did not care.

Papers rustled, and various devices beeped. Mary ignored the transformation of the Falconer House Library. She refused to be bothered by the signs of careless occupation by the police investigation team. Half-eaten pizzas stained cardboard boxes, while chip wrappers and endless paper cups empty of coffee littered one end of the once book-strewn table.

Keeping her mouth tight, Mary perched at the clean end of the table with Reynolds opposite and the Sergeant at right angles. Next to Reynolds a tripod camera rose on spikes from floor to head height. Its lens felt like a microscope trained on Mary soul. Let it, she thought. I prefer the machine to their uncomprehending faces. Let me hand over everything I do not know to their computer archive. Then she, Mary Wandwalker, could dig a hole and crawl in.

A cough dragged her attention back to the man. His head moved as if he were about to open jaws to bite her. What was Reynolds's problem? Oh yes, he'd addressed her.

"Jokes? What jokes?" Her voice rattled as if it came from a tin.

The bald man stared. Puzzled, Mary looked down at her hands, only to find a tight knot. That was surely his beige raincoat she could see about to slide off a chair under the window. The uniformed young man leapt to rescue his superior's garb. Meanwhile, Reynolds alternately grunted at Mary and at a printout in his right hand.

"Sorry," he mumbled after a minute. "So, you're the victim's mother, are you?"

Mary jumped yet managed to swallow the denial. It took everything she had to make the nod. Never, never had she been a mother. Her lungs expanded and contracted with George's dying breath. It had been one day ago but would last forever.

Reynolds tapped his fingernails on the shiny table. Mary noted clean curves. Her nails had dirt from yesterday. Reynolds cleared his throat and spoke again, this time more slowly.

"We need you to speak up for the camera's microphone, Miss Wandwalker. Let me put it again. The stabbing victim is Detective Sergeant George Jones of the Metropolitan Police, seconded to undercover Drugs six weeks ago. You're his mother? Come on, it's a simple question."

"Mother?" Mary struggled with the syllables. "No. I mean, yes. I am his birth mother. That is, I was." Mary had entirely forgotten that George was a policeman. "George was on assignment, I remember now. Do you, did you, know him, Chief Inspector?"

"Different Force," he grunted. "We ran the Oxford inquiry into psilocybin while Jones did Falconer house. Protocol." Then he changed tactic.

"Did you kill George Jones, Miss Wandwalker? Did you give him the psilocybin that made him unable to stop the knife?"

"No." Almost a scream, as Mary thumped her fists on the table. Then she looked up.

"*Psilocybin?* Like Perdita Falconer? And that attempt on Simon?"

"Quite," said Reynolds, stony faced. "A pattern. Psilocybin and the Falconers. It's why we let Jones take this assignment."

"A local officer could be recognized," Mary said wearily. Her face ached. She tried shutting her eyes. No, that brought back the wet grass and his blood. She shivered.

Reynolds drummed his fingers on the table. How to trap this clever woman into unguarded speech? Did she not know she was a suspect? His female sergeant shifted in her chair. Reynolds tried again for visual clues about George Jones's birth mother.

He saw uncombed hair, a bleached face, storm-colored eyes he could not meet. He recalled the redacted files on Mary Wandwalker, sent by someone called Jeffreys: autodidact archivist, skilled in sensitive material, classified services to an (un)grateful nation, clean private life. Bloodless bureaucrat, Reynolds concluded. Perhaps too easy an assumption. The murder of a police officer could provoke that, he realized.

Although trained to question witnesses immediately, and as hard as they could bear, Reynolds had a secret, one he had no idea his whole squad was privy to. Rather than decades on the job stamping out his sensitivity, it increased it. Few knew of his sister who, bullied as a child, struggled with agoraphobia.

"Cup of tea for Miss Wandwalker," he directed, inevitably, at the woman Sergeant. She grimaced, nodded, and shut the door behind her with a noticeable bang. The young man in the corner smirked.

"Let's start again, Miss Wandwalker," said Reynolds. His gentler voice was pure South London. "Your son, George Jones. Our records stipulate he was adopted, so how well did you know him?"

Understanding the question did not mean she could answer it, Mary discovered. Through Caroline and Anna, she'd known George. But Reynolds did not want to hear that, did he? She searched through streams of water on the windows, rain so thick that it faded the colors of the park and trees.

"Ah, sir?"

"What is it, Rameses?"

Mary frowned. Odd name, although the boy did look a bit Egyptian.

"If you remember Mrs. Jones's statement, she told us about meeting Miss Wandwalker recently and alone. George Jones did not know they met. Mrs. Jones reached out to Miss Wandwalker because the victim was in danger."

"Give me your iPad, Ramses. Okay, I see. So, Mr. Jones had not formally contacted you, his birth mother? He'd used intermediaries such as this ... um Mr. Jeffreys, your boss ..."

"Former boss. My employment at the Archive was terminated." Mary felt herself on firm ground when it came to the Archive.

"I stand corrected. Former boss, and Mrs. Jones herself. Ah, here's the tea. Could do with a cup on a day like this. Thank you, DS Summers."

"Pleasure, sir."

She lied, Mary could tell. She took the proffered mug in one hand. She then required the other to steady it. The tea was strong, warm, and sweet. One out of three was good enough.

Reynolds drank thirstily from the second mug on the tray.

"Better. Nothing like a cuppa, eh Summers? Right, Miss Wandwalker, if you would be so good. What we need from you is an account of the last minutes of the victim's life. We'll save the family stuff for later. Begin from when you realized something was amiss."

Amiss, what a word for a murder.

"Someone shouted. Or screamed," she said, keeping her eyes on her tea. The mug trembled, so she returned it to the tray, then began again. "Yesterday morning I woke up. I heard rain. Then came ... the noise, so I went out."

"This would be about 9 a.m. Full daylight?"

"I didn't check the time."

"Was the victim alive when you arrived?"

"No. Yes ..."

"Which is it, Miss Wandwalker?" He held his patience lightly. She appreciated that.

"It seemed he was already ... gone. Caroline thought so too. Then Anna said he was breathing. She snatched Caroline's phone and asked about an ambulance."

"Did you recognize the knife?"

"No."

The answer was instinctual. And not true, Mary recalled. She had a strong resistance to correcting herself. Interesting, she thought. There was a pause while Reynolds scrolled on his iPad, before raising an eyebrow.

"Really, Miss Wandwalker? You did not remember the knife? The chef's knife with the distinctive handle and sharp serrated edge?" He read out from his screen. "Last used at a tea party only days previously, at which Miss Wandwalker was present," then looked up. "Lady Solokov told us that you correctly identified this knife at the scene."

Anna, Mary gritted her teeth, refusing to speak. The woman Sergeant leaned forward and made a note on a pad of paper. The young man rushed over to check the camera after Mary's silent reply. He waved his superior on.

"In her statement, Mrs. Jones said that her husband was having an affair with Lady Solokov. She added that you and she saw them together. Is this true?"

Mary nodded again.

"How would you describe that encounter?"

Mary grabbed the third full mug and swallowed the cool brown liquid in one mouthful. She choked. Something had to be gotten straight for Reynolds.

"Seeing George and Anna wasn't an encounter. Not for me. George and I ... never spoke to each other. He didn't know me."

You are lying, a voice said from inside. He looked over to Caroline and saw you. *He knew who you were.* Mary refused to let those words leave her mouth. It was too raw. Her whole throat ached. Mary looked up to see Reynolds scowling, so she hurried on.

"Yes, okay, Caroline, Mrs. Jones, and I saw Anna Solokov and George embracing. They kissed, with passion. A sexual relationship, no question."

Reynolds shook his head. "All right. So let's return to DS Jones's final moments. The other witnesses say he spoke. While they do not recall the same words, they do agree that he spoke directly to you, Miss Wandwalker. Now, think carefully before you answer. What were George Jones's final words?

Mary could smell the blood, the shock of her own eyes in the dying man. Rain dripped from her dangling clumps of hair onto his cheek. Before he died. What had been said as her son's spirit married the sodden earth?

"He said 'Mother' to me, and then 'Caroline,' and then 'Anna.' Or those names the other way around, I cannot be sure."

Mary closed her lips firmly on George's mention of Falconers, the nest and the trap. That's personal, she thought. I don't care that it's wrong to keep things from the police. That's mine, ours.

Reynolds leaned back in his chair. "Well, well, Miss Wandwalker. How fascinating."

In the lengthening silence, Mary forced herself to look at him. He's trying to appear inscrutable, she thought. In fact, he's puzzled about me, can't make out my feelings. Join the club, Chief Inspector.

"What do you mean?" She gave him the response he clearly expected.

"You are sure about those words from Jones, George Jones? Those exact words?"

"I am." She pressed her lips together. This man was not Mr. Jeffreys. He could not read her mind.

To forestall any more probing, Mary switched her attention away from Reynolds's intensity to the window behind, now silvered with rain. Having narrated the death of George, she felt calmer. George's utterance of the nest and the trap belonged to a bigger mystery she did not yet understand.

One day I will, she promised herself. She would stake her life that those last words from her son would be solved by her. They were steppingstones into … whatever the wind and the stars and the valiant trees held for her. Deliberately, she turned back to the camera.

"I am sure George named Caroline and Anna," she repeated to the mechanical eye.

Chief Inspector Reynolds grinned and banged a fist on the table. "You hear that Rameses, Summers? I knew they were lying, both of them."

"Well sir …" began Summers.

"No cautioning me, Sergeant. I am going to tell our victim's mother what his wife and mistress claimed were his dying words." Reynolds rubbed his hands. A wedding ring flashed in the rain-dim light.

"Sir." Rameses looked shocked. Summers sat up straighter, then leaned forward.

Mary sat up; her body tingled.

"I know what they said," she said. It shot through with the force of lightning. "They accused each other, didn't they? Caroline said that George identified Anna as the one who stabbed him. Anna said George named his wife as his killer. Those statements are not true. He accused neither. I was there."

Telling this literal truth felt good. Mary drew energy from it. She recognized the earthy scent of her intuition; she was going to come up with a plan.

"I'm inclined to believe you, Miss Wandwalker. Although none of you three ladies agree on Jones's last words, we are allowing Lady Anna and Mrs. Jones to remain at Falconer House for the present. Although you, Miss Wandwalker, must realize the other possibility."

"That I killed him?" replied Mary, baldly. "And he named me. Yes, I see that you might think that. Nonetheless, no one points a finger at me."

"Apart from yourself, Miss Wandwalker. Apart from yourself."

CHAPTER 27
AN ASSORTMENT OF RED HERRINGS

By late afternoon, Mary was sick of being inside Falconer House. With accusations lurking like land mines beneath any encounter, she longed for the anonymity of the oncoming night. For once, I really do need fresh air, Mary decided. Tugging back iron bolts on the front door, she put all her weight into flinging it open. The massive oak groaned across the marble floor. That sound is the Falconer ancestors affronted, thought Mary.

Facing outward into the last of the setting sun, she was startled to discover she was not alone. With his back to the house loomed the dark silhouette of a man holding a cigarette.

"Fucking Falconers," said the man, sucking in tobacco like a lapsed addict.

His voice was loud enough to tell Mary that he was speaking to whoever had opened the door. Mary stood nonplussed. His charcoal suit melded him to the dusk. The last police car was vanishing into the gloom, leaving the rosy glow of their brake lights taken up by the red tip in the man's fingers.

Red eyes, thought Mary. Too many red eyes. She could see no car. How the man had traveled to Falconer House, Mary could not guess. Unless, she thought, with a dawning horror, he's been on the grounds for hours, waiting for the police to depart. Recognizing his voice made her feel marginally safer.

"Fucking Falconers and their babies," he said more loudly.

Mary stepped backward into the brightly lit lobby. Where were Viktor and Anna to deal with unwanted visitors? Mary was about to close the door so she could find the Solokovs when she heard thumping from the stairs. It was followed by trainers bounding across the marble. Before she could step away, a muscular young person knocked Mary aside in her haste to get down the stone steps. She pulled at the man's arm so that he waved his cigarette wildly. Then she flung herself onto his chest.

"Richard, Richard, you've come. I knew you would." The cigarette bounced off the step. Mary stepped on it, then promised herself to take it to a trash bin later. For now, there was a situation.

Revealing, thought Mary, watching Richard Bishop first resist, then accept Helga's embrace. Noting her own feelings, Mary fought a savage impulse to slam the door on the couple. But they were too interesting to ignore in the circumstances of the murder. She caught sight of Richard spitting out a mouthful of hair. He freed a hand in a gesture to Mary.

"Mary Wandwalker. Thank God. Please don't go. It's you I came to see."

If Richard had not looked so strung out, desperate even, Mary would have crafted an acid remark about student-teacher relationships. Instead, she dismissed her desire to slap Helga. With her long hair loose in the rising wind, its blue streak made Helga look like a wild woman of the woods.

As if sensing Mary's disapproval, Helga pushed herself off Richard's chest. Yet she would not let him go, rather dragging him across the threshold. Pushing the door shut, she hopped from one foot to the other in front of Mary and red-faced Richard.

"Ah, um Helga," began Richard. There was no enthusiasm in his tone.

Helga shot a tear-stained scowl at Mary before taking the main stairs two at a time.

"She's incredibly fit," muttered Mary.

"She'll be all right," said Richard. "I've known her for a while. She ..."

"You don't have to explain," said Mary. "No, Richard, really. I'd rather you didn't. Not now. I'm too tired for this."

She paused. "Why are you here? I don't suppose you found a contact for me. Someone I could ask about the Secret Service of 40 years ago?"

"A contact? Oh, that's right. You are looking for a chatty spook. No, sorry Mary, it's been mad at college this week…"

"Never mind." Mary bit back her retort. *Yes, there's been a murder.*

"I love you, you know."

Mary closed her eyes. It wasn't true, at least not in the way he thought it was true. More importantly, it wasn't something she could handle right now.

"Go away, Richard. You're not involved here. There's been a death, a murder. You should leave."

"Two murders."

Mary stared at him.

"You forgot Perdita."

Richard choked, then continued speaking to the assembled Falconer portraits. "No bastard here remembers that I'm the father who brought her up. I'm the one who bathed her scraped knees and helped her do her homework." He shifted his gaze until it came to the new painting of Luca. He took a step back, looking revolted. Then he swiveled to Mary.

"God, Mary, I don't *know* why I'm here."

He wrung his hands. People actually do that, she thought. Richard cleared his throat.

"Sorry, Mary, of course I came … well, for you. And because George Jones's death has got to be connected to Perdita's. When the police said stay in the area, I realized I had to be at Perdita's true home. She loved this place. And now I find you here."

He held his hand out. She stared down at his palm, gold in the lobby's lamplight. Flickering images, like flash photography, erupted inside. She was a volcano shooting out scenes of the Falconer family, living and dead; scenes set *here.*

"Of course," she breathed.

"Mary? Are you okay?" He pulled his hand back.

MURDER ON FAMILY GROUNDS

Mary became brisk. "Perdita and George. Of course, the deaths are connected. Even though Perdita died in college, it's all about *here*, this house and grounds. Don't you see Richard, that the murders are about Falconer House and who inherits? Perdita was the heir. After her death George was in line if Simon has no more children."

Mary bowed her head. Too heavy, the volcano died in a pile of ash. What did she care about a patch of mud with a big cold house on it?

Richard put his hands in his suit pockets. "I'm confused by this inheritance stuff. It's true, the story's out on social media that George Jones was your son and David Falconer's."

"Social media?" Mary said, shocked.

He tried to smile. "Let's find somewhere better to talk. This lobby's a hellhole with all those staring Falconers. Wait for me in the library, and I'll bring you some hot tea. Used to make it for Perdita when I brought her over. I'll fetch my suitcase later. My car's on the other side of the old stables."

Twenty minutes later, in the Library, now mercifully vacated by the police and cleaned by the students, Mary stirred sugar into her tea. She never took sugar. Richard insisted she needed instant energy, and she had to agree.

The rush of sweetness reminded her of the Falconer involvement with sugar plantations. Damn, she was nowhere on the problem of the Falconers and slavery. Hang on, that's not a real project, is it? The slavery thing was a pretense so that I could search for the Kestrel file. Mary held her head and groaned. Never in the Archive was ground so treacherous.

The Archive is where you escaped from family, soil, and blood, came from her inner voice. Mary swallowed the rest of her tea, then looked up at the grizzled man watching her.

"Fucking Falconers and their babies?" she queried.

"Perdita," confirmed Richard with a bitter twist to his mouth. "She should have been my daughter, Perdita Bishop. But no, she was never allowed to take my name. Even when she wanted to at age 12. Then they started bringing her here, emphasizing she was a Falconer by blood. Blood, ha."

Mary shut her eyes. George's blood on the grass swam before her. She shuddered. Not noticing, Richard sputtered the last of his tea and slammed down the cup. Mary flinched at the rattle. Richard wasn't finished.

"And now, George, your son is dead. Like you said, Mary, it's got to be the same crime, the same killer. At least that's what I guessed when I heard Jones was another Falconer."

Those words beat Mary like a drum. George Jones was a Falconer. Her head throbbed. This drum began when she first heard his name back in London. She might be accustomed to the drumbeat but not the heartache it caused.

It occurred to her that she and Richard could be wrong. Yes, George might have been targeted because of the father he never knew; because he, like Perdita, was a Falconer. On the other hand, Anna and Caroline possessed more immediate motives. She recalled both women around the dead body. Looking at Richard, his body still warm from Helga's embrace, her attraction to him took her to the two women involved with George.

"George Jones is still my son." No, that was not what she planned to say.

Richard paused. He picked up his cup, saw it was empty, and replaced it on the tray, gently this time.

"I knew you'd had a child," he said gently. "Even before George came to see me a month ago. I wanted to bring it up when we met at Solokov's ghastly party."

Mary sat mute. Richard sighed. "Back when we were together, you used to talk in your sleep. You broke off with me when I said you'd whispered about a baby."

Mary stared at him. "That's not how I remember it. I withdrew from our ... relationship when I found out about your wife and Per ... young daughter. She was starting kindergarten."

Richard frowned. Looking pained, he brushed his hair back from his forehead.

"Forget the past," he said. "Today I learned that your son died here at Perdita's real home. She loved Falconer House. Well, to tell the truth she felt most for the grounds. 'My family grounds,' she called them. It broke her heart when the estate was rented out, and she could not wander the woods as she used to."

Richard stared at something behind Mary. She hoped it was the ghost of Perdita Falconer. Come home, Perdita, she said silently. With a sigh, Richard brought his focus back to Mary.

"That's right, Perdita was the heir to the whole estate. Your George too would have a claim. You've got to be right about this. Someone's after the Falconer inheritance."

Mary heard the words and something else. A resonance, an echo, as if the earth shivered and older memories emerged from hiding. Tugged back to that garden party in 1978, Mary saw the Falconer family grounds in brilliant colors. Among the roses and summer frocks, a young Arthur Falconer in that ghastly lime tweed frowned at Rosalind Forrest. She only had eyes for Sir Daniel.

Something's *growing,* Mary thought, about George ... and Perdita. Before she could dig further into the past, she was brought back to the present by Richard seizing her hand.

"Listen, Mary," he whispered.

A door banged, followed by a crash, then shouts and exclamations from the lobby. Mary could tell by the echoey quality of the marble floor.

"Sounds like visitors," said Richard standing up.

"Not for me, the Solokovs."

They went to look. On leaving the Library, the voices separated into men and women, then familiar tones. Mary could even make out the tap of a cane. Could that be Arthur? And a woman's chatter, her slight accent surviving her habit of addressing company as if she were on the campaign trail. No, it couldn't be ...

"Belinda," said Richard, stopping. He glanced back at the closed library door, then his shoulders sagged. Mary wanted to laugh. Her tired body couldn't.

AN ASSORTMENT OF RED HERRINGS

The high-pitched voice lost its accent as it gained volume. "But I know Richard's here. His car's parked by that old stable."

Mary and Richard briefly shut their eyes. Instead of waiting to be discovered, Mary decided that the encounter with Belinda Choudhry MP would be on her terms. Edging toward the lobby, she found that Richard had taken her arm.

That woman has batlike radar, thought Mary. She'd spotted his vehicle in the dark just as before, at the portrait party, she'd homed in on her estranged husband. At least Belinda was not alone in the lobby. Apart from Viktor and Anna, there were other arrivals, as well as students clattering down the stairs. They'd probably been primed to collect suitcases.

Even so, stepping boldly forward, Mary was momentarily dazzled by the wool and silk purple sari before noticing Belinda's frown. Naturally Mary was ignored by the MP. Falcon-eyed Belinda zoomed in on her prey. Mary found herself withdrawing her arm from Richard's.

"Darling Richard. Here to welcome me. And you brought your spinster friend, Miss Wandwalker. How nice." Belinda's acid could melt a hole in the marble floor.

Mary jutted her chin. Richard and his wife are not my concern, Mary told herself. She withdrew as Belinda enveloped Richard, who tried backing away. His efforts only succeeded in Belinda pushing him toward a wall of portraits and away from Mary.

"Bel, are you still wearing that stuff," protested Richard, coughing.

Mary too almost choked on Belinda's perfume, as substantial as the body wearing it. Behind Belinda, Simon and Patrick smiled awkwardly at Mary, while Arthur was being helped into a chair by Johann. Mary did a double take, for Arthur now wore tan slacks with a navy jacket. Not a harmonious combination, but better than that psychedelic tweed, she decided.

"Delighted to be your host."

Everyone turned toward the smooth tones of Viktor Solokov. He posed to one side of a wall lamp that threw dramatic shadows on his blue-black suit and sharp chin. Next to him, Anna wore a sheath dress of the same color, a starless midnight sky. She gazed past Mary, giving nothing away. Even Belinda went quiet for Viktor, keeping her hand locked on Richard's wrist as they both looked warily at their host. Viktor's smile was more truly a gloat, Mary thought.

"Welcome, Falconers, Bishops," he bowed ironically to Belinda, "and Mr. McCarthy," to Patrick. "Welcome to this unplanned reunion of the extended Falconer family. You are here by special request of Chief Inspector Reynolds of the Oxford Police."

Registering the implied accusation, Mary took in Viktor's relaxed posture, and the way his eyes ranged among his subjects. Checking that no one's escaped his grasp, Mary concluded. Viktor Solokov's air of triumph chilled her. Anna was playing the perfect consort, a shadow to her king.

"Viktor's in bed with the police," hissed Patrick in her ear. "Means we're all suspects."

"You don't say," Mary murmured back.

Get me out of here, was Mary's instinctive reaction. She too surveyed the lobby. How can I leave Simon and Patrick, Arthur too? No, she realized with a slight shock, the truth is I can't leave George. It doesn't matter that they zipped him up in a plastic bag and put him in a fridge in Oxford. He's *here* and he needs me.

"So good to see you again, Miss Wandwalker."

That was Arthur, to her right on the chair, his blue eyes more human than Viktor's. Muttering agreement came from Simon and Patrick, although they did not meet her eyes. I must talk to them alone, without the Solokovs, Mary thought, shifting discreetly to Patrick's side. It was not to be, at least not yet. With his shiny suit flapping like a cape, Viktor crossed the floor to stand too close to Simon, Patrick, Arthur, and herself.

"Miss Wandwalker," he oozed with mocking intimacy "How gracious so of you to help make the Falconers feel at home. Not necessary, I assure you. We will all be together at dinner. Anna procured special caterers for tonight. In fact, my sweet, shouldn't you ..."

He made a dismissive gesture with one white hand. Anna rushed away; to the kitchen, Mary assumed.

"Sir Viktor, surely a strange time for extra guests?" queried Mary, wanting to dent his unnerving self-assurance. "I don't see ..."

"Not strange at all," contradicted Viktor loudly. "We Solokovs are assisting the police with their inquiries," he continued. "And of course, he said with a sneer for Mary, "we support the *family* in their grief."

Mary pressed her lips together. He knows, she realized. He knows that George is a Falconer as well as my son. He probably knows about the affair with Anna too. The police will have told him because it gives Viktor a motive. Before Mary could reflect, Viktor spoke again, this time indicating the Falconers.

"As you see, Miss Wandwalker, we have invited Mr. Jones's family to join us. We include Mrs. Jones, whose health is delicate. Johann has gone to fetch her from the cottage. That means everyone connected to the murder victim," he paused to survey the assembly with malice, "will be available for police questioning in one place, and for the rest of the time ..." He stroked his silk sleeve to keep the uneasy group on tenterhooks. "The rest of the time will be an old-fashioned English house party."

Mary could not believe her ears. Viktor clapped his hands. Everybody jumped, except for Arthur who glowered from his chair. Viktor gave him an ironic bow.

"Having finished preparing your rooms, the students will see to the remaining luggage. Now, if you please."

From their tight gathering in a doorway, figures in jeans, sweatshirts and messy hair darted forward to the cases and bags heaped by the door. Viktor watched, unsmiling this time.

"Dinner will be in an hour and a half, preceded by drinks in the library."

At last Viktor strolled to a door and disappeared through it. Mary found that she had been holding her breath. So too had most of the arrivals, she realized.

Before the newer guests could speak and Richard could prise Belinda's right arm from his waist, there was an incongruously small knock on the front door. Patrick opened it to darkness and Caroline, in her old raincoat. She dragged in a roller suitcase behind her.

"I'm to stay here too," she said, looking around until she found Mary.

Mary tried to look reassuring. "It's a house party, he said," she directed at the Falconers. "Sir Viktor's holding a house party for the convenience of the police. It's like an old-fashioned mystery novel."

Arthur nodded, looking worried. "Never mind Solokov. George is, was, family," he muttered.

"We've got to get to the bottom of this," added Patrick.

Shrugging, Simon removed his coat with the other newcomers doing the same. Helga and another girl rushed over to take their garments. Belinda threw a gold scarf at Helga's blue striped head. Grumbling among themselves, the students ushered the visitors up the grand staircase.

Who really benefits? Mary wondered. Then she paused to focus on her feet. Uncarpeted, the hardwood steps gleamed with polish. Mary trod very carefully. House parties still occurred among the rich and famous, she knew. Was Viktor behind this instance of elite socializing? Or had the Oxfordshire Chief Constable made a call?

Mary's grim mood deepened as she searched for suitable attire for that evening. What really counts, she realized, is whether the survivors of Perdita Falconer and George Jones are safer together. Or this "house party" could be another chance to for a killer to show the Falconers as "accident-prone?"

CHAPTER 28
AN OLD-FASHIONED HOUSE PARTY

Waiting to descend for cocktails, Mary sat on her bed and reviewed her impressions of the house party one by one. Belinda Choudhry MP she knew least. As mother of the murdered Perdita, she was sure to be a volatile addition. Mary cast her mind back 30 minutes to the awkward business of the bedrooms. The incident occurred while the students escorted the new guests upstairs. Mary dawdled at the rear. Interested in family interactions without gravitational pull of the Solokovs, more pragmatically she was avoiding Belinda and Richard. Therefore, she slipped inside her own room as soon as she saw the couple pause on another threshold. She guessed they were staring at the one queen size bed. Keeping her door ajar, Mary waited.

"Sir Viktor is mistaken. My wife and I are separated," she heard Richard say to the young person directing them to their rooms. The student merely shrugged and closed the door on them. After the door clicked, Richard and Belinda's fierce whispers took mere seconds before turning to shouting.

Waving Patrick and Simon farther down the hall, the student, an androgynous figure with colorless curls, set off after them. Meanwhile, Mary dodged out of her room and loitered as close as she dared to catch some of what Richard and Belinda were saying.

"No Belinda, we're not sharing that bed."

Trust Richard to sound strained while at the top of his voice, Mary thought.

"Look at the size of it," Richard continued. "We're not living as husband and wife, remember."

A muffled reply could not be deciphered. From the to and fro she guessed that Richard continued to argue. It was obscurely comforting. Telling herself not to get distracted by the Bishops, Mary then crept down the corridor in search of the Falconers. After all, Simon had been married to Belinda too. Turning a corner, she was relieved to glimpse a tousled head. A clean-shaven Patrick had a similar idea.

"Pssst, Pssst, Mary. In here, quick before that student brings Arthur. He's going to find the stairs a challenge with that leg." He beckoned. Mary's reaction was instinctive.

"Thank goodness we can talk," she said, shutting the door carefully to minimize the telltale click. Patrick leant to kiss her cheek. From the bed, Simon pulled himself into a sitting position and gave her a halfhearted wave. Wearing old jeans and a white sweater with grubby cuffs, he looked tired and unhappy.

"Good to see you, Miss W. Did you bring any booze? Whisky preferably. I bet that Viktor stashes the good stuff for himself."

Seeing a shortage of armchairs, Mary took a corner of the bed and exchanged glances with Patrick before addressing Simon.

"You didn't really expect me to sneak a bottle upstairs, did you?"

Simon pouted.

"Si ..." began Patrick, then threw himself into the only armchair, pulling it into a triangle with Simon and Mary. "Si ... I do believe you're winding me up."

Simon grinned.

"I'm just over the moon you finally removed that monstrous growth on your chin. Doesn't he look sexy, Miss Wandwalker? And don't mind this alcoholic."

Patrick leaned over and patted Simon's hand. His face became serious as he scrutinized Mary.

"We're so very sorry about this latest murder. Ignore Simon's levity. It means nothing. We're torn up about George. You must be devastated. I know Arthur is. He said it brought the death of Perdita home to him like never before. The old coot really wanted to get to know him."

Mary gulped. *So did I,* she realized. *I wanted to get to know my son.*

Simon grabbed Patrick's arm and pulled him to the bed to kiss him, then addressed Mary. "I never know what to say," he said gruffly. "I spout out the first thing that comes. It's usually about booze. Or winding Patrick up. However, Miss Wandwalker ..." He slowed, and his face looked older. "We don't make the mistake of thinking that George's death doesn't mean as much to you as Perdita's does to us."

This time Mary swallowed. Her back hurt, unsupported on the bed and not only her back. Her eyes ached too. A good thing she never cried, or she ...

"This light is too bright," she heard herself say, then her hands clasped her face. Tears leaked from between her fingers. All she could see was a black hole into which everything: Falconer House, the dark outside, the people in this house, everything, fell.

A male arm steadied her shoulders. A cloth dabbed at the drops falling from her chin. Mary pulled away to see Simon looking helpless with tissues. His blue Falconer eyes shone with unshed tears. *He has David's bone structure,* Mary recalled, *George's too.*

Patrick removed his arm from Mary and slid off the bed where he had been on Mary's other side. The bright light from overhead had been replaced by a glow. Must be a lamp, she realized with a dreary automatic response. She remembered seeing George in the lamplight of the cottage, George with Anna.

Mary nodded at Simon, who passed her the box of tissues, then gave her space. She dried her cheeks. *Don't make noise,* she said to the howl deep inside. *Not in front of three other people* in the room. Wait a minute, three? Yes, it really was Caroline standing closer than Mary liked. When had she arrived?

Mary had barely exchanged words with Caroline and Anna since they had returned from Oxford Police Station in the same police vehicle. Now Caroline peered at her as if Mary were a ghost. Not friendly. Caroline began to draw away. Instinctively Mary expected a shout, an exclamation, something that would hurt. She was right.

"Did you kill him?" The words came from Caroline. Nobody breathed.

"No, Caroline," Mary croaked. Her throat tasted salty. "Did you?"

"No. How could I?" said Caroline. Her voice cracked.

Her skin turned muddy in the lamp's soft glow, her eyes a darker green. She had more to say.

"The police think you could have killed him. Then you pretended to discover him with us."

In theory, Mary understood she was a suspect. The confirmation hit hard. She tried to remember Caroline and Anna huddled around the body. Try as she might, no images surfaced. Who among them had an alibi for George's murder?

"Caroline, were you and Anna together? In the time before he died?" Mary had longed to question both. Until now they'd vanished every time Mary glimpsed a designer dress or an old cardigan.

"Together, Anna and me? Oh no," said Caroline after a beat. "George did not spend the previous night at the cottage, even though he'd promised to." She sighed. "The last thing he said to me was that he had a plan to rescue Anna."

Caroline stared past Mary at the windows, where the lamplight reflected gold despite the dark. She moved closer to the bed, hunching over, before nodding to Simon and Patrick. Both watched the women, giving no indication they wanted to talk.

Sighing, Caroline took the opposite corner of the bed to Mary. She cleared her throat and spoke in an even tone.

"I waited up for hours and hours. All I heard was an owl hunting and the scream of a fox. Then I fell asleep on the sofa. When I woke, the dawn was shining around the curtains. That's when I went to look for George. I thought I saw Anna in the mist, but I wasn't sure. Then I found him on the ground. I found him *first*."

Her anguish, fused with anger, was hard to hear. "She came, Anna. Then you, or you and her. I don't know which. I only remember George dying."

With an exhausted sigh, Caroline deflated, slumping forward until her hands were on her knees.

"You should lie down, Mrs. Jones," said Simon gently. "Join us for dinner later or, if you like, we'll get one of the students to bring you a tray. Where's your room. Patrick will …"

"Of course," said Patrick leaping to his feet. "Si needs a rest too, as he is still recovering from the psilocybin. Come on, Mrs. Jones, let me escort you to your bedroom like the old-fashioned gent Si should have married. Instead, he got me, a messy artist."

"You are gentleman enough for me, Mr. McCarthy," said Caroline with a small smile. "I've one of the old servant's rooms on the next floor, along with the students. Anna never forgets that I am 'staff' because I help in the kitchens."

"Did I hear my name?"

Mary gulped. How had that young woman managed to open the door so soundlessly? For her all the doors creaked and scraped. She looked at the handle suspiciously, then back at Anna in a scarlet kimono. There was a suspicion of a jerk of the head before Viktor loomed behind his wife. The door swung wide open.

"Quite a gathering I see?" His tone was unfriendly, his blue eyes frigid.

"We were just … comparing rooms," said Mary, getting up, "before coming down for drinks like you said." That man made her nervous. Surely, he's looking to unnerve the company.

"If I had known you all wanted to sleep together, Anna would arrange it. After all, sexual adventures are your forte, aren't they, my beloved? Especially on the Falconer estate."

Suddenly Anna had no expression, no color in her face. Even her unpainted lips appeared translucent. She froze, statue like, while her husband laughed and left. His footsteps, too, made no sound.

"Anna?" said Caroline. It was a question receiving no answer. The young woman ran off in the opposite direction to her husband. Mary wondered if she had somewhere she could sleep alone. Perhaps there was a spare bed upstairs among the students?

"Definitely time to gather downstairs," Mary said. "We have to find out what's going on here. It's not over."

CHAPTER 29
NIGHTTIME CONVERSATION

Blessedly uneventful, Mary concluded, about drinks in the library followed by dinner. Only in looking back later did she detect tremors that foreshadowed the horrors of that night. In the absence of easy conversation, stiff requests for this and that gave way to dropped spoons, forced smiles and inane remarks about the weather.

Simon even choked after trying to eat his apple pie in one gulp. Arthur snapped at him, while Patrick pounded between Simon's blades. Neither Caroline nor Anna appeared in the dining room. One look at Viktor, and Mary decided not to inquire. Tomorrow would be better for questions, she told herself.

Only a couple of the students at a time would dine with the houseguests, Viktor announced. The rest would serve meals, taking turns with kitchen duty. Whatever catering Viktor Solokov had summoned from Oxford, proved "satisfactory," he said, to eager agreement from Belinda. No one else commented about the bean soup, grilled salmon, and apple pie with vanilla ice cream. After coffee had been offered and declined, the guests muttered excuses and departed upstairs.

That was before Mary's sleep was interrupted. Having dodged Richard's attempts to get her alone, Mary retired to bed. She woke after a couple of hours, due to cold and an aching back from the hard mattress. Finding sleep elusive, she pulled her coat on top of the blankets. Creaks and groans came from the old radiators. Mary shivered. Then she heard tiny taps at her door.

"Who is it?" she hissed, sitting up in bed, then grabbing her coat as her shoulders felt the draught. She switched on the bedside light. At least she wouldn't be assaulted in the dark. The door opened an inch.

"It's me, Patrick. Sorry if I woke you, but Si can't sleep. He's worried about something we forgot to ask you earlier."

Mary swung her legs out of bed. Fortunately wool slippers awaited her feet. At least the carpet blocked the gaps between the old floorboards.

"Come in if you must." Drat, I forgot to lock the door, she thought.

Patrick entered in jeans and a striped pajamas top showing under an olive pullover. His tone was tentative. "You were awake, I hope, Miss Wandwalker?"

"Sort of," Mary grunted. "I keep seeing ... his face."

Patrick padded over to squeeze her arm. He took the one chair while she put all the pillows at her back so she could sit up in the bed. A massive rattle from the radiator produced identical rueful expressions.

"Glad we can talk," Patrick said. "It's about the Kestrel, of course. What happened to George means more reasons to find the drug-dealing bastard responsible for Perdy's death." Patrick looked pinched. He added, "Simon's got a bee in his bonnet about Kyrill Solokov. Can't forget the treacherous swine got away with killing his grandfather. He's wearing me out saying there must be something from the 1970s Kestrel we can use as leverage on Viktor."

Mary groaned. "Couldn't this wait ..."

"They used psilocybin on George. Tried to poison Simon in the pub. Si's raring to catch today's drug-dealing Kestrel before he harms anyone else. It's got to be Viktor Solokov. Like father like son, you know."

Mary privately agreed about Viktor Solokov as likely candidate for the Kestrel. Nevertheless, she wanted to send Patrick back to bed.

"Apart from the Solokovs being a family and Simon's buzzing headwear," said Mary tartly, "we have little to link Kyrill, the 1970s Kestrel, to the drug dealer Kestrel today. My words in Perdita's note are a connection, not evidence."

She heard herself echoing Mr. Jeffreys and grimaced. "Despite Viktor taunting us to believe bad of him, we've no proof he's our Kestrel." To stop Patrick rebutting, she held up her hand.

"All I'm saying is that jumping ahead of ourselves won't help." The archivist in her spoke firmly. "What we *do* know is that George was on the trail of the Kestrel, the drug dealer involved in Perdita's death. It makes sense that whoever hides behind that name killed George, or had him killed."

Patrick nodded soberly. "Have you had a chance to have a look for Sir Daniel's Kestrel papers? Did they let you into the old study?"

"Yes and no," said Mary. Ironically sleepiness crept in from her chilled extremities, now that she had company. Patrick, however, leaned forward, his mouth open. Mary struggled to continue.

"Yes, in that I've sorted through what they told me were a complete set of Sir Daniel's papers. No, nothing on the Kestrel, so far."

She paused, recalling her frustration. "And no, I did not get into the study, which Sir Viktor uses as his private office. They told me the Falconer papers got consigned to the attic. I arrived to discover they'd placed the boxes in the next room to mine."

Patrick sat up, frowning. Mary glanced longingly at the bed.

"No government files," she emphasized. She saw that Patrick was about to object.

"I've been reading a diary kept by Sir Daniel's wife, Lady Margaret. Unfortunately, it's mostly appointments and brief remarks. What I've not had time for is Sir Daniel's correspondence. His letters may contain clues to the Kestrel's identity."

"You have copies of his letters?" queried Patrick, eyes gleaming. He was not as disappointed as Mary had been expecting. "You see, Si and I have been talking ..."

"Don't forget this is before computers. Officials like Sir Daniel made carbon copies," explained the archivist. "Do you want to examine the letters yourself?"

"I'll help you, to be sure," Patrick said, smoothing down his wiry hair. "Si, too, of course. The thing is Mary, Arthur says that Sir Daniel put his ... his sensitive papers somewhere special. Si's convinced that Viktor doesn't know this hiding place. Sir Daniel referred to it as his spy safe."

A very tired Mary leaned back. "You didn't think to tell me this before."

"Sorry, Mary. You see, we didn't know about the spy safe before we talked to Arthur ..." Patrick cleared his throat. "Actually, it was the night after George died. Arthur hasn't had a chance to tell you how much the death upset him."

Patrick peered at Mary's taut features. What has Arthur got to do with my son hung between them. Patrick nodded in sympathy. He's not a Falconer either, thought Mary.

"The thing with Arthur," Patrick began. "Well, you've got to see it from his side. First, he discovers his long dead brother had a son. That's a shock because Arthur's mother, Lady Margaret, never mentioned your pregnancy."

He shot Mary a rueful smile. Mary remained stony-faced. Patrick cleared his throat. "You see, it takes Arthur time to get used to things. Hence, those awful tweeds he wears."

Patrick hurried on. "For example, he never came to our wedding, Si's and mine. Arthur flat out refused. I'm over it, but Si won't forgive him. As you can tell Arthur's never had much of a relationship with Si. I mean, you've seen them."

Mary tried a theatrical slump. If Patrick did not get to the point soon, she might begin snoring. Unfortunately, he was

NIGHTTIME CONVERSATION

staring at the blue roses wallpaper. She shuffled in her seat. It got him started.

"Perdita wrote to him, Arthur. She often tried to smooth things over between her dad and Arthur. It was about a week before she got poisoned. Arthur made a trip to Oxford to see her. After having lunch together, Perdita arranged for him to meet George over a cup of tea. 'So much of David,' he said to us."

"Patrick," said Mary, lacking patience. "Can we do this tomorrow? Or, if you must, skip to the highlights."

"Oh sorry, Miss Wandwalker. What it amounts to is that Simon and I, Arthur too, are desperate to find the Kestrel. Arthur thinks the spy safe is in the lobby, which I guess means behind one of the portraits. The idea was Sir Daniel would lock his secret stuff away before he removed his coat. Sensitive papers could be grabbed as he left the house. Arthur even has a key from the 1970s."

Mary ground her teeth, audibly, she hoped. If only she'd known about this when the house was empty and searchable. Patrick noticed her mood.

"The reason I'm bothering you is that with the house so full, we can only search at night. If you already have the Kestrel file, there's no need."

"Not located any Kestrel file," said Mary getting up. "Yet." She placed an unambiguous hand on the bedroom door. "Goodnight, Patrick. Happy hunting." She had no intention of divulging her own plans.

Despite her exhausted state, she set her alarm clock for 4 a.m., the time the household was most likely to be beyond disturbing. *I'll find that safe*, she told herself as she threw herself into the bed, this time keeping her winter coat on.

CHAPTER 30
STAIRCASE

Still dark, the mantlepiece clock showed 6:30 a.m. when distant shouting woke Mary. Picking up her alarm clock, she glared, then shook it in disgust. At 2:21 a.m. the battery had died. Some investigator I am, she thought. What time is it anyway? Further castigation was interrupted by noise. Was someone *crying*?

Her head cleared. A man calling for help. Sounds like he's shouting into a void. Did no one else hear the yelling? Familiar voice … *Simon Falconer*. Without stopping for slippers, Mary opened her bedroom door and ran toward the stairs. There she paused, looking down.

Cold toes told her where carpet met the polished wood of the stairs. Holding firmly to the balustrade, Mary ignored the shock to her bare feet and descended until she found a fair head below. Doors slamming behind her suggested others were stirring. It could be too late.

"Who's up there?" Simon shouted. A red face swam into Mary's view.

"It's me, Mary Wandwalker. What's the matter."

Simon bent over. "He's gone. He's gone," he wailed.

Mary froze, then continued. Had something happened to Arthur? She made herself continue down the stairs. Sitting on the bottom step, Simon Falconer sobbed.

"He's dead. He's dead," he kept repeating.

Kneeling beside the body, Simon had pulled Patrick's head onto his lap. From the neck down Patrick sprawled on the marble lobby floor, one leg bent under. Dropping to her knees, Mary put two fingers on Patrick's neck. Later she would remember her relief as her freezing fingers stopped being quite so cold. Simon moaned.

"Shut up, Simon."

Her fierceness came from that woman who had stood over her son's body.

After an agonizing minute, she felt a tiny pulse, Morse code from another country.

"No, he's not dead," she said. The Falconer House lobby swam into view around them.

Shocked, Simon stopped making noises. He stared at Mary, then put his hand on Patrick's neck. Mary became aware of Helga, followed by Richard a few steps above. Other students were assembling at the top of the stairs.

"Not dead? Yes, I feel it. Patrick darling, Patrick, wake up." Simon Falconer bent over to kiss Patrick on the lips.

"Oh, for goodness' sake, he's not Sleeping Beauty," said an irascible voice from across the lobby. "Leave him alone until the ambulance gets here."

"Pa ...," said Simon. Mary could see him firing up. Arthur Falconer approached banging his stick. His mud-colored dressing gown had to be another old relic, noted Mary.

"You called an ambulance?" Mary wanted confirmation.

"Of course," said Arthur. "Simon makes a drama into a crisis. I left my phone in the library, so went to fetch it."

There was a muttering on the stairs. Three students mutely held out phones with flashing images of ambulances and police cars en route. Helga, her hair in bunches, crept forward until Mary motioned her to give them room. Arthur was taking up plenty.

"Knew we needed medics the moment I was woken by that appalling noise. Son, did no one ever tell you not to move a man who might have broken his neck?"

Simon's flush went white. Mary saw rage and horror warring in him. "Miss Wandwalker," he whispered to Mary. "Have I ... have I ...?"

"I think his neck is fine," said Mary. She had no idea about Patrick's condition. Enough crimes of passion at Falconer House. Glancing at Arthur, she saw angry tears in his blue eyes. He wants a fight, she realized. He's spoiling for a row with Simon. All those pent-up frustrations have been building for years.

She felt Patrick's neck again.

"His pulse is stronger," she said firmly to Simon. He nodded shakily. "Stay just as you are, holding him," Mary said. "What's the ETA on the ambulance?"

No one replied. Mary looked up at Richard and Helga. They were holding hands. Not now, she said to herself, sternly. "Richard, your phone?"

Richard started. He must have been in a daze. "Oh, right, oh. I'll get my phone." He vanished up the stairs. Helga tried to follow. She gave up as Richard detached his hand and pushed through the crowd.

Mary motioned to the students to step past Simon to the main part of the lobby. Johann unbolted the front door and peered out then shook his head at Mary.

Where were Viktor and Anna? Mary wondered. There was a clatter as Arthur tried to work his phone with one hand and failed.

"I'll help you, Arthur," Mary called.

"Don't leave me," said Simon to her. "Please don't leave me until the ambulance comes." Simon's face had aged in the last few minutes. Even his fair hair, tousled from sleep, seemed to be fading. Under his scarlet dressing gown Mary could see his muscles straining to keep Patrick's head and torso still.

Arthur sank into one of the lobby's hard chairs. He spoke into his phone.

"Seven minutes. The ambulance knows the way," he said.

Because of George, Mary immediately thought.

"Because they were here for the corpse of my son," she said. Her eyes met Simon's and saw understanding there. She was surprised how good that felt. A hand descended to her shoulder and a stick appeared by her knees.

"I met David's son, Miss Wandwalker. I liked him." She would not look up at Arthur. Simon needed all her concentration.

"My son too," she managed. There was a pause.

"I'm sorry about ..."

Mary did not to know whether Arthur regretted his parents not responding to pregnant Mary or was expressing sympathy for George's death. The front door banged open. Mary, sitting on the floor with her back to it, knew it was Anna. She turned her head to see Anna Solokov in a man's jacket too shabby for Viktor. Narrowing her eyes at Mary, she addressed the students as if there was no injured man in her lobby.

"Why aren't you eating breakfast? Viktor went early to Oxford. He will be waiting for Johann with packages. The minibus is ready," she said loudly.

The entire lobby sank with several degrees of cold. The students disappeared, leaving a tableau of Simon holding unconscious Patrick, Mary kneeling, and Arthur standing affronted with his stick.

"You look like the last scene of a play," commented Anna. "Why is Patrick asleep?"

"He's unconscious," said Mary. Fury made her teeth ache.

"Oh, my God." That was Caroline at the top of the stairs. She hastened down in pink slippers. Her man's dressing gown had seen better days. Must be George's, Mary thought. Even that tiny detail hurt. Seeing slippers made her own icy feet twitch.

"Ambulance, I can hear it," said Arthur. Now they all could: from a faint siren to full assault on their ears. Anna moved aside, glaring at Mary while two green-suited paramedics rushed over to Patrick.

"Needs a full body scan," the man grunted as the woman put a blanket over Patrick.

"I'm coming with you." Simon rose unsteadily. Yes, he must be stiff all over, commiserated Mary silently.

"Miss Wandwalker, could you, ..." Simon began.

"Miss Wandwalker, stay right here. Keep watch," Arthur finished. His eyes met Simon's. The younger man glared. He stepped toward Arthur, then swung on his heel, following the stretcher outside. After a couple of bangs, the purr of the engine rose to a cough. It was followed by a grinding of gravel as the vehicle departed.

"Patrick ...," began Mary.

"Don't believe it's an accident," muttered Arthur. "And he's not even a Falconer."

CHAPTER 31
HOUSE PARTY ON FAMILY GROUND

At the comment about Patrick not being a Falconer, Mary froze. She shot a glance at Arthur that made him turn away. He mumbled something. It could have been "sorry," thought Mary. Surely Patrick counted as a Falconer after all these years?

His tumble might still be an accident. Yet in retrospect that dangerously polished staircase looked like an inviting opportunity. The Kestrel or any of his minions only had to watch and wait. Was it possible that Patrick, his back turned, had been mistaken for Simon, or even Arthur?

With a rattle from the windows recalling Mary to her chilled legs, she planned to go upstairs for her clothes. Before she got to the second step, someone pulled her arm, making her stumble backward to the lobby floor. Her bare feet aching from the cold, matched the painful grip of olive fingers with blood red nails.

"Anna, let go. That hurts. You'll make *me* trip. Didn't you know these stairs are a death trap?"

"What happened to that artist?" said Anna through her teeth. She let Mary go, regarding with scorn the older woman rubbing her arm.

"We don't know," said Arthur loudly, approaching. "Simon found Patrick unconscious at the foot of the stairs. Perhaps he slipped and fell."

Ah, he's lying to her, thought Mary. Good idea.

Anna swung around to scowl at Arthur. He took a chair close to the stairs.

"Lady Anna, why don't you go and supervise the students," said Mary.

Anna's head whipped back. Again, Mary saw two people looking out of Anna's eyes, the ruthless operator and the traumatized woman. Anna stepped backward away from Mary. Her gaze swept the room as if she were programmed to detect danger. Then she nodded inscrutably and disappeared in the direction of the dining room. Mary and Arthur stared after her.

"Did Simon really find Patrick the way you said?" asked Mary.

"That's my best guess. By the time I could manage the stairs, Simon was having hysterics over Patrick's body. He ignored me. That's when I went to find my phone."

Mary dragged a chair next to him while Arthur cleared his throat.

"Being Simon's father was always about the 'scene of the crime' so to speak." Arthur grimaced. For a second, he looked the same age as Simon did before he left with the ambulance. I suppose Arthur Falconer's not that much older than I am, Mary thought.

"Why did you stop me going with them? Simon wanted support."

"Simon's spent his whole life demanding support," said his father. He banged his stick. "He's had nothing but support for 40 years. Support at an expensive school; support in a do-nothing job for the Conservative Party that his wife got him; support in rehab — three times — and support over the death of Perdita." Arthur shook his head. When Mary did not react, he seemed to see her for the first time that morning.

"Sorry, Miss Wandwalker. You've had your own loss. George Jones was a fine man. I only met him once, and I could see David in him. It was as if his ghost came back after all these years."

Arthur uttered the last sentence into the blue-veined marble that covered floor of the lobby. Portraits on both sides nodded back, or so it seemed to Mary. Mary decided she could stand a couple of minutes more without shoes. Resting her feet on her heels helped. Her insides warmed at Arthur's words. Bloody Falconers, she said to herself, almost affectionately.

Arthur continued. "Why am I unloading more grief on you? You never knew Perdita. You see, my granddaughter was the best of us, loving, intelligent, thought for herself, not *of* herself. Called me Grandpa Arthur, after Simon kept calling me Arthur. She was the Falconer jewel, our hope of something better for the future of the family."

Arthur took an unlit cigar out of the pocket of his dressing gown and started to chew the end. Mary wondered if it was a substitute for gnawing Simon. She caught sight of a sticking plaster on his lower jaw. Should ask Simon for shaving tips, she thought.

"You blame Simon," she said without thinking. "You blame him for Perdita's death, don't you?"

"Drugs," muttered Arthur. "Magic mushrooms. I don't care how Perdita got them. Simon was always the druggie. He paved the way."

"Surely not," said Mary, without conviction. Then she remembered Jamie, the perceptive dreadlocked nurse at Cardinal College. "No, really, Sir Arthur …"

"Arthur will do. Friends call me, Art."

Mary blinked. "Um, Art then. Listen." She fixed him with her Archivist expression. "You've got the wrong end of the stick with Simon. You know, don't you, that Perdita was poisoned by an overdose of psilocybin from magic mushrooms? No one believes she took it voluntarily."

"But Simon …" spluttered Arthur.

"Simon did a fantastic job putting Perdita off drugs," said Mary firmly. "I know that's the truth because I talked to the nurse at Cardinal College. He said that Perdita was definite that drugs were not part of her life. It was her father, Simon, who taught her from his own experience. That's why no one believes she did it to herself. Simon got that right."

"Simon did something right?" Arthur's face relaxed. A ghost of a smile wafted to Mary.

"Indeed, he did. Now you must excuse me, Sir ... Art. My feet are freezing on this marble."

He stopped her, touching her hand. "You're right Miss Wandwalker. I too should dress. At breakfast, we'll call Simon about Patrick. Afterward you and I will search for that damned Kestrel file. I'm sure there will be clues about Kyrill Solokov. They will be damning, given what he did to my father. We'll distract Lady Anna."

"Distract her, how exactly?"

"You'll think of something. She said Viktor's in Oxford. The police will be back for more interviews about George and Patrick's tumble. We've got to take any chance to find the spy safe."

He grinned. She found herself reciprocating. They wouldn't risk saying it out loud. Patrick's fate was agonizingly uncertain. While they could only *wait,* they could not *only* wait, Mary reckoned. She and David's brother would search Falconer House for Sir Daniel's lost Kestrel file.

CHAPTER 32
BEST LAID PLANS

News from Simon at the hospital came while Mary Wandwalker and Arthur Falconer lingered over breakfast. Neither wanted to make a move to search for the Kestrel file while Anna was tramping in and out of the dining room, chivying students. She informed a loitering Johann it was his turn to do the morning dishes.

Arthur tried to reach Simon three times before he got a reply. He placed his phone on speaker while Mary sipped coffee in the chair opposite.

"Hello, Pa." Simon sounded subdued.

"Get on with it, Simon. You're on speaker for Miss Wandwalker here. What's the news on Patrick?"

"Good," said Simon. He does not sound happy, thought Mary. They could hear Simon clearing his throat.

"Good as can be expected. Patrick woke in the ambulance and tried to get them to bring us back. No chance, given he'd been unconscious so long, said the paramedics. At the hospital they found a cracked rib. Yet they're more worried about the bump on the head. Nothing on the scan, so they are keeping him there for observation."

A gulp came from the phone. Arthur and Mary exchanged glances as Simon spoke again, hoarsely. "They chucked me out. They said I was bothering him too much, getting in the way of the docs. Absolute quiet is essential for the next few hours. I will get a taxi back."

"Give Patrick our love," Arthur grunted. There was a silence.

"That's rich coming from you," came the haggard voice.

Mary's eyes widened. Time to intervene.

"Did Patrick say what happened? Did he slip at the top of the stairs?"

"Miss Wandwalker, I'm glad to hear you. Maybe I misled you saying he woke up. Patrick can't talk much. Says his head hurts too much."

"Ah," said Mary, thinking fast.

"Miss Wandwalker? Do you know something?"

"No, Simon, I don't. Let's speak when you are back at Falconer House."

There was a click, and Arthur's phone went dark. Its owner looked at Mary with curiosity and, yes, an old pain.

"Really, Art, don't stare at me like that. I don't *know* anything about Patrick's fall. It just strikes me that if it was an accident, he would have said so when he asked the medics to turn around. Unless he's lost his memory, and Simon did not say that, there must be something more."

Before Arthur could reply, the door to the breakfast room, which had been ajar, crashed open. A loud voice preceded the brightly clad woman.

"More what? What did you say, Mary Wandwalker?" Belinda stormed with huge dark eyes. She stood behind a chair in an orange sari, affronted and … she looks afraid, thought Mary.

Mary drew up her neck to meet the MP on her ground.

"Ms. Choudhry, you've heard that Patrick McCarthy is in hospital. We are waiting for Simon to return with more information." Mary did not let her eyes go to Richard Bishop, who entered quietly in the wake of his estranged wife.

There was a pause. Belinda Choudhry narrowed her eyes at Mary, then took a seat at the other end of the table.

"Where's breakfast?" the MP demanded. "Lady Anna ignored me when I asked her what was going on. I never eat before 10. Sit with me, Richard. Not with *her.*"

Mary groaned inwardly. Whether or not Belinda knew about Mary's recent night with Richard, she was taking no chances. Belinda's strident tones filled the room. With an imperious wave, she ordered her husband to join her. However, Richard walked the opposite way around the room to take the empty seat by Mary.

"What's the real news on Patrick?" he said quietly.

"Good — ish," replied Mary. "He woke but has a broken rib and a head wound that will keep him in the John Whitcliffe for now. Simon's on his way back."

"He woke up?" queried Belinda, her tones too high as well as too loud. "You mean he's talking? Is he talking to the police?"

An anonymous student dashed into the room with a plate of scrambled eggs for Belinda. They smelled lukewarm. Mary wrinkled her nose.

"We could visit," said Richard looking uncertainly at Mary, then Belinda.

Just who are the "we" here, Mary wondered.

At this interesting moment, Helga erupted into the room, stopping at the gathering, then seizing the coffeepot and rushing out.

"I wasn't finished with that coffee," said Mary to Helga's retreating back. "Oh well, Arthur, are you ready?" She indicated the stick that Arthur had left by the door. Before he could get to his feet, Belinda addressed Arthur.

"*You* must be glad that Patrick is out of the way."

Arthur paled.

"Bel, don't." That was Richard, standing as if to protect the older man. "In fact, come with me, and we'll get breakfast in Oxford. We can go to the Randolph Hotel. You know you like being seen there."

Belinda ignored him. Arthur took a few steps toward the MP, as if prepared to receive a blow.

"You didn't go to the wedding, Simon and Patrick's," continued Belinda. "I don't know why you bothered to come to *my* wedding with Simon. You never supported our marriage, not even when Perdita, your only grandchild was born."

She stabbed her plate of scrambled egg before leaning over to grab the ketchup. So violent was her shake of the sauce bottle that a bright red glob splashed onto the table. Mary winced and rose for a cloth. She would not tolerate anything that looked so like blood. Not today, not with the smell of blood lingering on the lawn outside.

Richard glanced at Mary and moved to a seat nearer his wife.

"Belinda, that's enough goading Arthur about weddings. In the circumstances it's pure spite." He glared for a few seconds, then leaned back, his forehead sweating. Mary could even smell it.

Mary had never seen him this upset with Belinda. She's not really speaking out of spite, Mary thought. Looking at Belinda so taut and upset, this was more like fear. Belinda's eyes met Mary's, and there was a split second when Mary saw an appeal. Then it was over, and Belinda, having given up on her eggs, was preparing to leave.

"Richard, drive me into town," she said to him. "Take me to a proper breakfast at the Randolph. Then we'll visit Patrick. After that I have constituency work for the rest of today. You'll bring me back here." She paused then turned to Mary. "I'll remind the Chief Constable about the murder of George Jones. It must be cleared up quickly. Parliament sits next week, and the PM wants me in the House."

She swept out, with Richard behind. He tried and failed to catch Mary's eye. Mary felt a yearning she refused to show. Resolutely, she forced her head to stay focused on the window. Too much was happening at Falconer House to indulge whatever it was between herself and a man still involved with another woman, maybe two others. So absorbed was Mary that she did not hear the door open.

"What house is she talking about?"

Arthur and Mary swung around to the door that connected to the kitchen. In old jeans and an oversized sweater, Caroline stood with a plate of toast triangles, a mug also precariously balanced. She used her other hand to shut the door behind her. For the seconds it had been open Mary caught the sound of younger female voices. It sounded like Anna was berating Helga.

So concentrated was Mary on listening that it was Arthur who limped over to Caroline to rescue the rattling mug.

"Good to see you, Mrs. Jones," he said. "Have you heard about my son-in-law? Although Patrick fell victim to the Falconer staircase, they say he is doing as well as can be expected."

"What a relief that must be," said Caroline with the best smile Mary had yet seen. "I rang a friend at the hospital to see if I could get any details. Nothing wrong on the head scan. Such cases usually make a full recovery, my friend says."

Mary frowned. "How did you ..." she began.

"Yes, I know I'm not a relative. However, I've done voluntary work at the John Whitcliffe. A few nurses are friends."

"Thank you," Arthur said with simplicity. He turned to Mary. "You heard Belinda say that I declined the invitation to Simon and Patrick's wedding. I want to tell you both why."

"You don't have to explain. ... I saw, I mean it must have been hard seeing them happy. George said you never had their chances."

Caroline knew the right things to say, thought Mary.

Arthur threw a measuring glance at Mary. She mused on the oh-so-recent Equal Marriage Act. After centuries of invisibility, persecution, prejudice, and exclusion, same-sex couples could finally love with the legal backing and optional extravagance of any other couple getting married. An elder generation might well be consumed with envy, Mary thought.

Caroline put down her mug of tea to briefly squeeze Arthur's fingers. He smiled. To her surprise, Mary detected a stab of jealousy.

"I want to explain," Arthur repeated. "You two belong to George, David's son. That means you're family now."

Caroline took a seat next to Mary. They exchanged glances at the notion of being part of the Falconer family. Mary recalled denying it to Patrick and Mr. Jeffreys. That seemed so long ago.

While Arthur pondered his next words, Mary caught the echoes of continuing anger in another room. Anna and Helga rowing about some domestic matter of no importance, she decided. Much later, Mary realized she could not have been more wrong.

Meanwhile, Arthur wanted the full attention of the two women. Both were happy to give it.

"It comes down to selfishness," he pronounced. "I'm a selfish old man. My not being at Simon's wedding to Patrick was inexcusable. My doctor diagnosed depression. I knew I brought it on myself by envying Simon living the life that I should have had." His mouth twisted before he swallowed and went on. "My wife urged me to attend the celebration with her. She's a good woman. I yelled at her that I would only spoil their day. The truth is I could not bear to see my son happy."

"Arthur, you are too hard on yourself," said Caroline quickly. "I've had depression all my life. Don't blame yourself for feeling that way. You did not have Simon's chances. The world has changed."

"Not that much." He shook his head. "They legalized homosexuality in time for me. I could have pursued real relationships, not married a woman because my father told me to. I was too afraid of him, even after he died. And then it was the 1980s." He nodded at Mary.

"AIDS." Mary remembered. A dark, grim time. She'd lost friends.

"People I knew, a few lovers, it was a death sentence in those days. So many died. I hid in the closet. My wife, Ingrid, supported me, said I should seek my happiness but ..."

He let his words trail off, trying to smile at the two women. "Perdita's death felt like the end." He took a breath. "She had introduced me to George. Your George," he said to the two of them as if George had been their gift. "He got back in touch, and I realized here was another Falconer."

"*Service through Family*," said Mary dryly. "It's the Falconer motto, isn't it?"

"Yes, my father never stopped insisting that the first duty of a son is to produce heirs for the estate. Even Simon, who never met him, felt the pressure to marry for a child. Now I've lost the granddaughter I adored and a nephew I hardly knew."

"He respected you," said Caroline, unexpectedly. "George told me about meeting you when he found out you are his uncle. He hoped the three of us could get together and you could tell us about David."

Caroline put a hand over her mouth. They sat in silence for a while, until Arthur thumped the table, knocking over the salt.

"I've had enough," said Arthur loudly. "Enough of this English nonsense with heirs. It's grotesque that Perdita was born so someone with Falconer genes could inherit this house. That kind of *Service Through Family* is a travesty."

"Not George," said Mary, thinking. "Born to inherit the estate that is. He was illegitimate."

"Ah, I've been thinking about that," said Arthur. "No longer true, Miss Wandwalker. Since 2014, when the law changed, bastards ... sorry Mary, illegitimate children have the same rights."

"Oh," Caroline breathed. "George an heir. Does that mean? *What* does that mean?" She turned to Mary. She motioned to Arthur. He had more.

"The Falconer estate is entailed 'heirs of the body,' where most traditional trusts specify male heirs. It meant Perdita was as much an heir as any boy. Our girl could have inherited, and

George, under this new law, also had a claim. In fact, after Perdita, George Jones *was* the Falconer heir.

"Both George and Perdita are gone," whispered Caroline to the table.

"Who inherits now?" asked Mary Wandwalker, refusing to dwell on the image of George. She would be pragmatic, assertive. She would be Mary Wandwalker. Caroline appeared only mildly interested in the future of the Falconer estate. Arthur winced, as if Mary had prodded an old wound.

"Don't know," he growled. "Although I've been wondering about …"

They were interrupted by unnecessarily loud footsteps. Anna banged the door open to the distress of aged wood paneling. She brought a summons for Caroline. The police wanted her right away.

CHAPTER 33
NOT THE KESTREL FILE

Although Anna made it sound as if Caroline was about to be charged with her husband's murder, her tone proved misleading. Deliberately so, in Mary's opinion. More accurately, the police planned to reinterview all Falconer House guests plus the Solokovs. Mary wondered about Patrick's so-called accident. Were they now treating it as attempted murder? The house resumed an atmosphere of imposed order. Those not immediately summoned to the library for more questioning made themselves scarce.

Mary and Arthur waited until forensic operatives finished dusting the offending staircase for fingerprints. Only then did the intrepid detectives begin the hunt for Sir Daniel's spy safe.

"Given all this white plaster, it's got to be under a portrait," said Mary.

"Agreed," said Arthur. "An obvious safe would have been emptied long ago." He tapped his cane over to his mother's portrait. "You know, I always liked this one. Pity McCarthy changed his style to milk the uber wealthy like Solokov."

"Yes, pastiche 18th century does not suit Mike McCarthy's talent. Whereas this one of Lady Margaret feels much more authentic. I noticed it when I came to the Solokov party," agreed Mary. "There is something I can't quite put my finger on ..."

About to say more, she stopped and put the side of her head on the wall to examine the thickness of the frame.

"Miss Wandwalker," Arthur sounded hoarse. "Miss Wandwalker, have you found the spy safe?"

Arthur dropped his stick and stepped forward to help Mary lift down the portrait. Both gasped, almost letting go of the painting. Carefully placing Lady Margaret facing the wall, they put their fingers all around the tiny door in the marble finishing.

Mary's jaw dropped. Arthur was all business. He pulled out a keyring, found a tiny key, unlocked the door, pulled out a brown envelope, locked the safe, and was helping Mary rehang the portrait before she dared breathe. Their luck held. No one bothered them while they pulled two chairs to a secluded part of the lobby where, behind a golden pillar and a statue, no one could see them unless deliberately searching.

Thank God for Solokov's bad taste, thought Mary. Made so ostentatious by the new gilding, the lobby dazzled traffic to and from the house. The result was secluded corners and this discreet space behind the stairs. Without comment she and Arthur divided the handwritten pages from the envelope. Mary recognized Sir Daniel's scrawl from the carbon copies of letters upstairs.

"Nothing about the Kestrel, so it can't be the file we're looking for. These are private letters."

She heard stiff paper unfolding followed by a sniff, then an intake of breath. Mary felt as if something cold had blown on the back of her neck. Arthur craned over a single piece of paper. He sighed, then rubbed his eyes. Mary stiffened, knowing she should ask what he'd found. Or perhaps she should take him somewhere more private.

While she was prevaricating, Arthur cleared his throat.

"You need to read this." He passed her a photocopy of a single page stamped as from the John Whitcliffe Hospital. When Mary saw the name under the logo, the paper trembled. Fearful of interruption, she perused it very fast, then crammed it in her handbag for concealment.

Arthur looked at her. Mary had to ask first.

"You saw the name, didn't you? Results from an autopsy on David."

Arthur looked away. He tapped his stick quietly in front of them both. "Yes, Miss Wandwalker. It's what we, Patrick, Simon, you, and I suspected. This photocopy is a page from the medical report on David's death. You remember what we discussed when we found that psilocybin tin with his name on it."

"But not with his writing. That wasn't David's tin," protested Mary. Her stomach hurt at the thought of David. Had he driven into that wall because drugs silted up his mind?

"Agreed," said Arthur. "David did not do drugs. If both of us are sure, his brother and his ... girlfriend ..."

"Fiancée," snapped Mary.

"Fiancée, sorry. Then we can rule out a self-inflicted overdose. Like Perdita," said Arthur, strongly. He swallowed. "And yet, we see from this page of the autopsy that my brother had so much psilocybin in his blood that ... well, enough for him to lose control of his car. His death was no accident."

"Murder," croaked Mary. "David was murdered!"

CHAPTER 34
DAVID FALCONER

Arthur Falconer kept a respectful silence after Mary delivered her conclusion on the death of her would-be husband. His fierce expression comforted Mary.

Before either of them could go on, the sound of shrieking metal made them hold their breath. A bolt that needed oiling protested. There was a crash from a door carelessly banged followed by soft footsteps from trainers. Someone was arriving.

"Hello, Pa, Miss Wandwalker. Why's my grandmother's picture crooked?"

Simon was too pale. The black around his eyes even suggested he'd been the one to fall down the stairs. Mary realized that the dark blue jogging gear, several sizes too big for him, must be what they gave him at the hospital. He'd gone with Patrick in a scarlet dressing gown.

She jumped up to straighten the proper Lady Margaret in her simple wood frame. Meanwhile, down the stairs came Caroline, looking exhausted from police questioning. Somewhat to Mary's surprise Arthur held out the photocopy report to her. After Caroline's eyes widened, Simon snatched it.

"Hush," said Arthur as Simon seemed about to expostulate. "Walls have ears."

Or students spying for the Solokovs, Mary thought.

Simon appeared to be struggling between impatience and sympathy, Caroline pulled up another chair and patted Mary's hand.

"Looks like David Falconer died in a way later used on our George," she said.

"And Perdita," hissed Arthur.

Mary roused herself to deal with such muddled thinking. "Strictly speaking," she said, the precise archivist, "George died from stabbing. We've no idea how he came to have psilocybin in his body."

"He'd never take it voluntarily," said Caroline, stung. "Or knowingly. Not after ..." and she dropped her eyes after glancing at Arthur.

"Not after psilocybin killed our Perdita," concluded Arthur. His fists clenched, then uncurled as he caught sight of Simon's frozen expression.

Confirmed, thought Mary. All three Falconer deaths involved psilocybin. Two of them may be 40 years from David, yet they are connected by a drug manufactured from the same magic mushrooms on the Falconer estate.

Deep inside Mary something old and sweet began to ache. An old wound seeped blood: David. Now David's death all over again, together with George's. These griefs would bury her in the mud outside where her son fell.

There was a long silence in the lobby, punctuated by the distant sounds of several vehicles drawing up at the front of the house. Mary's bones could detect the reverberations. Yes, another swarm of police would soon engulf Falconer House.

"More police," said Caroline, unnecessarily. "Probably to speed up the interviews. I'd better go back to Inspector Reynolds." She stood up, hesitating over Mary.

"Mrs. Jones, I thought you'd been interviewed this morning," said Arthur.

"No, they gave me a break. This time they want everything, every tiny detail about the last few days and George." She gulped, then looked briefly at Mary. "They want lots about our marriage too."

"I see," said Mary, feeling as if one of her Archive staff were in trouble. "I'll come with you, Caroline." Then she had an idea. "Or what about a lawyer? You have a right to have one with you when you are interviewed. Sir Arthur ... Art, don't the Falconers have a firm of solicitors in Oxford?"

"Definitely," said Arthur. "Our family lawyers are good with criminal cases. We used to meet them at the police station in the old days when ..." He narrowed his eyes at Simon, who shrugged. "I'll make a call and ..."

"No," said Caroline, loud and defiant. Mary blinked. "No lawyers coming here. No more strangers, I can't bear talking about George and ... Anna. Not to more people who did not know us. Maybe a duty solicitor if we go to the station, but here in this house ... not until we know why George died." She turned to Mary.

"Don't come, Miss Wandwalker. You're needed here with Arthur and Simon. I can do this." She padded away in worn slippers.

Mary watched her go. "Mrs. Jones is clearly unwell. I don't understand clinical depression. Perhaps she just needs a rest."

There was a hollow laugh from Arthur. "I know those blues. Mrs. Jones would prefer to climb into bed and never come out. I bet she can barely make herself eat or leave her room. That she came to talk about George is courage indeed."

Mary stared at him. Caroline's haunted face swam before her.

"Oh. I see, sort of. I've never suffered that way. But she is a murder suspect. To refuse a lawyer makes no sense."

"It might," broke in Simon. "If she feels that a prison cell would be a refuge from having to go on living without him." He stared into his own pain.

These Falconers with their impractical attitudes lost Mary. She was about to say so when she recalled Caroline's slow, determined climb up the stairs. Could she have murdered George? Mary thought. I don't really believe so. But I can see how the police would. Why did she tell me to stay with Simon and Arthur?

"David Falconer," said Simon, interpreting Mary's thoughts. "She knows he meant as much to you as George did to her. As Patrick does to me," he said pointedly to Arthur.

Arthur scowled at his son. That grimace made Mary very tired. Be patient, she told herself. But she did not feel patient.

"Stop it right now. I've had enough," she ordered. Yes, her Archive persona was coming in handy today. Both men stared at her with those blue Falconer eyes. Mary had to go on.

"Given what is happening to your family, it is way past time you got over your … your stuff." Her lame ending made her more cross. "Someone's killing Falconers, and you two are stuck on who came to whose wedding. We haven't even found that bloody Kestrel File yet."

"Hey, Miss W. We're not that petty," Simon protested. His flushing made him resemble his father even more. "You don't know the history."

"Just a minute, Simon." Arthur rattled his stick, gaining their attention. "Miss Wandwalker understands that I was a terrible father."

His heart is heavy, Mary thought. Mine is sinking into the ground.

Arthur addressed the stunned Simon. "I admit it, Simon. I neglected you. Later I was jealous of you. If we are to be picked off by a killer, then I want you to know how much I regret letting you down."

Simon began to stammer. "Pa, I never said any of that to Miss W. Neglect? Jealousy? What are you talking about? And no one is going to kill you. I … I won't allow it."

"I'll leave you two," said Mary. She was eager to check the news from Mr. Jeffreys. Should he be encouraged to join them, given that the perils of Falconer House were increasing by the day? The two Falconers in the dining room had other ideas.

"No," they said as one.

"Miss Wandwalker, you have to stay," said Simon. "I need a witness."

"You're involved," said Arthur, unexpectedly. "Not in my bad parenting, of course, but certainly in what is going on here. After all, you are family."

Mary looked at him. Lady Margaret, Arthur's mother, had denied her appeal to be part of the Falconers, denied her when she was heavy with dead David's son. Arthur nodded with comprehension.

"Family," he repeated.

Mary saw his mute appeal. He's scared, she realized. And he is right to be. Arthur is David's brother. Also, he met George, and he liked him.

"Thank you," was all she could manage. Simon seemed about to speak, so she stopped him. "Arthur wasn't so much a bad parent as a sufferer of unfortunate timing," she said firmly. All right, she'd started this.

"Simon," she said, fixing him with the Wandwalker stare. "Your father had his family devastated by what we now know to have been a double murder — first his brother, David, and then Sir Daniel, his father. Even before those horrors, Arthur was under pressure not to live the life he wanted."

Mary stopped and glanced at the elder Falconer. There was something terribly vulnerable and intimate in the way he was looking at Simon. She had the sensation of soaring above Falconer House, of seeing a small boy with a ball and a father who turned away.

"Once he saw that you also were gay, he stayed away to protect you from his unhappiness. You've got to understand that Arthur lived through the worst of AIDS. He would have been terrified for you. By the time medical treatment improved I expect he was exhausted. Of course, he felt jealous of your happiness with Patrick."

Mary gripped the table in a moment of bleakness.

"Hell and damnation, Simon Falconer, *I'm* jealous of your happiness with Patrick. I lost the love of my life 40 years ago. So, I punished myself by sending away our child. Now he too is dead. Between the two of you, you've got what I lost forever: Simon, a loving spouse, and you, Arthur, a child."

Then Mary thumped the table as she'd seen Mr. Jeffreys do. "Falconers," she continued, sternly. "Pull yourselves together. People are dying. The police don't have the family history to solve murders 40 years apart."

When Mary ceased speaking, Arthur and Simon looked almost comic, both raising their eyebrows and folding their arms. Did I really tell Sir Arthur Falconer and his son to pull themselves together? Who am I to pontificate on a lifetime of bitterness? I don't *do* families.

"Mrs. Jones is right. I'd refuse a lawyer too," she said, getting up. "In fact, I *am* refusing a lawyer. This situation is too … personal."

Noting pursed lips (Arthur) and slow grin (Simon), Mary Wandwalker marched out, head held high. The aroma of fresh coffee from Simon's mug drew her to the kitchen. After more coffee, she planned to prod the police into a more productive direction than Caroline.

Unless, of course, she reflected, I'm chasing a mirage, the Kestrel is a distraction, and Caroline killed her husband after all.

CHAPTER 35
PREGNANT CONVERSATIONS

Having failed to locate Detective Inspector Reynolds, Mary came to another staircase at the end of the corridor of guest bedrooms. This one could not be called "grand." One-third of the width, its dust-colored carpet was threadbare. The way to the servant's bedrooms, Mary deduced, now the abode of students and Caroline Jones. I wonder ...

It was Helga she wondered about, nipping up the winding stairs to find a similar corridor with double the doors of the fancy rooms below. Try as she might, Mary could not stop herself rerunning Helga's encounters with Richard Bishop. Surely two murders justified a bit of snooping while the students braved the windy streets of Oxford. However, it was sounds from a woman older than Helga that froze Mary outside the door.

Could it possibly be Caroline? Caroline *laughing?* While another voice spoke too low for Mary to separate into coherence. The doorframe shook. Someone was jumping up and down. Extraordinary, thought Mary. She gingerly put her hand on the door handle. It opened with a loud crack. Mary put her head around the door and gasped.

Caroline was alternately leaping up, then sitting back down on the narrow bed to hug Anna. The young woman looked somber in the sparse room. She wore a brown smock clearly meant for a much larger figure. While Anna glowered at Mary, Caroline shone. Even her freckles sparkled.

"Go away," said Anna.

Mary came farther into the chilly room, shutting the door behind her.

"Mary, Mary, you'll never guess," gushed Caroline.

She's feverish, thought Mary. That flush and sweat is not a good sign.

"Are you ill?" Mary said, alarmed. Are you mad? was what she thought.

"Wonderful news," gushed Caroline. "George is having a baby. Mary, just think. You'll have a grandchild."

Mary's shock was not pleasant. For a second she hated herself, then realized that something did not add up.

"Caroline, please calm down. Sit down. How long have you been pregnant?"

She was relieved to see Caroline stop dancing around. Her too bright eyes dimmed. Taking a shuddering breath, Caroline subsided onto the bed next to Anna. She squeezed the younger woman's arm. Mary fetched the desk chair to sit facing the strange pair, Caroline quivering, and Anna subdued.

"Not me pregnant, silly," said Caroline, happy to correct Mary. "Anna is. She's having George's baby."

Mary felt the room rotating. She was on a roundabout. Putting her hands to her throbbing forehead, she squeezed. Caroline and Anna swam back into focus. Anna raised her head to Mary, black eyes giving nothing away.

"How do you know it is George's," said Mary with a deliberate lack of tact. Anna not reacting was starting to set off alarms.

"I know." Anna's voice was barely above a whisper.

"George is having a baby," repeated Caroline, resolutely. "He's not entirely gone."

At that remark Mary examined both women. Caroline's enthusiasm worried her. She looked as if she was running a temperature. By contrast Anna was shut down, power switched off. After a long pause, Mary knew what she had to say.

"No," she said. "There is no baby."

"Yes, yes there is," gabbled Caroline. "Anna said you'd say that. Here's the pregnancy test. See, it's positive."

She waved a small white stick at Mary who took it with a frown. Yes, there was the blue line, that flag for joy, or horror, or both. Could it be true? Am I about to be a grandmother? She recalled her own pregnancy so long ago. Her heart froze and crumbled into family ground.

Caroline picked up Anna's hand and kissed it. She turned back to Mary. "All the doctors insisted my mental health was too fragile for children," she said quietly. "It was a huge disappointment to George. Now with him gone ..." She swallowed. "He'd be so happy. *We'd* be so happy."

Anna got up. Dodging around the bed, she arrived at the big wardrobe. Wrenching it open, she began to rifle through old coats. The smell of mothballs crawled over to Caroline and Mary. They stared at Anna's back.

"Come back, Anna," Mary managed.

Anna stopped. She did not turn back to Mary and Caroline. From outside the room came the tramp of official feet. Voices tossed cheerful remarks about lunch arriving from an Oxford pub. By contrast, Mary heard screeching from the window.

She dodged past Anna and stared at a broiling sky. A cluster of bare trees shook branches in a wild dance. Around them, rooks jumped into the wind, crowding the sky with big black wings.

Anna resumed fingering through the wardrobe. With that ghastly smock, she could easily melt into the old clothes, thought Mary.

"That is no doorway into Narnia," said Mary from the window. "Go back and sit next to Caroline."

For the first time, Anna obeyed. It told Mary everything she wanted to know.

"Narnia, I love that book," interjected Caroline with delight. "Where the children fall through the wardrobe into the magical land. *The Lion, the Witch and the Wardrobe*, I read it every year to the second graders when I taught school ..."

"Stop it Caroline," said Mary softly. "You *know* we have to do this."

"Saw the film," muttered Anna.

Mary returned to her chair. Caroline looked anguished, Anna mutinous.

"Anna, look at me," said Mary. Anna did as she was told. Her skin was sallow, earthy. Dark sickle moons shadowed her eyes.

Mary's voice was gentle, even more gentle than with weeping interns in the Archive. "There's no baby, is there, Anna?"

Silence. Caroline's hands trembled. She put a hand over her mouth.

Anna sniffed, waited, and at last spoke. "No baby." She kept her eyes on Mary. "I can't. When I was a child, men ..." She stopped, then began more loudly. "Things were done to me. I cannot get pregnant."

She jutted her chin, daring Mary to comment. Instead, Mary saw how Anna's words dug through her youth and beauty to something very different. For a second an old woman confronted her. Neither Anna nor Mary paid attention to Caroline.

"Noooo."

Caroline doubled over in pain. Before Mary could reach her, Caroline shot to her feet. In one swift move, she bent down and slapped Anna's face. The young woman did not respond except to rub the red mark on her cheek. With a wail of fury, Caroline sped from the room. The door's *bang* reminded Mary of the day they met. Then Caroline had slammed the front door on the spectacle of George and Anna.

Mary took a deep breath. She looked curiously at Anna, who appeared ... *relieved*. To Mary's surprise she offered a faint smile to the older woman. Mary realized that Caroline's blow had returned Anna to her everyday personalities. The devious criminal and the trafficked woman flickered mockingly at Mary.

"DNA," said Mary, uncompromisingly. She would hang on to essentials. "So easy to check these days. No getting away with a fake pregnancy in a murder investigation. What with George being a cop, the police are going to check up on a sensational adulterous pregnancy. You'd have to take a DNA test. The police or ... maybe someone else ...?" Mary raised her eyebrows. Anna's scowl deepened. "Someone else would insist on discovering paternity. Finding out you are not expecting would rile D.I. Reynolds. They'd charge you with wasting police time."

Anna tossed her head, becoming remote again. The woman's no fool, thought Mary. So why try to deceive Caroline?

"How did you fake the test?"

Mary scooped up the white stick from the indentation on the bed left by Caroline. Before Anna could reply, they heard a different set of footsteps; lighter, uneven. Someone was galloping up the stairs toward them, someone confident moving about the house. Mary was getting ready to insist on an answer when they were interrupted by a loud crash.

Is everyone addicted to slamming doors, thought Mary crossly? A hand seized the pregnancy stick from her fingers.

"There it is. I've been searching everywhere. Anna. You stole my pregnancy test. I don't know why you want it, but it's mine. I need it." Helga, breathless and angry, ignored Mary entirely.

Anna lifted her head in weary defiance. Yet Helga and the white stick had already vanished. Another bang rattled the doorframe.

"Ah," said Mary Wandwalker. "So that's how you faked it."

Again, Anna was about to respond when yet more footsteps pounded toward them. These were louder. Since Helga pulling the door behind her had failed to latch it, it bounced open.

A woman entered wearing a pleasing dark red dress. Ignoring Mary, she cupped Anna's face in her hands, kissed her passionately on the lips, then dashed out. Anna smiled, a cat who had secured her cream.

Now I know what is meant by dumbfounded, thought Mary.

"Caroline?" croaked Mary. Her throat was tight. "That was Caroline? I don't believe it."

"Oh yes," said Anna. "That was Caroline. She's been giving me the eye since she moved in. I must go to her." As she glided across the room, Anna let her enigmatic smile grow triumphant.

Bloody hell, I need to lie down, decided Mary.

CHAPTER 36
GIVING THANKS

At 10 the next morning Mary and Arthur Falconer were perched on the hard chairs in the lobby. A few minutes earlier, Mary, with occasional help from Arthur waving his stick, dragged four wooden seats into an intimate circle. Not in the main thoroughfare, but neither were the chairs hidden away. Rather, Mary and Arthur had prepared a rest spot for a man entering Falconer House after several days in hospital. Very soon Simon would arrive with Patrick. He had called his father from the hospital car park.

"Isn't it time for another text?" muttered Mary as Arthur monitored his phone.

Mary tapped her foot. Caroline and Anna vanishing after the revelation of yesterday morning caused little comment, partly due to Viktor Solokov being away in London, yet mainly because of what the police found a couple of hours later. Searching the grounds of Falconer House, a junior officer stumbled across a door set into the earth floor of a disused brick shed. Prizing it open revealed a psilocybin laboratory in what had once been an icehouse. For the rest of the day the area buzzed with police and white shrouded figures of indeterminate sex.

Mary's pressing questions got herself barred from the site. She mentally kicked herself for not suggesting an icehouse to Inspector Reynolds. Of course, a grand historic house would have an underground chamber lined with straw to keep blocks of ice through the summer. How else could frozen desserts be served in the centuries before fridges?

Minus the straw, an icehouse was ideal for illicit distilling. It was unfortunate that the glass apparatus, drying mushrooms, and bottles of wine revealed nothing identifying any specific person at Falconer House. Mary heard a couple of cops saying that Reynolds was waiting on fingerprints and forensics before risking interrogating the Solokovs.

"Sir Viktor has too many high-up cronies to tackle him without evidence. Wife too."

Meanwhile, Mary fumed. What about the danger to the surviving Falconers? Mary could not quash suspicions about Patrick's so-called "accident." She didn't buy it. The Kestrel was a bird of prey. Who might be next?

Now waiting in the morning gloom for Patrick and Simon, Mary searched her recollection for clues. With the students in Oxford and Viktor shut up in Sir Daniel's old study, she decided to broach the subject with Arthur.

"This house gives me the creeps," she began. "What if the Kestrel ..."

"Four minutes," said Arthur. "They'll be here in about four minutes, Miss Wandwalker. Don't forget Simon said that a lorry overturning on the Ring Road blocked traffic out of Oxford." He chewed on his lip. Then in a lower voice he said, "Worrying won't help."

Mary leapt up, crossing the marble floor to the house entrance. If she did not do something, she might start shouting. Arthur didn't deserve it. *Something bad would happen today if she did not intervene.* She could feel it in the muggy air. Since high windows ensured neck strain, if one wanted to peer down the drive, she decided to open the huge door.

Made of large oaks that once stood in the park, the door was the only part of the facade that survived the classical remodeling in the 18th century. David had told her that as they drove up, she now recalled. Oh, David, Mary sighed, then tackled the rusty though oily bolts. Then she peered at the statues of scantily clad Roman gods in each corner and met Arthur Falconer's nod.

GIVING THANKS

Despite the opulence of the lobby, Mary felt a prisoner. The door was a means of escape. Arthur pottered over, clattering his stick. Together they swung the heavy oak wide onto ... nothing at all.

Mary gasped. Fog swirled everywhere, concealing everything. From the vanishing of trees, garden walls, to the swallowing of the driveway and gravel, fog seemed to have consumed the whole world. *Everything has gone, including George*, thought Mary. Arthur stood silent beside her.

"Don't go out there," she admonished. "We don't know where the danger lurks." Mary prepared to retreat.

A bony hand gripped her shoulder. "Wait," whispered Arthur. "I hear something."

They both stuck their heads into the fog. A chilly film covered Mary's face and hair. From the corner of her left eye, she could see drops forming on Arthur's nose and chin.

"Nothing," she said with a shiver. "Can we...?"

"There, there," hissed Arthur, dropping his stick in excitement. "It's Simon, bringing back Patrick. No doubt about it."

Mary saw the glowing orbs before she heard the crunch of tires. Two golden eyes carved tunnels in the swirling mist. From them emerged a black body. The four wheeled creature swung around, panting steam from its exhaust pipe.

"That's not Simon's car," said Arthur, dismayed. Mary, on the other hand, ran her fingers through her gray bob and checked her cashmere jumper for breakfast crumbs. The beast stopped breathing. Stubby wings stretched from the sides to disgorge two passengers.

"I knew it," crowed Mary, invigorated. "Only Mr. Jeffreys would arrive in a London taxi."

"Fare for two hours. That's extortionate," grumbled Arthur.

Stretching his limbs outside the taxi, Mr. Jeffreys filled a stone-colored suit one shade darker than the fog. Paying no attention to Mary and Arthur, his features looked somber as he waited for a man with tousled white hair to climb out with a

MURDER ON FAMILY GROUNDS

small suitcase. Mr. Jeffreys then bent to retrieve his own bag and speak to the driver. A moment later the black beast began to cough more smoke, before vanishing back into the fog.

The two men heaved their luggage up the steps to the house. Mary had an odd impulse to help Mr. Jeffreys, which she suppressed. Never would she admit relief to see her former boss. The white-haired gent with him hesitated. Mary and Arthur stood aside.

"Mr. Jeffreys, I know but who is this old guy?" said Arthur in an undertone to Mary. "Hang on, he looks familiar."

"Perhaps it is the family resemblance," returned Mary, now she'd put the man into the right context. "He's Mike McCarthy, Patrick's father, the portrait painter. He did that painting of Sir Viktor hanging inside. I was here for the unveiling party."

It was so long ago, a lifetime. George was alive then. *You fool,* came her inner voice. All right, but I can't tear myself apart now. I must protect George's family. My family. Mary put her hand on Arthur's arm.

"Oh, I see. McCarthy's come because of Patrick's accident," said Arthur into Mary's ear. He misjudged his volume: The words seemed to bounce around the lobby.

"No accident," said Mr. Jeffreys. He dropped his bag with a thump, then turned to face Mary.

"Mr. McCarthy and I do not believe in accidents at Falconer House."

Mary and Arthur stood aside. Spotting the chairs, the two arrivals thumped down. Arthur joined them, leaving the chair for Mary who addressed Mr. Jeffreys.

"You are not being very discreet. No accident? Now, who would hurt Patrick?" she queried innocently.

Not wanting to give anything away in front of the unknown quantity of Mike McCarthy, Mary spread on her most bland Archive face. It was Patrick's father who flushed. Before anyone could say more, footsteps approached with the crack of expensive leather. A man in a white suit sauntered toward the newcomers. The four instinctively tensed.

GIVING THANKS

"More guests for Thanksgiving dinner?" said Viktor, his sneer audible as well as visible. "Delightful. My wife is nowhere to be found."

Mary suppressed her shiver. Was that a threat?

"Viktor, old chap," said Mike McCarthy with an attempt at normality from artist to patron, or so Mary deduced. "You're doing Thanksgiving here at Falconer House? That American thing? Nice of you to invite us. However, I'm here to see my son. Then off back to London."

"Not quite," said Mr. Jeffreys, sounding more deadly than Mary remembered. She shot him a frown. Mike McCarthy gulped. Mr. Jeffreys gave Mary a slow nod. Then he moved his gaze from Mike McCarthy to Viktor and back again. "Mr. McCarthy will be staying on due to er ... unfinished business with the Falconer family."

There was a tight pause. Mr. Jeffreys gave Viktor his most public smile. Viktor Solokov inclined his head. Mr. Jeffreys continued.

"Do I understand that you are inviting us to Thanksgiving dinner tonight? An American celebration?"

"My mother was American," said Luca, inscrutably. "After she died, I continued Thanksgiving in her honor. This house was where Rosalind Forrest was particularly ... joyous."

There's something he's saying and not saying, Mary thought.

"How appropriate," she intervened. "For today we give thanks for the safe return of Patrick McCarthy. After his so-called *accident*."

Viktor's silent response reminded her of a fish on a slab, one cold eye gazing into infinity.

"Seven p.m., drinks in the library and formal dress," he said to no one in particular. "Don't be late, because ..." he paused for effect, "I have an announcement that will affect all of you. It concerns the Falconer family and this estate."

Leaving his audience stunned, he vanished, his icy breath hanging in the warm air.

"Was that Viktor talking about *our* family?"

The voice came from the doorway.

"Simon, thank god," said Arthur, getting up to embrace his son as if he had been lost for decades. Perhaps he was, thought Mary, as Simon gave his father a quick pat on the back before leading in Patrick with a huge bandage around his head.

"Son," said Mike McCarthy, rushing over to Patrick and pulling him onto a chair. "Tell us how you are. I wanted to get to the hospital last night, but Jeffreys said ..."

"Leave me alone, Dad," said Patrick quietly.

"He should be in bed," said Mary. "Can you manage the stairs, Patrick? We're so happy to see you."

Her eyes met Mr. Jeffreys's, noting his sardonic expression.

"Of course, he can manage the stairs," said Simon in a robust tone. He doesn't like not being the vulnerable one, thought Mary, amused.

"No one's answered my question about Viktor," continued Simon. "What's he up to? He mentioned some big news about the Falconers?"

"Tonight, at the Thanksgiving dinner," came a young female voice from the opposite direction of the lobby. It was Anna dressed in a scarlet ball gown. At 10 in the morning, Mary noted. She's been playing dress-up ... for Caroline?

Next to Anna, Caroline glowed in jeans and a big sweater. The sweater must have been George's, Mary guessed. Had they just arrived from George's ... Caroline's, cottage?

"Did I hear we are having Thanksgiving?" came unmistakable public speaking tones, this time from a ballooning pink dressing gown at top of the stairs. Belinda, of course. I'd forgotten about her, though Mary, Richard too. Mary swung her head from Belinda to Richard standing behind her, to the imperious gaze of Anna, then back again. Wait a minute, was Caroline winking?

Mr. Jeffreys coughed.

"We've established that Sir Viktor Solokov wishes his guests to join him in a Thanksgiving dinner in honor of his

American mother. Can I suggest that we get Mr. McCarthy, Mr. *Patrick* McCarthy," he said, nodding ironically at Patrick's father, "to where he can rest?"

"Come up to bed, darling," said Simon, putting an arm under Patrick's shoulders. Mary caught Belinda scowling as she gave way for the pair. Mike McCarthy dragged his suitcase up behind his son. Mr. Jeffreys made to do something similar, when Mary took his arm.

"Leave your bag. Anna will get the students to deal with luggage when she's sorted your room. Come with me. I know where they keep the good coffee. We've got to talk."

He smiled, showing his perfect teeth.

"An excellent idea, Miss Wandwalker."

CHAPTER 37
MIKE MCCARTHY

Not updated was the best that could be said of the Falconer House kitchen. Mary grimaced at the peeling paint and stale odors that never seemed to change. Preoccupied, she brewed a pot of Kenya Peaberry coffee from Oxford's Covered Market, all the while conscious of Mr. Jeffreys uncomfortably balanced on a stool at the wooden table. His body language suggested anthropological interest and mild concern.

When did I get so involved with this house and the Falconers, Mary pondered? Was it when I heard about George? Or was it when he said, "Mother," as his life drained into the earth? As if he could read her thoughts, Mr. Jeffreys nodded soberly.

After pouring two mugs of coffee, Mary took hold of the fridge's vertical handle and threw herself backward to open the door: a trick she'd been shown by Helga.

"You know I take my coffee black?" said Mr. Jeffreys, with deceptive meekness.

"Naturally. The milk is for me," said Mary. She sat down with her mug. A smell of onions arose from the unvarnished table. Mary cleared her throat instead of gagging. She tried not to wonder about the food hygiene habits of the students, and Anna Solokov.

"Well, Miss Wandwalker, you wanted to talk."

Mr. Jeffreys was not a patient man, Mary recalled. Well, he deserved to wait, and she deserved time to ponder. She recollected he did not know about Helga's pregnancy. That must fit in somehow. Then there was the strange passion between Anna and Caroline. No, there was something even more troubling. Mary looked up at the man she continued to find provoking even though he was no longer her boss.

"Mike McCarthy?" she said. "Why did you bring him to Falconer House?"

"Mike McCarthy present and correct, Ma'am," said a cheerful voice from behind Mr. Jeffreys's bulk. Mary almost fell off her chair. Instead, she stood up as Mike McCarthy sauntered into the room as if very much at home.

"Oh, am I disturbing something?"

He did not wait for a reply. Brightening at the half full coffee pot on the cooker, he swanned to the sink's draining crockery, took a mug, and filled it before pulling out another stool from under the table.

"Sorry, to barge in Ms. W.," he winked. "Patrick doesn't want to talk to me. Plus, we both know your Mr. Jeffreys summoned me back to the estate for more than a social call. Let's get it over with, old chap."

He must be more nervous than he looked, thought Mary, because his hand holding the coffee trembled. A trickle dribbled onto the table. Mary leapt for a cloth.

"Too late for this old beast. Table's been here forever," said McCarthy as she scrubbed at the stain. The coffee mark barely registered alongside traces of food, drink, and knife nicks from chopping and slicing. McCarthy spoke again, this time more slowly.

"I used to sit at this kitchen table in Margaret's time. In those days no one peeled a carrot without a board to protect its surface. This bit of wood meant something to her. She'd polish it herself whenever things got too much. Looking back, I can see she cared for the whole house far more than Sir Daniel, who was born here."

Mary shot a glance at Jeffreys, and he raised an eyebrow: Wait, listen, she deciphered. McCarthy placed his hand flat on the unvarnished surface, then raised his fingers to his nose and winced at the smell of onions.

"One winter afternoon Margaret, Lady Margaret Falconer, told me a story she got from an old servant. How this table came from the biggest oak tree in the park, in Sir Daniel's grandfather's time. One night there was a tremendous storm: a once-in-a-century tempest, the papers said. No idea of global warming in those days. Struck by lightning, the old oak split down the middle."

A stubby finger caressed a smooth yet slightly raised knot. "The gardeners left the half with more roots to grow for another 50 years. The rest ended up as this table. It's served generations of Falconers and their staff. Strong roots, oak trees; Falconers too."

The hairs on the back of Mary's neck rose. Mike McCarthy had joined Viktor Solokov, Anna, and even Mr. Jeffreys in saying something disguised as something else. She wanted to be irritated. Hell, I *am* irritated, she said to herself. Even so, she could detect Mr. Jeffreys's warning to be patient without glancing at him. George Jones was dead. Perdita Falconer was dead. They were way beyond the luxury of irritation. She would feel her way forward.

"You knew David's mother, Arthur's too?"

Mike McCarthy gave Mary a hard look. Old pain, she thought. There's something there, something he's not telling us. Before she could insist, she heard a rustle of paper along with a scrape of a stool on the worn kitchen tiles. Both Mary and McCarthy watched Jeffreys taking small items from an inner pocket.

Sacrificing a handkerchief, Mr. Jeffreys wiped a plate. On it he spread the page from David's autopsy report. He turned the plate so Mary and McCarthy could both examine it. Mary swallowed hard then crossed her arms. Her accusing look at Jeffreys shifted to the other man. Mike McCarthy stared in horror at what remained of the evidence of David's poisoning. He reached out a forefinger to touch it, then drew back as if scalded. Mary caught sight of ingrained paint in his nails, knuckles, and palms.

This time Mike McCarthy had to force out the words. "You found it. After all these years, you found it in that wretched spy safe of Sir Daniel's."

He pulled his gaze from the paper as if it hurt to separate from it. Speaking to Mr. Jeffreys with defiance, he continued, "If you've been snooping around, I suppose you've got the tin too. I know that didn't end up in spy safe behind the painting, not enough room. Yeah, I see you know that tin. You've had the contents analyzed, eh Jeffreys?"

"Psilocybin," confirmed Jeffreys in his darkest voice. "Murder weapon for David Falconer and ... more recently, the kind also used on other members of the family."

Mike McCarthy's lip trembled. One hand shuddered; he lifted the other to still it. To buy time, he sipped his coffee. He's hiding something, Mary realized. How come he knew about the box and the paper? Why is Jeffreys looking at me like a slow pupil at school?

That tin of psilocybin with David's name on it. How could Mike McCarthy know about that? Ah.

"Mr. Jeffreys, you've heard back on *both* tests, the tin and the contents," she accused.

Mr. Jeffreys showed his smile again, the one with teeth. Go on Mary.

"Mr. McCarthy, I'm guessing your fingerprints are on the tobacco tin. Probably the photocopy too. *You* hid them both. Did you copy the report on David in 1978?"

"Call me Mike, please," McCarthy said. "Lady Margaret begged me to do it." He lifted his eyes to the cereal boxes at the other side of the kitchen. "Make the photocopy, that is. Hiding the tin came later. I saw it after Sir Daniel hotfooted to France, leaving Margaret desperate to understand what happened to David. That kid drove brilliantly, she said. Margaret could not accept the accident story." He sniffed and slurped. Mary dared not interrupt the flow of his thoughts.

"Right as he was leaving for France, Sir Daniel insisted on an autopsy for David. The results were to be kept under wraps until he returned. Of course, when he did come back, it was in a coffin. By then secrecy about David's death became part of covering up the truth about Sir Daniel's."

"But there was a point where Sir Daniel was only missing, and Lady M wanted answers about her son. She and I became friendly when Sir Daniel opened the Falconer estate to art students doing plein air sketching. So, knowing I had a friend who became a police artist, Lady M implored me to use my contacts. He'd been up at Oxford with us and knew the local squad. I got an hour with the lab report." He gave a bark of bitter humor. "God rest the '70s. I had to run around the City Centre looking for a photocopier."

McCarthy's hands were now fists. There was more, and it was harder to say. They would wait. With a glance at his unyielding companions, McCarthy stumbled on.

"We planned to show the report to Sir Daniel when he returned. Then we ... well, Sir Daniel died over in France. Too devastated to carry on, Margaret called me. She made me watch as she threw the photocopied file into the drawing room fire, told me to forget everything. What she didn't know was that I'd made two copies."

He made eye contact with Mary. "You see, David was a pal. We met in the Cardinal College Bar, then bumped into each other on the Falconer estate. I had a phase of trying to make my own watercolor paints from earths and plants there. Gave up that nonsense afterward, but David liked my trying to do something ... oh, *grounded,* I think he said. He even suggested to his mother that I paint her. She followed up on that, eventually." Mike gave Mary a crooked smile. "Last phone call, David said something about my designing a wedding invitation. So, I found I could not destroy the psilocybin result. It was his truth."

Mike McCarthy paused and sipped his coffee. "I stuffed this one page in the spy safe months later. Margaret gave me some letters of Daniel's to put there. Those letters nearly killed her. When I realized they were letters to that Rosalind woman, I knew why. Margaret said she would not erase that part of his life, but I was to keep the safe key and give it to Arthur after her death. Passed it to him at Margaret's funeral."

Lady Margaret would have had to sign the Official Secrets Act, Mary realized. She'd be forbidden to talk about how Sir Daniel died. That would probably extend to David's mysterious drug-fueled car crash. Mary shivered. Margaret Falconer'd gotten the truth about David with the help of Mike McCarthy. Now it was about keeping secrets, *family* secrets. Well, Margaret, thought Mary. I'm family now. I guess that means it's time for me to accept the apology you wrote on my letter.

Tell Mary Wandwalker, I'm sorry. Margaret Falconer had scribbled that in her very last days. Mary put her elbows on Margaret's kitchen table and briefly covered her eyes. She looked up to find Mike McCarthy watching her.

"I'm an artist. I don't like burning history." He indicated the photocopy with his mug. Mr. Jeffreys pulled it away from within splashing distance.

"This page tells the truth about why David crashed his car. I wanted to follow the psilocybin clue. So even though I was now *persona non grata* at Falconer House, I had a quick shufti outside. In the old stable, I saw the tin under a mess of broken glass and a Bunsen burner."

He peered at Mary. "I could go on, but not today. You see, Margaret was no longer talking to me. It was two years before she got in touch about the portrait. The past was out of bounds." He squinted at the tobacco tin. "Should have thought about fingerprints. How d'you know they were mine?"

"They are on file," said Mr. Jeffreys without emphasis.

"Ah, I'd forgotten that DUI in '96. See how old sins come back to haunt us, Miss Wandwalker?"

"Perhaps more than you realize," said Mary. Patrick's depiction of Anne of Cleves glowed in Mary's recollection. Something about its daring and complexity stuck to Mary's sense of Patrick, Simon's husband. Now she faced that man's father, who did not appreciate his son's art.

"Mr. McCarthy, have you never wondered why Patrick's portraits fuse paint with collaged documents? They are obsessed with history, just like you keeping that paper about David."

McCarthy's jaw dropped at Mary's insight. Mr. Jeffreys looked amused. He lifted his empty coffee cup at Mary, as a salute and a question.

"The coffee is over there, Mr. Jeffreys," she said. "Help yourself."

Without comment he got the pot and shared the remaining brew.

"Don't give up your day job, Jeffreys," muttered McCarthy, his humor sounding forced.

Trying to be jaunty again, Mary noted, although she saw he'd taken her remark about Patrick's distinctive style to heart. She was not fooled by his evasions. There was something about his relations with the Falconers, with Lady Margaret in particular, that he did not want to talk about.

"No," said McCarthy, "don't look at me like that, Miss Wandwalker. I'm not telling you the rest of my story just yet. That Viktor Solokov is up to something. He called me yesterday. I thought it was to touch up his bloody portrait again. In fact, he wanted to talk about the death of George Jones — said my unique connection to the Falconers meant I should be here for Thanksgiving dinner tonight. He's plotting something."

He eyed Mary. "Viktor said Jones was your son, yours and David Falconer's, Miss Wandwalker. You must be in shock. I have a feeling, call it artist's intuition, that tonight's revelations are going to be … well, rather interesting."

With that bombshell, McCarthy exited the kitchen, leaving Mary forlorn. So, tonight's a big deal.

"It will soon be over, Mary," said Mr. Jeffreys.

She thought his gentle voice more unnerving than his commands.

"It will never be over," Mary said.

CHAPTER 38
READY FOR DINNER?

This is the best you're going to get, Viktor Solokov, reflected Mary as she smoothed down her gray wool dress with the sky-blue trim. The gong for drinks reverberated in her ears. Nevertheless, Mary hovered in front of the mirror. In for a penny, she thought as she pulled her most vivid rose lipstick from her handbag.

Wan from George's death, anxious for the Falconers, and finding Falconer House increasingly uncanny, her legs were leaden at the prospect of sitting through a formal Thanksgiving dinner. Whatever Viktor Solokov planned, it could not be good for the Falconers he resented, the wife he showed no sign of loving or respecting, or either of her lovers. Mary blinked, realizing she was now counting Caroline among those involved with Anna. How did that happen?

Foreboding made her look longingly at the bed she'd made that morning. No, you don't, she said to herself. I've saved Government ministers from career-ending mistakes, defeated bullies and crooks among my staff, so I can do this evening for George. Struck by the oddness of that realization, Mary abandoned self-examination. Swiftly she exited the room. She had almost reached the fateful staircase when she heard her name.

"Pssst, Mary. Over here."

Mary tensed. Looking up and down the corridor she could see no one. Probably a gust of wind blowing through her overactive imagination, she concluded. A second gong for drinks urged from below.

"Here, behind you."

Mary swung around. Nothing visible in the corridor's dimness. The other guests must have descended, she'd thought. Patrick was going to get up for the dinner, Simon confided earlier. Also, Mary had detected the strained voices of Belinda Choudhry and Richard Bishop as they passed her bedroom.

"Who's there? Stop playing games." Mary was affronted rather than scared. A pale shape emerged from the dark, and Mary shrank back.

"Sorry, I'm putting the light on. It's Anna."

Warm lamplight streamed from an open door. The pale figure was Anna in a silvery evening gown. Behind her Caroline's head peeked from inside the bedroom.

Mary took a few steps toward them. "Anna, whatever…?"

"Can't stop this minute, Miss Wandwalker." Anna moved rapidly toward Mary, speaking sotto voce as she slipped past. "I'm late for meeting Viktor. Go see Caroline. We've something to show you. For George."

With a swish of gleaming satin Anna zoomed down the grand staircase more rapidly than the lady of the manor should, thought Mary. Anna flirted with danger. Mary could still see in her mind the crumpled figure of Patrick.

"Here, Mary, come inside," said Caroline.

"Does it have to be now?" grumbled Mary, switching on corridor lights as she approached Caroline. "Can't it wait until after dinner?"

"No," said Caroline, grabbing Mary by the arm, then not letting go until depositing her on the bed. "It can't wait. Not with Viktor's big surprise everyone's talking about. You must read this page."

She thrust a cardboard-covered packet at Mary. "Just skim it. We want you to have this information before Mr. Jeffreys."

Mary sighed, opened the folder, and then sat very still, staring at the names.

"*This* is the famous Kestrel file Sir Daniel kept. Simon and Patrick were convinced it would be in that spy safe. All we found were letters to Rosalind Forrest and ..." she paused, "that page from the report on David. We've been looking all over Falconer House for more on the murdering Soviet spy. How on earth...?"

"It wasn't hidden in Falconer House. We found it in our, my cottage, under the floor. Too much creaking whenever Anna and I got out of bed. So eventually she got a knife and prized up the board. Anna is so resourceful."

Mary shot a hard look at Caroline. She noted that swollen eyelids from crying had given way to a new strength about the jaw.

"Good," Mary said, nonspecifically. "I was about to give up. Ah."

"Yeah," said Caroline. "That's the bit that we wanted you to see."

Mary bent over the faded typewritten pages. "I see," she said, after scanning to the end. "Most illuminating. Really, we should have guessed this. The Kestrel's motives were hidden in plain sight. These murders truly are a family affair." She met Caroline's shining eyes. "Now let's go down to Thanksgiving dinner."

In a kaftan of dull red with a gold border, Caroline led the way down. So began the most bizarre and twisted evening in all of Mary Wandwalker's life.

CHAPTER 39
THANKSGIVING

After drinks, after the inevitable turkey (too chewy), with mountains of potatoes (too soft), and carrots with sugar over them (too hard), and gravy (too lumpy), Mary resigned herself to enduring rather than enjoying the pumpkin pie. To her surprise it was moist, fudgy, and spicy, with buttery pastry and topped with clotted cream. Her eyes met Helga's. The girl's expression flickered momentarily into a smile.

Helga made the pie, Mary remembered Anna saying. So why is she so tense? And why are Helga and Johann the only students around tonight? Mary would find out in approximately four minutes. A rustle went around the table in shivers and coughs. It was starting.

Viktor Solokov, resplendent in a fawn silk jacket and black bow tie, rose to his feet. Silence descended like an invisible blanket. Most of his guests suffered from stress-induced indigestion to a greater or lesser degree. Although those big slices of pumpkin pie don't help, thought Mary. I'm giving up on it even if Helga did make it.

Viktor took a fork and struck his water glass. The insistent clinking set Mary's teeth on edge.

"Ladies and gentlemen, Falconers, and guests, I have an announcement. Listen carefully, it affects every single one of you."

He clamped his lips shut, prolonging the suspense.

With minimal head movement, Mary glanced around the dinner table. For the first time she noticed that the arrangement of silver on the table left everyone visible, exposed. No flowers hid strained expressions. There was one-inch-high centerpiece close to Viktor. It's plaited autumn leaves, berries, and single unlit candle made the whole table look like an open field. Only by bowing their heads could the men and women escape their host's scrutiny.

Weariness and wariness characterized the assembly. Patrick's enormous bandage looked too tight. It made tufts of hair stick out at right angles. Ah, Simon changed the bandage, Mary realized. Patrick drooped his head until it found Simon's shoulder.

At the head of the table, Viktor was flanked by Belinda, her face frozen. Richard, on Viktor's other side, darted a worried look at his estranged wife. Before now, he'd tried to catch Mary's eye once or twice. She ignored him in favor of inconsequential remarks to Arthur on her left and a few exchanges with Caroline on her right.

Mr. Jeffreys, looking out of place among the Falconers, had eaten his meal calmly, with one eye on Viktor. At the opposite end of the table to her husband, Anna bolted her meal and attempted to flirt with Mike McCarthy, sitting next to her. His attempts at gallant banter reminded Mary of his evasiveness in the kitchen that morning.

Just what had McCarthy decided not to reveal? Could it have anything to do with Viktor's big news, news she could anticipate, thanks to the Kestrel file. Not prepared to risk leaving it in her bedroom, she had stuffed it into the handbag sitting at her feet.

"My news," repeated Viktor coldly. Yes, he was waiting for everyone to look at him, only at him. Arthur knocked over his wine glass and merely gazed at the red stain seeping over the white cloth, as if in a trance.

Viktor smiled. He's enjoying this, Mary pondered. A sadist. Viktor takes pleasure in inflicting pain or creating fear. She glanced at Anna, who stuck her chin higher and looked past her husband. Anna was gritting her teeth. So was Mary. Viktor began to speak in a high, clear lightly accented voice.

"Guests and owners of this fine English estate, it is time for me to join the Falconer family. I have all the necessary DNA proof." He stopped and glared at Mr. Jeffreys. "Should you be so vulgar to require it. I, Viktor Solokov, am the son of Rosalind Forrest and Sir Daniel Falconer. You see before you Sir Daniel's third son; heir to the estate after Mr. Simon Falconer here."

As Patrick's head shot up, Simon choked over his glass of water, spilling some onto the snowy tablecloth. He mouthed "Rosalind" in horror at Mary. Patrick's arm went around Simon's shoulders. Mary put a hand on Arthur's arm as he gasped.

Mary Wandwalker remembered Rosalind Forrest. In Los Angeles-styled glamour, the woman stood at Sir Daniel's side that day in 1978, acting as hostess. Lady Margaret was at the Devon farm. It had all been there in plain sight, Viktor's parentage, in those blue Falconer eyes. These eyes found the current owner of Falconer House.

"You will be pleased, Sir Arthur, that the line will not die out. I offer you yet more Falconers. You see, I am to become a father."

Arthur's jaw gaped as heads swung back to Anna Solokov sitting stonily opposite Arthur.

"No, not my barren wife. My barren and faithless wife."

The words cracked like a whip. Mary and Caroline flinched. Anna did not.

"Helga, sitting here, sister of Johann, carries my twins. The scan shows a healthy boy and girl. How fortunate that changes in the law mean that we 'bastard' children may inherit this estate."

As Viktor quoted the term for illegitimacy, it seemed the word would shatter into sharp blades of glass. No one dared respond. More pieces of the puzzle fell into place with his suppressed rage. Mary glanced at Mr. Jeffreys. He had guessed about Viktor being a Falconer. But neither of them had foreseen the addition of Helga. Mr. Jeffreys pursed his lips at the young woman sitting opposite. The blue streak in her hair was the only touch of color about her. She wore a beige smock. Her eyes had become dark smudges.

"Viktor's referring to the 2014 change in the law," whispered Caroline into Mary's ear. "It equalizes the rights of all children, born in wedlock or not. Anna thinks Viktor put pressure on the Conservatives to speed up the change. He made a huge donation and cozied up to Belinda, who was on the right committee. He's been plotting this for a long time."

You don't say, said Mary to herself. Oh yes, this has been plotted for a long time, and not only by Viktor. Not four years, more like 40, she thought, catching Mr. Jeffreys nodding. Under the table she slid one foot from her shoe so her toes could feel for the file poking out of her bag. Got it.

Arthur and Simon do not yet understand that the Kestrel is two men set on revenge, not one.

As Viktor gloated at the head of the table, Mary surveyed her companions with growing alarm. Noting the tremor of Arthur's hands and Simon transfixed by the silver dishes in front of him, she decided to act.

"Um, Sir Viktor," Mary said loudly.

Viktor scowled, evidently nonplussed by the interruption of his big moment. The diners swiveled their shocked expressions to Mary. Like a tennis match, she thought, how absurd. She experienced a moment of déjà vu, the faces of Simon, Patrick, and Mr. Jeffreys long ago in that Barbican flat. Glimpsing a half smile from Mr. Jeffreys, she felt a surge of energy. Like her hostile host, Mary stood up to address the company.

"Sir Viktor, you've forgotten to mention your real father, the man who brought you up, Kyrill Solokov. Your stepfather, otherwise known as the Kestrel, taught you to hate the Falconers. This is *his* revenge on the whole family."

Mary sniffed. "No doubt discovering the woman he loved was pregnant by his enemy made his hatred personal. He decided that his revenge would not die when he did. So, he ensured you became *his* child. He formed you, educated you, ruined you."

Mary's voice grew louder. She commanded the room. Viktor stared, unable to stop her.

"Did Kyrill, I wonder, decide to make you his instrument before you were born? Did you never wonder why he supplied so many drugs to your mother? By punishing her, he gained total control of you."

Viktor leaned over the table as if he could skewer Mary from 10 feet away. "Don't talk about my mother," he yelled. "She was more a mother to me than you to George Jones."

For a second Mary saw him contract into a gleaming blade. It came for her heart, as it had come for George. She blinked. Then her fingers found her dinner knife. Another hand gripped and pulled her back. Caroline, Mary shook herself free and stood tall.

Viktor hissed. "I or my children will inherit," Viktor repeated, staring through Mary.

Not yours, Mary Wandwalker. Not your son, hung between them.

There was a general scaping of chairs, dropping of spoons, and two glasses fell to the carpet, rolling in spilled wine. Mary could see members of the house party joining the dots. Viktor as Sir Daniel's son was bad enough…

"Did you kill my daughter, my Perdita?" That was Simon, still seated with Patrick's arm around him. Mary instinctively turned to Arthur. Tears ran down both cheeks. She picked up his stick and put it in his hand.

Very slowly, Viktor inclined his head to Simon. It was not quite a nod. His gloat gleamed. Long suspected, here was all but confirmation that Viktor was today's drug dealing Kestrel. He had also taken on his stepfather's role of killer. The horror on Patrick's face was painful to witness. To quell the murmuring, Mary hurried on.

"Viktor Solokov, you claim to be a Falconer by blood. It's not enough." Mary did not know what she wanted to say. Words felt like lumps of Falconer earth from a grave.

"No, you've spilled too much Falconer blood to be part of... *our family*."

Now Mary could say it. "You are no Falconer. You are a Solokov. Kyrill Solokov married Rosalind Forrest in Los Angeles shortly after your birth. After the disastrous end of his spying career, he dealt in drugs, then other kinds of organized crime. That's the kind of businessman you are, nothing but a gangster."

Viktor bent over to bang his fist on the table. Mary ignored him.

"Some of you," she looked at Mike McCarthy and Helga, "might not know that Kyrill, the Kestrel, was a KGB double agent. He betrayed and murdered his British handler, Sir Daniel Falconer. When Rosalind Forrest announced she was having a child by Sir Daniel, the Kestrel's fury fueled a revenge plot that lasted 40 years." Mary's mouth went dry. "My George was the latest victim."

A snapping noise made Mary pause. Viktor thumping the Thanksgiving table so hard the setting of twigs, autumn leaves, that one white candle like a bone, jumped. Without taking his eyes off Mary, he was breaking everything: twigs, the candle, even the wooden letters that had spelled "Thanksgiving."

"Snares and lies," he said between his teeth. "The Falconers are a trap, not a nest. Kyrill said it again and again. They trapped Kyrill, and my poor mother. He told me everything."

Viktor threw bits of wax and wood to the floor, making Belinda shake. She crouched over her plate. Mary glanced again at Mr. Jeffreys, then, seeing his slight nod, resolved to continue. After all, Viktor had said it, hadn't he?

"'After one golden day I'd see that the Falconer family is a trap, not a nest?' Is that what he told you?"

As Mary quoted from her own letter of 40 years ago, she realized she could no longer feel the hurt that made her write it. Too many other hurts had been dug up recently.

In the pause, Patrick took Simon's hand on the tablecloth. Mary recalled that "trap not a nest" also came from Perdita

THANKSGIVING

Falconer's so-called suicide note. Who wrote it? Viktor or one of his minions, the so-called students? Mary had more. She placed her hands on the table and leaned forward.

"Back in the 1970s, it was a different time. Perhaps Sir Daniel did use his family and this beautiful house to …" Mary hesitated, "seduce Kyrill into thinking it a nest, Rosalind too."

Definitely to seduce Rosalind Forrest, she saw Simon mouth to Patrick. She had to finish quickly before Viktor detonated.

Mary raised her stormy eyes to meet Viktor's blue fury.

"You won't get away with any of this. To Kyrill it was not enough to kill Sir Daniel in France. Sir Daniel's son, David, also had to die. Through you he could destroy the whole family. Grandson George Jones and Sir Daniel's great granddaughter Perdita must pay too. That's what Kyrill made you promise before he died in 2011."

Mary felt bleak. She held a knife and had to drive it home into this smiling terrible man.

"Not Kyrill's son by blood, but you inherited his hate, his criminal organization, and his non de plume, the Kestrel …"

Mary was interrupted by a howl as Viktor crashed both fists on the table.

"For crimes of drugs and trafficking," continued Mr. Jeffreys, his bulk suddenly standing. Everyone pushed back their chairs. Fear ran round the room like a fox with its tail on fire. Fear hardened into stone: Viktor had a gun.

Mary's vision contracted to that black hole in the black gloved hand. No fingerprints. He thinks of everything. The gun pointed at Arthur, who rose shakily to his feet with the aid of his stick.

"Are you going to kill me in front of my family?" he asked.

"You cannot inherit Falconer House if you kill for it," said Mr. Jeffreys.

Everyone held their breath.

The gun shifted infinitesimally. After a rise and fall of the chest his chest, the gun disappeared into the fawn jacket pocket. Viktor's next words cut.

"I can't inherit Falconer House if I am *proven* to kill for it." Viktor watched for the impact of his words. Horror spread from face to face.

This is what he wanted, thought Mary. He wants to inherit, and he wants us to know he killed for it. If we cannot prove it, he gets everything, including destroying the Falconer family.

Including killing George. Another kick to her chest. She saw Viktor looking at her with those blue eyes. She willed herself not to sit down. This is not about money. It's revenge by destroying the Falconer family.

"Perdita," whispered Simon. "You killed our Perdita."

"And George, my husband," added Caroline, putting her arm through Mary's.

"Prove it," hissed Viktor, a snake with demon blue eyes.

There was a distant bang of a door, then a tramp of feet getting louder. Viktor did not move, despite the entry of several uniformed men behind him. He smiled to show this was all part of his plan, then he waved at the officer in charge.

"Chief Inspector Reynolds, you have joined us just in time. Please arrest my wife over there. Anna Solokov murdered her lover, George Jones."

Caroline gave a sob. She made a move for Anna. Mary held onto her hand. Ignoring Caroline, Anna darted for the nearest door and catapulted into two more police officers. One produced handcuffs, clipping them onto Anna's wrists. Anna tensed for a few seconds and then drooped. She avoided looking at anyone as she was led away.

"Don't take her like that. You have no evidence," called Mary in outrage. Anna was not guilty of killing George. In her bones she knew Anna's relationship with George was more complicated than that.

"On the contrary, I have an eyewitness who saw the young woman stab your son," said Reynolds, his face grave. He shook Viktor's hand. It seemed to be some kind of signal, because Viktor flashed his white teeth and left the room.

Mary choked, then helped Caroline back into her chair. Reynolds scrutinized the company until he found his quarry. "Ms. Choudhry, please remember to be at the station by 9 a.m. to review and sign your statement," he ordered. Reynolds flicked a glance at Mary that she found hard to decipher. Dawning comprehension on the faces of Falconers, however, irritated Mary. She wondered why.

Belinda nodded blankly in Reynolds's direction. The Chief Inspector backed out of the too bright too fissile room while Richard got to his feet. Police cars began to purr in the distance.

"*Belinda, what have you done?*" bellowed Richard across the table at his estranged wife. Everyone jumped. Even Mary. She'd never seen Richard this angry. Belinda hugged her shoulders. She began to shake. She's going to break, thought Mary. This is all wrong.

Richard staggered to the sideboard for a fresh linen napkin to wipe his sweat. His cheeks were scarlet.

A tiny tinkling sound came from the bangles on Belinda's plump arm. She stretched a hand to Richard. He stared back.

"I know you're lying," he whispered. After a moment he went to a chair as far away from Belinda as possible. Helga slid over to Richard to grab his hand.

Mary heard a sob. Johann slipped in the open door to help Belinda stumble from the room.

No one followed her, Mary noticed.

"No, no, no," wailed Caroline into Mary's shoulder. "Anna did not kill George."

This is all wrong, thought Mary. This is Viktor Solokov. The Kestrel is doing this.

CHAPTER 40
REGROUP AT THE RANDOLPH HOTEL, OXFORD

Shocked into sobriety, the remaining guests at the wrecked Thanksgiving dinner exchanged glances. Distant roars dying to the sound of wind marked the departure of the last police car, with Anna handcuffed in the back seat. Mary whispered to Johann, who vanished, returning to report that Viktor could not be found in any of the communal rooms of Falconer House. No one dared suggesting tapping the door of the bedroom marked "Solokov." Mary looked inquiringly at Mr. Jeffreys.

"It would appear," he remarked, suavity regained, "that Falconer House is not healthy for anyone named Falconer. Nor if married to one." He nodded at Patrick.

"We're getting out of here," said Simon. "Right now. That means you too, Pa."

Everyone started to move. Several persons darted out of the dining room in search of coats and outdoor shoes. Mary took Caroline upstairs to collect essential belongings. Simon did the same, leaving his white-faced husband in the charge of his stunned father. Mr. Jeffreys produced a briefcase and said he was ready to depart. Mike McCarthy reappeared with a suitcase.

Only Belinda Choudhry wanted to stay at Falconer House, or so reported Richard Bishop. She'd locked herself in their bedroom. Richard said he would leave without his belongings. He was too tight-lipped to comment further on Belinda.

The leaving party would decamp to Oxford. Despite the lateness of the evening, Mr. Jeffreys secured three rooms at the Randolph Hotel, while Mary sorted rides in the available vehicles. Since Arthur said that he had a friend who would accommodate him in the city, Mary decided to share with Caroline, silent since Anna's arrest. Patrick and Simon would take another chamber, leaving Mike McCarthy and Mr. Jeffreys the last available bedroom in the hotel.

Richard announced he would go to his rooms at Sumer College. When Helga begged to accompany those leaving Falconer House, Johann made a rude gesture at his twin. After yelling something in Hungarian, he stamped away. Helga threw her arms around Richard and burst into tears. Patting her head and wincing in Mary's direction, Richard promised to get her a room in Sumer. She was their student after all.

"We'll meet over breakfast at the Randolph," announced Mr. Jeffreys. "For a council of war," he added.

"Not before 9 a.m.," added Mary, thinking of the lateness of the hour. It would be well after midnight before the leaving party could settle into their respective beds, surely longer before they would fall sleep.

Mary was right. Apart from Mike McCarthy, who snored like a steam engine, as Mr. Jeffreys later confided to Mary, no one else who witnessed Viktor's performance got a good night's sleep. Mary Wandwalker devoted hours to thinking long and hard about Belinda Choudhry. Something troubled her about Belinda's claim to have witnessed Anna Solokov commit murder.

Mary wanted to discuss the arrest of Anna with Caroline. However, the woman in the other twin bed would not respond. Curled into an inert ball, she was a millstone. Mary tried not to worry. She guessed Caroline had gone back in time to the cottage. She had gone home to George, or to that day she shared with Anna. Sighing, Mary returned to the unreal events of the evening.

Later, as the long night gave way to Oxford's early traffic, the millstone melted. Caroline began to speak. Mary listened without comment as Caroline conveyed what she had learned about Anna's life, from George, and then Anna herself. At last, exhausted beyond measure, Caroline turned over and slept.

Mary rooted in the bottom of her handbag for a piece of paper folded and unfolded too many times. For her own sanity, she made additions to the Falconer family tree. "Service through Family," my eye, she muttered. I guess I am still a documents person.

Mary Wandwalker's additions

Falconer Family Tree (motto: *Service through Family*)

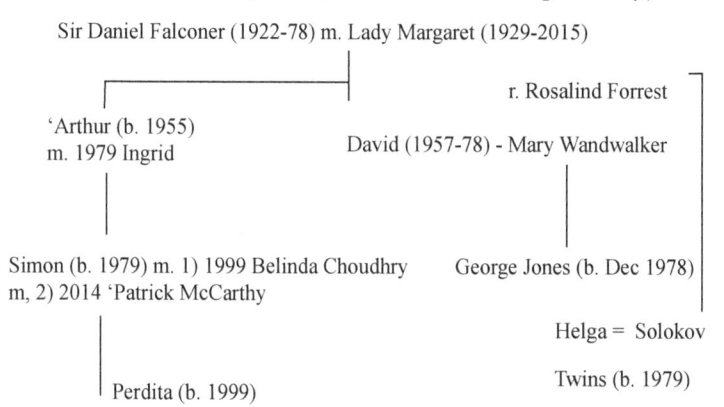

Sir Daniel Falconer (1922-78) m. Lady Margaret (1929-2015)

r. Rosalind Forrest

'Arthur (b. 1955) m. 1979 Ingrid

David (1957-78) - Mary Wandwalker

Simon (b. 1979) m. 1) 1999 Belinda Choudhry m, 2) 2014 'Patrick McCarthy

George Jones (b. Dec 1978)

Helga = Solokov

Perdita (b. 1999)

Twins (b. 1979)

When it was close to dawn and she was still unable to relax, Mary had an idea. Gathering up her clothes without putting on the lamp, she dressed and crept down to the Randolph kitchens where preparations for breakfast had barely started. Fortunately, Mary Wandwalker was adept at making coffee in a strange kitchen. After checking with the night receptionist, she gave a brisk knock on the door that housed Simon and Patrick.

"Do you always get up this early?" complained Simon as Mary rummaged in the cupboard and plugged in the capsule coffee maker.

"Have a sip of this before yours is ready?" she said, offering Patrick some from the flask she had commandeered.

"Tea for me, please Miss Wandwalker. Something to do with my head. I can't take coffee right now. There are tea capsules as well. English Breakfast is good."

Mary handed the full coffee mug to Simon who slid off the bed in search of sugar. She found the right tea. Reassuring, she thought, how the mud-colored brew brightened to burnt orange by the addition of milk from the room fridge.

"Thank you, Mary," said Patrick, taking a sip. "I think I know why you're here. It's Belinda, isn't it? I was going to talk to Si about what we do next."

Mary sat on the bed, swiveling to face the two men who had pulled the duvet up to their respective chins. They look like twins, she decided, so comfortable together and both needing a shave. Twins made her think of Helga and last night. She winced before draining half her coffee and placing the mug on the bedside table.

"Yes, I'm here about Belinda. She's being blackmailed," she said. "It's the only explanation for her lying about seeing Anna kill George. Anna didn't do it. I just know. Or, if you prefer, it was in the way George said her name as he was dying. He said 'Caroline' too. He was speaking to me, and it was not an accusation. They are innocent. Well," she said, hearing herself speak that word of Anna Solokov, "you know what I mean."

Patrick grinned. Simon stirred his coffee. Mary continued.

"So, Belinda is lying. Either Viktor has something on her going way back, or there is something new. Is Ms. Choudhry a corrupt Member of Parliament?"

"No," said Simon without hesitation. "My ex-wife is not corrupt. Or not more than your average Conservative politician supporting the causes of big donors and suchlike; cash for honors. Not pretty, of course, but not unusual."

"So, her previous dealings with Viktor do not make it worth lying to the police about witnessing a murder," said Mary. "The blackmail must be about something big because she will have to testify under oath in court. That's perjury."

"Anna Solokov could be involved, even if she didn't wield the knife herself," Simon speculated. "Didn't Jeffreys discover she was part of organized crime in Europe?"

"Viktor's money comes from organized crime," corrected Mary, thinking of Mr. Jeffreys's recent emails. "He ran prostitution rings with drugs on the side. Anna helped run Viktor's operation, which began with his father, but it's not what you think."

Mary took a swig of her remaining coffee. It gave her time to ponder how to explain Anna.

"Caroline's been telling me more details of Anna's life. She began as a victim. Anna doesn't even know her real name since she was trafficked for sex as a child. Crime became her way of escaping that trade."

Mary shut her eyes briefly, recalling the halting conversation in the dark. Caroline had spoken of Anna's life as if it were her own: raw and painful.

"God," said Simon. "Child trafficking. Horrible."

"Would that ... that sort of past tends to suggest ... I mean, she could lash out," began Patrick.

"Not so likely, if you know Anna," returned Mary. "Okay, *I don't* know the woman. I doubt anyone really knows her, despite what Caroline thinks. My sense is that Anna's a survivor before everything else. George ..." Mary stopped. Not that lump in her throat again. "George was no threat to her. If anything, George was part of her survival."

"I don't see it," said Patrick, worrying at his bandage. Simon took hold of his hand.

"Leave it, my love. I'll get you a new one in a minute. Remember what the doctor said. Now about Miss Anna, I see Miss Wandwalker's point. Whether Anna was duping our George for Viktor or helping him solve Perdita's murder so she could get away from Viktor, neither suggests murderous intent."

"As I've said, I really don't see her killing George," stated Mary. "Which means that Belinda is lying. And I have an idea why."

"Ah," said Patrick. "I think you've already guessed the situation, Miss Wandwalker."

"Are you ready to talk about it?" Simon sounded anxious.

"And are you sure it was Belinda who pushed you?"

"Since last night I am. That ghastly perfume Belinda wears. As if that dinner was not appalling enough, I almost threw up when she passed my chair. That same pong hit me right before I fell."

Mary gave a huge sigh and reached for the last of her coffee.

"So, I'm right. It was Belinda who pushed you down the stairs."

"Yeah. When I woke up, I remembered feeling hands on my back. They were small, a woman's. Decided not to say more until my head cleared. The perfume clinches it."

"No one but Bel wears it these days," said Simon sadly. "'Poison,' I think it is called, from the '90s. I source it on the internet for her birthday and Christmas. It was her mother's favorite."

"How do you think Viktor found out?"

"That boy," groaned Simon.

"Who, Johann?"

"Him. He hung around the hospital. Patrick and I were talking pretty freely. You've seen how my voice carries. Finally, I noticed a cleaner hovering around us. He scarpered, but even from behind I could see that red streak. Viktor must have sent him to spy on us. Hearing about Belinda attacking Patrick, Viktor seized his opportunity. If Viktor put pressure on Belinda, she'd crack."

"Who's cracking. Not you, Patrick, I hope?"

It was Richard. He peered around the door Mary forgot to close properly. Entering in a brown sweater over jeans, he brought his own paper cup of coffee. Mary thought he looked relaxed for the first time in days. Warmth flooded from her belly toward him. Something older and wiser inside told her to hold back.

"Hey, Dick. We're talking about Belinda," said Simon. "You know, your wife."

Richard's face changed. He pressed his lips together while pulling over a chair.

"Belinda," he said, "that's why I'm here. In fact, Simon, Mary, if you don't mind, I'd like to talk to Patrick alone."

"Too late, Dick, old man. We know. Miss Wandwalker knows. Your wife tried to kill my husband."

Richard tensed his whole body on the hard chair. "Simon, don't. Just, don't." He licked his lips. "Surely, we can sort this out between us." He looked hopefully at Patrick. The injured man raised himself a little from the covers and nodded at him to go on.

"She didn't mean to kill you," Richard said, nervously.

"Is that what she told you?"

Simon was working himself up, Mary could tell.

"Oh, for fuck's sake."

Without warning Richard rose and threw his empty coffee cup across the bed to the wall, two feet from Simon. As it was cardboard, there was little damage. Jumping up, Mary saw what looked like three brown tears sticking to the gold wallpaper. They glittered, then began to run down.

Simon's jaw dropped. Patrick breathed heavily. He hung onto the chair's back and bent over. Mary wanted to go to him, but before she could move, Richard crossed to the closed door and leaned against it. He swung round to Simon.

"*You bastard. You utter bastard. All my life, all my fucking marriage, I have been second best to you, Simon bloody Falconer, heir to a grand estate and a long line of bastards.*"

His strangled tones shocked Mary.

"Second best," Richard repeated. "So, you see, I know how Belinda feels," he said fiercely.

Simon could not look at Richard, whose voice reminded Mary of her own scorched earth. He had more, a lot more.

"It was not all right, *Simon,* for you to marry Belinda and leave her after Perdita was born. You excused that by saying that you could not be your father, the closeted Arthur. Never, never *once* did you consider how Belinda felt. It was not all right,

Simon, for you to not notice how much she was in love with you. You, *Simon bloody Falconer,* are her one and only. She was second best for you, and I am second best for her. *Look at me."*

Richard stamped his foot. Even on carpet he made an impressive noise. Simon gulped. Beginning again, Richard's tone made Mary tremble.

"Perdita, our beloved Perdy. She had to be a Falconer for you, *Simon.* It killed her. I'm not allowed to grieve for my daughter, yes *daughter,* am I, Simon, the selfish Falconer?"

Patrick shot out a hand to restrain Simon. They had to let Richard continue.

"*I* was only her mother's husband. The man who shared the night watches when Perdy was a baby, the man who took her to and from school. Who helped her with her homework, who worried about her staying late at parties."

Richard paused for breath. Mary wondered how much of this she had always known.

"*You* were in and out of drug rehab. Effing Belinda was too busy being an MP to impress her father. Did you know that Choudhry never forgave her for being a girl? No wonder Belinda never forgave Patrick for marrying you. I'm only surprised she did not lose control before now."

"Richard," said Mary, not knowing what she wanted to say. "Richard, please."

The man she'd once had a love affair with drew himself up to face her. Richard now spoke to her alone.

"Mary Wandwalker, you're the only woman I've been with who could convince me I came first for her. But it's too late, isn't it, my lost love?"

Mary looked away, embarrassed. There was a sound of the door unlocking. Richard moved sideways, glaring at Simon.

"Too late for what?" Mr. Jeffreys pushed open the door. "You know you can be heard in the hall."

Behind Jeffreys, Mary caught sight of Caroline. And was that a stick she could hear on the landing? Arthur?

"Too late for what?" repeated Mr. Jeffreys. He'd heard some of Richard's rant, deduced Mary. Nevertheless, Mr. Jeffreys turned back to help Caroline bring in two extra chairs. Arthur followed them, his expression troubled and yet with a healthy color. Mary caught Simon looking relieved at the interruption. Then he brightened to mischievous.

"Dear Pa," he called as the newcomers sorted themselves. Richard remained standing so Mr. Jeffreys took his seat. "Dear Pa," Simon repeated. "How is your old friend? The one you've been visiting on and off for 40 years. Isn't it about time we accepted him as one of the family?"

"Not now, Simon," grunted Arthur. "I met Jeffreys in the lobby, and we've had a chat about Belinda. *We* think ..."

"No," said Mary very loudly, surprising herself. Everyone stopped fidgeting. "You're all going to listen to *me*. I've got something to say to you Falconers."

She paused. No longer Miss Wandwalker of the Archive, Mary felt she could channel a storm. The one that began as smoke on the horizon at the Barbican restaurant.

"You Falconers, and that means you too, Richard ..."

Simon and Arthur flinched. Richard merely gaped.

"That wretched motto: *Servitum per Familiam,* Service through Family." Mary stopped. Make them wait. "The Kestrel may be two evil men, but there is truth in this family as a trap instead of a nest."

"I say," exclaimed Simon. "Aren't you on our side?"

Mary stared at him. Simon dropped his gaze. The other men looked thoughtful, while Caroline gave Mary a tremulous smile.

The room was silent. Expectation thickened as daylight began to creep up the thick russet curtains.

CHAPTER 41
MOTHERS

With six people in a hotel room designed to house two at most, and mainly for sleeping, the air reeked of coffee and testosterone. Mary pointed Richard to the window. He turned to investigate. No good, he mouthed, the windows were sealed.

Patrick spoke as if each word hurt. "Please, Miss Wandwalker, tell us what you mean. Do you really believe the Falconer family is a trap?"

"That's not the point ..." began Mary. Mr. Jeffreys gave Mary a hard look, just as Arthur broke in.

"If this isn't about Belinda ...?" began Arthur Falconer.

"It is," retorted Mary. She glared at the Baronet, and the Baronet subsided. "God knows I'm not a fan of Belinda Choudhry MP. She hates the sight of me."

"Because of you and me," interjected Richard. Mary waved at him to stop. That was not the conversation she needed to have right now.

"Listen to me, especially you Falconers. There is no way in hell you should turn Belinda in. All of you are forgetting something. She and I share one thing: We are mothers of a dead child. How long has it been since Perdita died?"

"Two months, one week and three days." That was Patrick.

Silence jelled the air. Caroline gave Mary an encouraging smile.

"On the other hand," said Mary, forcing the words out, "Belinda is *not* like me. She brought up her child. She loved her for 19 years before Perdita was coldly murdered. Even what turned out not to be true, that Perdita might have killed herself — that would have ravaged Belinda's heart."

"It did," broke in Richard. His glance at Mary was deeply sad.

"Mary, you loved George as your child. I know you did," said Caroline in a small voice.

"Not. The. Same," said Mary painfully. She owed Belinda that. Then she forced a lighter tone. "Maybe it is because I did … do care about George that I can see how much worse it was for Belinda." Mary darted her skewering look at Simon.

"Simon. Belinda will always be Perdita's mother."

Simon flinched. At last, he nodded. "Yes. I see."

Mary continued. "Patrick, you and Belinda both love Simon. In a moment of madness, she pushed you." Mary took a deep breath. "You are the injured party. What are you going to do?

In the pause, Mr. Jeffreys slapped his knees. His chair creaked like all chairs sentenced to be under him, Mary reflected. She knew he followed her reasoning.

Patrick gave the room his crooked smile. "Don't worry, Richard. There's no question of pursuing charges against Belinda."

"What?" expostulated Arthur. "She tried to kill you. She could be in league with Viktor. He wants to kill Simon *and* me. He almost said he's planning to do it. Or, Belinda is working with Anna Solokov. What do you say to that Miss Wandwalker?"

"Anna did not kill George." The shouting came from Caroline.

"I agree," said Mary at her most brisk. "And, Art, I agree that you and Simon are in danger. Although I think Viktor enjoys terrifying people almost as much as hurting them. Given that he wants to inherit the Falconer estate, he is likely to wait a while before attacking more Falconers."

"How reassuring," said Simon, tartly.

"If you want to stop Viktor Solokov, you will listen to Miss Wandwalker." When Mr. Jeffreys spoke in that tone, everyone took notice.

Richard took a step toward the bed and Patrick. "You want Belinda to retract her statement about seeing Anna kill George Jones." He stated quietly.

He's worn out by his outburst, decided Mary. She smiled to reassure him.

"If Belinda's lying about seeing Anna do the murder, then yes, of course, we insist on a retraction," said Mary. She put out a hand. "No, Caroline, I don't think Anna did it. I'm on the side of truth."

"I'm on the side of love," muttered Caroline under her breath. She got a few askance looks, especially from Arthur.

"Look at the time," said Mary. "In an hour and 10 minutes Belinda Choudhry will sign her witness statement at the police station. Retracting after that risks a charge of wasting police time."

"Or possibly worse. I don't want Bel getting interrogated about her relationships to the family, such as her first marriage," agreed Richard. "Patrick, can you and I go and get her from Falconer House? Best if she's gone before the police pick her up."

"Certainly," said Patrick. He swung his legs out of bed. "*Oww*," he grabbed his head in both hands. Despite turning his face from Simon, it was no good.

"Patrick, stay where you are. You're not well enough for a crazy race to Falconer House."

Patrick got to his feet, steadied by Mr. Jeffreys. Richard was now at the door, jiggling car keys.

"But you're going anyway," sighed Simon. "I'm coming too. I suppose breakfast is out of the question?"

Mr. Jeffreys was already tapping a text into his extra-large, extra-dark phone.

"In five minutes, hot sandwiches will be delivered to the hotel entrance," he announced. "My driver will meet us. I'm joining the trip to Falconer House to make sure that Viktor Solokov won't try to prevent access to Ms. Choudhry. On the road, I'll get in touch with our very own Chief Inspector Bert Reynolds."

A strange beeping noise erupted from the floor near the bed.

"Your phone, Si," said Patrick. "Might I ask you ladies to withdraw so that we can get our clothes on?"

"Oh, of course." Caroline lunged for the door. Mary Wandwalker did not. Distracted, she maneuvered around chairs to the window. Not full daylight yet, just a stream of cars with their blazing yellow eyes. Surely there is something I should be doing, she thought. Who's not here?

"Who else was at that ghastly Thanksgiving dinner last night? Ah, Mike McCarthy shared Mr. Jeffreys's room. He must still be asleep."

"McCarthy's headed back to London," said Mr. Jeffreys after a glance at his phone. "But there *is* someone missing, Miss Wandwalker. I rather think she's used to being overlooked."

"Helga," said Mary and Richard at the same time. A look of understanding passed between them. Mary nodded.

"Fine," she said. "I'll go to Sumer College," said Mary. "She knows more than she's told us. I think she knows who killed George."

I think I know who killed George, she said to herself.

"I mean Helga knows who actually did the stabbing," Mary explained. "Viktor as good as told us that he's behind both murders. Oh, sorry, Patrick. You want privacy. I'm just going."

"Wait," Simon called imperiously. "I've got seven text messages about *you*, Miss Wandwalker."

"What? Not possible."

"It is if your phone is permanently switched off, and you don't check your texts." Simon grinned while pulling on his jeans. "Someone called Jamie Sanders says he's been trying to get hold of you for days. Asks you to come to his clinic as soon as you can. You're not…"

"Not ill, no. Nothing like that," said Mary thinking rapidly.

Jamie Sanders, yes, she remembered. He's the nurse at Cardinal College. Now she recalled sensing he knew something more about Perdita Falconer. Not wanting to upset Perdita's father at this moment, Mary smiled her most reassuring smile and slipped out of the room.

First Cardinal College, and then Sumer, she promised herself. While she hoped for a good, nay, a *forgiving* outcome to the reunion of Belinda, Richard, and Patrick, she had no idea of what lay ahead in two very different colleges. So why do I feel I'm getting close to the real Falconer family ground, she wondered.

CHAPTER 42
YOUNG AND IN LOVE

My goodness, Jamie's office is even more cramped than that hotel bedroom, Mary reflected. I'd also forgotten about those stone stairs. Her thighs ached. Sitting and perching her handbag on her knees, she gazed expectantly at the dreadlocked young man.

"Miss Wandwalker, you got my messages," said Jamie. "You are lucky to catch me this early. My office hours don't begin for 50 minutes."

He's nervous, thought Mary, noting the bouncing knee and the way Jamie was looking anywhere but directly at her.

"Yes, sorry about the delay," she said treading carefully. "I'm not mobile phone literate."

Jamie began picking bits of lint off his sleeve. Whatever his problem, she did not have time for this.

"Mr. Sanders, last time I said I was here for my son. Am I? Am I here for George Jones?" She paused. "He was murdered. Did you know?"

Jamie stopped fidgeting. He spread his hands on the desk. Beautifully trimmed nails, thought Mary. He's a nurse, and his hands show it. He stretched one hand over Mary's cold fingers. She looked up. His face now open ground that invited her in, she tried to smile. The young man began to talk.

"Jamie, call me Jamie. And yes, I heard about George. That's when I decided to examine my records. Although, to be honest, I did not need the computer to remember Perdita Falconer."

"This is about Perdita?" Mary felt oddly relieved. No new revelation about George, thank goodness.

"Yes, Perdita. You see, I wasn't entirely straight with you, Miss Wandwalker." He hesitated. "Perdita, she was special. Not like the other students; she was kind, considerate. Alone among Cardinal students she tried to see what it was like for me here."

"Yes, you suggested that last time." Then she realized Jamie's problem. He had dangerous ground too. "You liked her, didn't you? Really liked her. Were you in love with her?"

Jamie sat up straight. Now his hands clasped together. His voice came from far away. "I did love her. I can see that now. But nothing happened between us, you must believe me."

"Of course, I believe you," said Mary. She could see that was not enough and so she repeated it in a gentle voice. "Jamie, look at me. I know you are telling the truth when you say nothing happened."

"It's strictly forbidden," said Jamie. "You know about doctors and patients not overstepping boundaries. Well, they drill it into us college nurses too. And for someone like me in a college like this …"

He waved his hand to his dreadlocks, neatly tied back as always. Mary understood that she was catching up. A Black male nurse in a college of rich white students would be a magnet for suspicion. In those windswept quads reeking of centuries of white male privilege, just chatting to Perdita would be enough.

Young enough to be Mr. Jeffreys's grandson, he faced the same prejudice that landed him in that midnight fountain all those years ago. Mary hated injustice. Racism was the worst kind.

Looking at Jamie, it occurred to her that he would have been an ideal boyfriend for Perdita Falconer. His groundedness would have steadied her. He could help navigate the shifting sands of her family. They would have faced the uncanny atmosphere at Falconer House together. Mary sighed. It hurt to see sadness in the young man.

"Jamie, I'm so sorry. Did you ever… say anything?"

He sighed. "Not exactly. Perdita asked me out for coffee. She said her family was getting more complicated. Could we find time to talk longer than my office slots? Yet there was more. I could see it in those amazing violet eyes. She felt a connection."

He turned his head toward the window. "I turned her down, Miss Wandwalker. I said no to coffee. Said it was not allowed, would get me into trouble. She left immediately."

Jamie turned back. The words spilled from him.

"I never saw her again. So selfish of me. If I'd gone for that coffee …"

"Don't ever think that," Mary snapped. Jaime was shocked into silence.

"We can't do what might have been," she said.

My heart is broken, she thought. If only I'd known how little time I had. If only I'd gone to meet George. If only. *Words that kill.*

"Sorry," Mary whispered. "I gave George away when he was born. Did you know he was a sort of cousin to Perdita? That's probably what she meant by her family getting complicated." Mary took out a handkerchief and blew her nose. Jamie was a very good listener.

"I never got to talk to my son, you see." Except as he was dying, she reminded herself. There is something there I must go back to. "He's my 'if only.'"

"Miss Wandwalker?"

She looked at him and saw anxiety. "Sorry, Jamie. Is that what you wanted to tell me? About you and Perdita, I mean?"

"No, not about that. I need to explain that my sister met Perdita. She was saying goodbye when Perdita arrived early. What I didn't know until a couple of days ago is this." He swallowed. "My sister got a text about her train being delayed. So, she decided to hang around Cardinal Main Quad and take pictures of the students going to lectures. She planned to show them to our Mum and Dad. They can't believe what this place is like. Okay. I'm digressing." He took a breath. "Some of the shots include Perdita."

Mary sat up. About to speak, she saw Jamie had more to say. He gave an awkward smile.

"Maybe Sis was struck by Perdita or instinctively sensed something between her and me. Even then she forgot these last shots until news of Mr. Jones's death mentioned Falconer House. That's when my sister realized Falconer was the name of the girl she'd met in my office. See here, I enlarged and printed out the pics with Perdita."

From a file drawer, Jamie pulled out slightly fuzzy photographs about six inches square. I must have seen photos of Perdita in Simon's apartment, realized Mary, because she instantly recognized the graceful sweep of dark hair, the wistful smile. Did she know, Mary wondered? Did she have a premonition? Then she stiffened, picking one image to hold closer to her face.

"When exactly were these taken?" she rapped out.

"Oh, didn't I say? I got my sister to double check the time stamp. Eight hours after these were taken, Perdita was found dead on her bed. Yeah, I saw that one you are holding. Even though it is in the background, we can see the bottle. Port, isn't it? The drink that was laced with the drug that killed her?"

"More than that," said Mary, very grim. "Tiny as it is, I'm sure that label has a picture of Falconer House. Big houses used to blend their own port like Oxford colleges still do. I bet Viktor Solokov found a stash of old bottles in the cellars. Ah," she stopped and pulled out her reading glasses. "Yes, indeed. I can identify the person handing the bottle to Perdita."

For a moment Mary shut her eyes. Was it really going to end this way?

"Jamie, this is evidence. The police found a psilocybin lab at Falconer House. They probably poured the poison into the port before replacing the cork and seal. Not difficult for a killer with chemistry students at his command."

"I guess this means the police," said Jamie, subdued.

Mary bit back her retort. No need to get into Jamie's reluctance to talk to the police. No doubt he worried that the pictures on his phone could be misconstrued.

"We'll go to the police together," she said. "Later. Right now, I must find a young woman who is pregnant with twins. She knows more about these pictures than we do. Her knowledge means her life is at risk."

"Definitely, coming with you," said Jamie. He rose. "I'll cancel my office hours for this morning. Don't argue, Miss Wandwalker. I refuse to let another woman I respect walk out of here alone when she's in danger."

Mary opened her mouth to reply and was stopped by a knock on the door.

"Come in," called Jamie, buttoning up a leather jacket over his green uniform top and jeans. It was a small office, and so Mary stood aside to let the person enter. A disheveled long-haired young woman in jeans, a pajama top, and a scarf staggered through the door. White-faced, her breath came in gasps as she collapsed into the chair.

"Helga," Mary said. "Thank goodness. I was about to come to Sumer to find you."

"The Randolph Hotel told me you were here," she whispered. "Miss Wandwalker, I'm in terrible trouble. You're friends with Richard Bishop. I hoped ..."

She swayed, murmuring "dizzy." The voice came from far away, thought Mary. She really is in trouble.

CHAPTER 43
HELGA'S CHOICE

A chapel bell bonged the hour from somewhere over the Cardinal rooftops. Traffic hummed distantly, like purring cats, and a lonely seagull screamed overhead. Meanwhile, a pregnant young woman with a blue stripe in her ponytail wobbled in her chair. Helga's eyes were shut. Déjà vu all over again, Mary reflected. Once she'd been a pregnant and scared Oxford student. *No, Helga's not like you,* came that voice from inside. *She's not free.*

It was a realization that shocked Mary. Shocked her that she had not put it together before. Helga moaned. She stretched out a hand. Mary took it.

"This is Helga, Jamie. She knows about that picture on your phone," Mary said to the Cardinal nurse. "Oh, and she's having twins." Helga moaned louder. Still holding on to Mary she opened her eyes.

"Don't feel well."

It was Jamie's office, so Mary let him take charge. At least for the moment, she decided.

"Lie down on this couch, Miss. That's right, so I can examine you. I'm a nurse. You'll have seen my name on the door."

"Jamie Sanders," whispered Helga. Short on floor space, one wall of the office was taken up with a medical daybed. Mary helped Helga unwind her scarf and unbutton her top.

"You're freezing. Don't you have a coat?" scolded Mary.

"Left it last night. You know, after that…"

"Ah," said Mary, recalling the rush to grab belongings after Viktor's announcements and Anna's arrest. "We would have waited for you to fetch your things."

Helga blinked as if it had not occurred to her.

"Let the young lady get her breath and get warm," interrupted Jamie. "She needs to relax so I can feel her abdomen." Mary took a tiny step back.

"Don't go," shrieked Helga, trying to get up.

"I won't, I won't," Mary assured her. "I'll be here. I promise." Helga subsided and allowed Jamie's hands to feel her belly.

"Perdita said the Cardinal nurse was the best," said Helga.

Jamie took her blood pressure, listened to her heart, tapped her stomach, and watched her breathe — all with professional speed and consideration. He'll make a great doctor, thought Mary, if he gets the money for medical school.

"Thank you, Miss er…"

"Helga. Just Helga. Our mother died when we were 5. Mr. Solokov said we were not to take his name."

"Viktor Solokov is your *father.*" Horrified, Mary took the chair again, angling it to face Helga. Echoing loud and strong in her mind was Viktor declaring himself the father of Helga's babies.

"No, silly," Helga whispered. "*Kyrill* Solokov was our father. Our mother was one of his girls in Berlin. I know people say he might not have been our father, but he made condoms the absolute rule. Saved on doctors' fees, he said. Before she died, our mother said we were Kyrill's. Neither he nor Viktor denied it. Didn't stop them putting us to work."

"Like father, like son," muttered Mary. "So, if Kyrill is/ was your father, you and Viktor … I mean, your babies, it's still incest. Viktor is your brother, half-brother."

"No, Miss Wandwalker." Helga sounded irritable at the old woman not getting it. "You forgot what Viktor said back at Falconer House. Kyrill was Viktor's stepfather, not father. Sir

Daniel Falconer is Viktor's father. Viktor always says he got the Falconer blue eyes from him."

"Oh, please," exclaimed Mary. "Give me strength, Falconers and their babies. Dammit, I'll have to amend that family tree *again*. You should probably know this, Jamie."

Mary extracted the family tree from her bag and picked up a biro from Jamie's desk. "So let me get this right, Helga." She drew a couple of uneven lines and added names, guessing at the dates.

Mary took a deep breath, archivist again. "Correct me if I'm wrong, Helga. Kyrill Solokov, KGB spy in the 1970s marries Rosalind Forrest when she is expecting Sir Daniel's child. That makes Kyrill stepfather to Viktor Solokov, who *does* take his name. After the Berlin Wall comes down, Kyrill takes to running prostitutes and drugs. All this time he is training Viktor become an instrument of revenge on Sir Daniel's family."

Mary noticed Jamie's startled expression.

"Yes, Jamie, it's positively gothic. My guess is Kyrill, a KGB hit man, lost too much to be wholly sane. To pretend to defect, he had to deny the world he grew up in, lose his home. When the woman he desires betrays *him* for Sir Daniel, she's picked the man Kyrill most hates. Sir Daniel did not know that he was the means of Kyrill losing his soul. Taking Rosalind from him broke any humanity Kyrill had left."

Mary bent closer to Helga as the idea came. "Who knows if the KGB really did order the murder of Sir Daniel? Kyrill could have acted alone because Daniel Falconer, with his women, his family, his historic house and lineage, summed up everything Kyrill had lost. To cap it all, the world lost to Kyrill vanishes forever when the Soviet Union falls. Everything Sir Daniel represented won in 1989, or so it appeared at the time."

Mary stared at the white wall above Helga. "I see it now. Part of Kyrill's revenge on the Falconers is what he did to Viktor. He turned Sir Daniel's son into a trafficker of sex and drugs. How well he succeeded."

She glanced down at Helga. "Kyrill begot children like you Helga but could not care for them. I almost feel sorry for him."

"Erm, Miss Wandwalker," began Jamie, pulling out some wipes for his hands. "I'm not sure I'm following. Miss Helga here is okay for now. However, it sounds like she is under too much stress. I take it the father of her babies is not supportive."

Mary gazed at him. "Hardly. Last night in his house we fled for our lives."

Now I feel ill, thought Mary. That bastard Viktor has David's eyes, from the same father, Sir Daniel Falconer. And I mean bastard in the moral sense. In a world-weary tone, Helga tried to explain.

"It's true that Kyrill and Viktor were closer than most fathers and sons. Even so, Viktor and me: It's not incest, technically."

Mary slapped her forehead. "Falconers and their babies," she said again, making both Jamie and Helga stare. "Or should I say masters and slaves?"

Helga shrank back. "I don't know what you mean," she said in a small voice.

Mary sat ramrod straight. "George. Viktor killed George, who was so like him: a Falconer by blood yet lost to that cold, rich house." Helga shifted on the bed.

"I don't know what you mean," she repeated, sulking. Her color had improved, Mary noted.

"Miss ... er Helga," began Jamie, washing his hands in the tiny sink. "It sounds like you are in a complicated situation. If there is any possibility of consanguinity ..."

"What? Con ...? Who?"

"Incest, consanguinity means connection by blood," said Mary, getting impatient. "Jamie wants to know if there is *any* chance that Viktor is your father, as well as the father of your babies."

Helga winced. "None," she said, shortly. "Viktor swanned around a posh university in Switzerland at the time we were conceived. In fact, I only met Viktor later, much later, when his father gave him control of us sex workers. Kyrill died in 2011 which is when ..."

"Viktor started *his* plot against the Falconers," said Mary. At the repetition of "Falconer" Jamie frowned at his horizontal patient. At Mary's warning look he put his finger on his lips and took out his phone. Pressing it several times, he placed it on a bookcase, where it would be hidden from Helga's view. Mary let out a breath. If only Helga would let out what she knew about the murders.

"Um, Helga, I do want to help. Rest for a few minutes while we talk."

"All right, Miss Wandwalker. You're my best hope."

"Oh," said Mary at her crispest. "In that case, tell me all about it. You mentioned trouble. Do you mean a problem with Victor?"

The young woman shifted on the couch and put her hand to her stomach.

Mary had planned to search for Helga at Sumer college. Sumer was where she'd encountered Helga before. Mary sighed. Helga and Sumer meant a secret she'd be very wise to keep from Viktor Solokov.

"God, Helga, I don't believe it. Have you ...? Your twins might not be Viktor's. That's it, isn't it? Richard Bishop might be the father."

Mary seized her second revision of the family tree from the desk and stuffed it into her bag. What was the point of trying to document things when people were so ...? So, what, Mary? she asked herself. So unpredictable? No, Helga was predictable in looking for something beyond what she was born into.

Helga lay very still. A tear spilled onto each cheek. Then she nodded. Mary told herself that this was no time for sentimentality. Her thoughts flew over troubled ground.

"Given Viktor's ... priorities, he is bound to make you do DNA tests when the babies arrive."

"Before then," whispered Helga.

Mary did not want to have to say it, yet she must. "Are they Richard Bishop's babies?"

Helga gulped. "I don't know. *I really don't know.*" She scrunched her face up and cried. "Miss Wandwalker, what can I do? Viktor will kill me. He'll kill the babies too if they're not his."

What Helga should do was obvious to Mary. Clearly confiding in the police was not on her to-do list. How to get the girl to see this for herself?

Jamie stood up, gesturing at the door.

"Perhaps it would be easier to talk to Miss Wandwalker alone?"

"No!" called Mary and Helga simultaneously.

Jamie sat back down. At that moment the morning sun reached the window. It warmed the top of Jamie's dreadlocks, making Mary think of furrows in a ploughed field. Sunshine then shot onto Helga's hair, making the blue stripe sparkle. Her dull, uncolored locks glistened with tiny flecks of red, gold, and green.

"Why Richard?" muttered Mary. She'd not intended to speak this thought. Helga took the question seriously.

"It was Anna's idea. She's not bad to us, really. Told me to find a man who could get me out of the life. Like she'd done with George Jones."

Dumbfounded by Anna yet again, Mary was floored by this vision of the affair with her son. She felt a cool touch on her wrist and looked down at Jamie's hand. His knees almost touched hers in the small space. She managed a smile.

"He is dead," she said into his concern. Stupid, she told herself. Jamie already knows this. She swallowed hard. "My son, George, died because he tried to get Anna out of the life? You do know he was my son, don't you, Helga?"

"I'm sorry," Helga whispered.

"Murdered, he was murdered, Helga," said Mary sternly. "I need to know what you know."

HELGA'S CHOICE

The girl flinched, even lying down. Mary continued through gritted teeth. "Murder can't be walked away from. Just like you can't walk away from Viktor. He'll find you if you run. Richard can't protect you if Viktor believes you have his babies."

"Or if Viktor thinks I cheated on him and they're not his," said Helga in a small voice.

"You have no choice, Helga. You must go to the police."

"No, no. I've seen what he does to women who ... do that."

Helga began to pull herself into a seated position. She started to look around for her coat and scarves. Mary seized all of Helga's outdoor things and thrust them behind her chair onto the stone floor.

Helga's watery eyes met Mary Wandwalker's implacable gray.

"You can't make me talk to the police."

"No," said Mary. "I can't." Her frankness startled Helga. But Mary wasn't done. "However, you and your babies will never be safe until Viktor is in prison and his criminal network dissolved. You've got to stop protecting him."

Mary's expression became implacable. "Start by telling us who killed my son."

Helga shivered and hugged her thin chest. She looked at Jamie in appeal.

"Answer Miss Wandwalker," Jamie said in his gentle voice. "She's right."

Helga shook her head.

Stalemate. How did the police do interrogations? Mary wondered. How did Mr. Jeffreys? That colored stripe in Helga's dull hair, the sunlight on her knees,stirred a memory.

"It was Johann, wasn't it? Johann, your twin killed George. That's who you're really protecting. I bet he killed Perdita too, on Viktor's orders. Jamie, hand me back those photos."

"Nooooooo." Helga curled up on the bed in a fetal position, hands clamped on her face.

"Take your hands down and look."

Mary was surprised when Helga did as she was told. Taking the photos and sitting up, she put them down one by one.

"Yes, that's me," she finally said. "I'm handing the port bottle to Perdita. That's Johann in the background. I swear, I swear to you, Miss Wandwalker, we did not know it would kill her."

"Oh, come on," demanded Mary, the Archivist disciplinarian. "The police found the psilocybin lab. It had to be you and Johann. You chemistry students made the stuff as well as distributing it."

Helga put her hands over her eyes. "Miss W, you don't understand," sobbed. "Yes, we distilled the psilocybin. Then we injected it into wine bottles from the Falconer estate, and more that Viktor bought. Once on a trip to London he told us to spike a bottle of whisky in a pub, 'The Dragon and the Raven,' I think."

Simon's poisoning, and those others, Mary thought. She did not want to do anything, not even flick an eyelash, that might stop Helga's story.

"Mostly we took the drugged wine to parties, or otherwise offered bottles as gifts from Sir Viktor. Students twigged it had something special added and wanted more. That's how we set up the distribution for the psilocybin. The drug is very strong but safe. All students at Falconer House work in the business."

She stopped and swallowed, speaking in a smaller voice. "We have no choice. Viktor said it was this or sex work, like before. Drugs are a better way to make money, and go to parties."

Mary nodded. She felt sick. To get it over, she spoke for Helga.

"Then one day Viktor gave you a bottle especially for Perdita Falconer, no one else. Perhaps he did not tell you it had been spiked twice. Viktor said none of you were to drink it."

Helga nodded. "He said — he always said — that the Falconer family was a trap, not a nest. On Viktor's orders, Johann repeated it to Perdita when I gave her the bottle."

HELGA'S CHOICE

Mary held her breath. She'd been right. Viktor Solokov *did* want the Falconers to connect his crimes to those deaths 40 years ago. Now she had to ask.

"Do you know if Perdita wrote …"

"She laughed," said Helga, wonderingly. "Perdita laughed at the idea of her family as a trap. Wouldn't have it at all." Helga paused. "I wrote the suicide note."

A tear raced down her cheek and dripped from her chin. "Viktor dictated it to me," she admitted. "After telling me to steal some of her handwriting for practice."

Mary's mind was racing. Viktor handed the fatal bottle to Helga and Johann. Even so, evidence of his intent to murder was sketchy. She had to probe further.

"Helga, listen to me," she began. "Viktor has an alibi for George's, my son's stabbing," she said. "The police cannot break it. I think it was Johann who killed George because Viktor told him to. Your twin would do anything for Viktor, wouldn't he?"

"Johann's my family."

For the first time, Helga's voice came from somewhere deep down. This is the girl's family ground, thought Mary. This is her truth.

"I know. I know what it means that he is your family." Mary paused. How to say this next bit? "To save yourself and the babies, Viktor must go to jail. You can put him there, *but only if you tell the truth about Johann too.*"

Helga looked at Mary imploringly. It was Jamie who broke the silence.

"It's not a choice between your babies or your brother."

The two women stared at him.

"It is between saving your whole family or throwing it into a grave. Think about it, Miss er … Helga. If your brother killed someone on the orders of this monster, what next? A command to kill you or your children? Tell the police everything, and they will offer your brother a deal to put this Viktor Solokov behind bars forever."

"A deal, yes," said Mary with relief. "And I know just the person who can ensure that Johann gets the very best deal. Mr. Jeffreys has a lot of influence with the police. Helga, this is the only way. There'll be a deal for you as well. You won't give birth in prison."

Helga hung her head. Mary and Jamie waited. From outside a bell banged the quarter hour. No one moved in the tiny office. Finally, a regular thudding could be heard from outside. Footsteps tapped the stone steps to Jamie's door. Oh no, not now, thought Mary. Another student with an embarrassing rash or a stomach pickled with alcohol. Such innocence.

With silent grace, Jamie unwound his long legs from his chair, went to the door and whispered.

"All right," Helga said while his back was turned. "All right, Miss Wandwalker, the police it is. I'll tell them everything. You're right. Johann stabbed George because Viktor insisted he do it. That is what Johann said afterward. And now he can't sleep."

Relief choked Mary. It was earth, her family ground. It rose from that morning in the mist when George looked up with her own eyes, her storm gray eyes, not the Falconer blue. When he said: "Hello, Mother."

CHAPTER 44
FAMILY

The end came fast. No, it took forever, thought Mary Wandwalker, reviewing the long hours with Chief Inspector Bert Reynolds's team. Mostly she met with a gray woman in unflattering glasses and unwise crimson lipstick. She'd been assigned to get Mary's statement organized, while Reynolds bobbed in and out with news of the arrests. To Mary's relief, he'd barely hesitated over Helga's claim that Johann stabbed George Jones on Viktor's orders.

"Viktor Solokov's obsessed, Reynolds said.

"He'll do anything to destroy the Falconers and inherit Falconer House," added Mary. Mr. Jeffreys used to praise her succinct summary of complex agendas.

"Get a picture of Solokov and Johann to all the airports," Reynolds snapped to the underling in the interview room. "If half of what these ladies are saying is true, he'll have a number of passports and an escape plan."

"Thank you for believing us," said Mary, somewhat surprised.

"Belief is in the evidence," grunted Reynolds. "Your son, Jones, was one of ours. I lied when I said we hadn't met. We keep personal stuff away from the investigation. In fact, I briefed Jones myself on the rumors about the source of Solokov's money."

He bent his head in acknowledgement of Mary.

303

"Ms. Belinda Choudhry accusing wife was too convenient. A crime of passion? Highly unlikely with Lady Solokov. Drugs got Jones sent there in the first place. Now you say the murder comes down to family. I'll buy it. Jones was a good man, a great officer. You can be proud of him, Miss Wandwalker."

He nodded at both Mary and Helga. Mary's throat ached. She turned away hastily, thanking the stars that Belinda's lashing out could remain within the family. Reynolds turned to the real witness. "Thanks to Miss ..."

"Helga," said the young woman.

"Thanks to Miss Helga here, we may get justice for Jones. Unraveling the Solokov empire will be a bonus. Are you all right, my dear? Do you need a rest before continuing with your statement?"

"Bathroom," squeaked Helga, trying to rise.

Mary took hold of her arm. "Morning sickness."

Reynolds ran to open the door. Mary got Helga to the Ladies with seconds to spare. A woman officer materialized outside the stall.

"The Chief Inspector sent me," she explained to Mary. "I'm trained to support pregnant witnesses. He's sent for the doctor. The Chief says can you come back for essential details, so he knows who to arrest. We'll do proper statements later, when Miss Helga is feeling stronger. I'll look after her now. You go back, Miss Wandwalker."

"Thank goodness," said Mary, hoping Helga could not hear. She took a few deep breaths in the corridor before returning to the interview room, where she found Reynolds with the red-lipped gray woman. She fiddled with silver buttons on her uniform. Nerves, Mary presumed. Although they were bent over laptops, Reynolds looked up.

"Cameras picked up Johann entering Sumer College. Said he was looking for his sister. We've dispatched uniforms to pick him up."

Mary was sitting down with a coffee when another officer dashed in, a disgustingly healthy-looking young woman with pink cheeks. So short was her blonde hair that it had to have been cut with an electric razor.

"Gov, that MP is here with her husband. Ms. Choudhry won't sign her witness statement. She's retracting saying she saw Lady Solokov killing Sergeant Jones."

Reynolds waved her away. "No time for that. Send Ms. Choudhry to her solicitor. All we need is a signed letter dropped off at the station. Then we'll consider it closed."

The door shut behind her, and Reynolds's tiny smile met Mary's silent query.

"Never get involved with politicians if you don't have to," he explained. "Especially Conservatives. Too tortuous, and it always ends up that they have buddies on the Parliamentary Police Committee."

Mary nodded understandingly. She was about to ask Reynolds what else he required from her when the laptop facing away from her emitted a series of pings.

"Ah," said Reynolds. "Check that out, will you Samantha. And," he scowled at her, "do something about your vampire lips. You look like you've been biting our witnesses."

Taking out a tissue and rubbing her mouth, the woman glided from the room. She waited until Reynolds had his back turned before making a rude gesture. Mary tried not to laugh. She coughed, then raised her eyebrows at Reynolds.

"Yes, it's good news," he confirmed. A grin softened his worry lines. "Our Hungarian henchman, Johann, is in custody. My officers are rounding up the other students for questioning. Even better, we've a sighting of Solokov at Birmingham International."

"Nearest airport to Oxford," commented Mary.

"It is if you are trying to get to Pacific islands with no extradition," confirmed Reynolds. "That's the passport he seems to be using."

"He's abandoned everyone he made do his dirty work," remarked Mary. "Anna, Johann and Helga: all expendable in the Solokov version of family. Well, Inspector, at least you can release Anna Solokov. She didn't murder George Jones. No one accuses her of harming Perdita Falconer."

"Ha," said Reynolds, leaning back in his chair. "Well now, Anna Solokov is a complicated lady. You could say the authorities know too much, or, rather, too little about her." He pursed his lips. "Sorry, Miss Wandwalker, no can do. Bigger powers than Oxford police have plucked her from my hands."

Mary did not like his grim smile. "Surely Anna ..." she began, then stopped, unsure of how to continue.

"Surely Anna Solokov, or Anna Vronsky, as she used to be, is not her real name," countered Reynolds.

Mary experienced a sinking sensation. Below the floor tiles it was mud, no quicksand. Reynolds, she could see, had more. He rustled his papers. Mary knew he was preparing to impart bad news.

"Once arrested, she refused to speak," he read from the printout. "She had to be compelled to give her fingerprints. Not a good sign."

Mary had a mental vision of two police officers holding Anna down while another two worked on her clenched hands. This was going to get worse.

Reynolds coughed. "Interpol has a BOLO on Anna Vronsky, or Tatiana Petrov, or Giulia Rach, plus half a dozen other names. BOLO means Be-On-The-Lookout. I'm afraid that's only the start for Anna Solokov. Minutes later four arrest warrants popped up, and there are seven, no ..." he busied himself with the screen, "11 now if you count the speeding ticket in Montenegro. Your Miss Anna has been a busy lady. She'll be tied up with the European authorities for some time."

Reynolds watched the effect of his words on Mary. She wanted to brush away his unspoken sympathy.

"Some time?" she said. "You mean weeks?"

"I mean years."

"No," Mary said, shocked. "That's not right. From what I've had from Caroline, that's Mrs. Caroline Jones, Anna is more victim than criminal."

FAMILY

Reynolds put a hand to his forehead and groaned. "Mrs. Jones, oh da ... dash it. I forgot about her. Heaven preserve us. She's out there in the waiting room. Won't leave until she sees Anna, she says. We must release her, she says."

He waved at Mary. "Miss Wandwalker, we won't have your paperwork until tomorrow. In the meantime, please, I beg of you, take Mrs. Jones away."

Mary got up. "Caroline is my son's widow. She was with us at Falconer House, was there when Viktor gloated over becoming a Falconer heir. Surely, she can help you?"

"Yes, she can. We have her statement. But she won't accept what we tell her about Anna Solokov's past. Insists that she can exonerate her. She's driving my sergeants crazy by refusing to understand the difference between evidence and hearsay. Recounting unlikely stories that she claims Anna — and George — told her is no good. Take her away and come back tomorrow."

Reynolds sounded like a man out of patience. Mary buttoned her coat. "When I come back, I too will want to discuss Anna Solokov."

She left with dignity and the realization that she, as well as Caroline, could not let Anna drown in the muddy waters of the European judicial system. Reynolds was forewarned.

The next morning Mary was greeted at the police station with both good and frustrating news. Good was the arrest of Viktor Solokov the previous evening. Frustrating to Mary was that Reynolds had gone to London to consult on the political ramifications of the case. Coward, Mary thought immediately. Then she had to admit that Viktor's public position as a major donor to the governing party, not to mention Belinda Choudhry's entanglement, could provide the Chief Inspector with enough reasons to get the case straight with his superiors.

Mary was left to the gray detective sergeant whose lips glowed an unrepentant scarlet. Lipstick caked too thick, thought Mary. Of course, she made no comment. Together Mary and the Sergeant prepared the statement which would help convict the drug trafficker, murder-ordering, prostitution-organizing, Knight of the Realm, Viktor Solokov.

"He's a whoremonger," Mary said to the gray lady. By now it did not matter that her lipstick bled into the Sergeant's age lines. Mary felt cheered by the defiance. Anna would appreciate the bloody color, she thought, and smiled. Mary noticed that the Sergeant was staring.

"Whoremonger," Mary repeated. "We don't use the word today. I remember it from my undergraduate studies in literature. Viktor Solokov and his stepfather, Kyrill, coerced young people into prostitution, controlled them, took their earnings. Even Kyrill's own children, Helga and Johann, were 'put to work,'" she said.

"Slavery," muttered the woman, bending back to her computer.

Oh, yes, thought Mary. It is slavery. On plantations slave women had no choice about sleeping with the masters. Their children were sold like any other slaves. Viktor Solokov brought slavery home.

CHAPTER 45
WE WHO HAVE LOVED

Mary repeated the point about slavery a month later when, just before Christmas, she and Mr. Jeffreys arrived for lunch at Falconer House. After the wholesale arrest of the Solokov household, Arthur, Simon, and a fully recuperated Patrick decided to move in. In December, Oxford University suspended classes for vacation. Those Solokov students not remanded in custody were abroad trying to reconnect to their families with the support of local charities. After a simple meal of omelets, followed by fruit salad prepared by Arthur, and to Mary's surprise, Simon, the five of them gathered over coffee in the library.

With the atmosphere subdued, Mary held off on the questions she had about the future of the Falconer family and estate. Given the complexities of arrests, multiple charges, and the trial ahead, she could sense the pain of recent events. It hovered among them like the hovering mist she'd noted earlier. It embraced the lawn and the tree under which George had perished.

But more than the death of her son haunted Mary Wandwalker. It was the word "slavery" spoken by the woman who gave nothing away apart the defiance of her red lips. Patrick told her how glad the Falconers were that Perdita dismissed the notion that her family was a trap instead of a nest. Yet the phrase Mary overheard 40 years ago continued to resonate. She could see now that it had been true — true of Viktor Solokov's so-called "family."

"Slavery," Mary said. "Here at Falconer House. That's what Viktor practiced. We didn't see it. Not until Helga began to talk. Viktor made this house into a trap. It masqueraded as a nest for vulnerable young people."

For a while no one responded.

"Again. Slavery again," said Arthur, lighting a cigar after everyone else had declined. Now attired in cheerful green wool, his chin shone free of stubble and sticking plasters. Mary was fascinated. She had to tell herself to concentrate.

"Slavery again, Miss Wandwalker. Our fight about the Falconers owning slaves may have been a ruse to find the Kestrel papers, but Patrick here dug up incontrovertible proof. With the help of Jeffreys and the Archive."

Mr. Jeffreys nodded and darted a glance at Mary. Not prepared to reveal her feelings, she looked away. Simon stared gloomily at the fire that would soon require more wood. Patrick, however, appeared rested, so Mary addressed him.

"Are you going ahead with those portraits? The ones with slaves as well the Falconers."

Patrick grinned. "Definitely. Did you hear I've been promised an exhibition in a major gallery in London?"

Mary shook her head.

"It's all thanks to my father, who turns out to be serious about changing his own style. No more 18th century Mike McCarthys to flatter the rich. The main reason for his visit this afternoon is that he wants to spend time with his Lady Margaret Falconer. Says it will help him recover what he once had. If it all works out, we'll do a joint exhibition, really open up the portrait form."

"The main reason?" Mr. Jeffreys used that deceptively gentle voice that Mary knew well. *He knows something*, she thought.

"Erm …yeah, well, my dad wants a word with Miss Wandwalker. So please do stay until he turns up."

"I suppose so," said Mary. "Remember, I am invited to the cottage for afternoon tea."

"You invited yourself," reminded Mr. Jeffreys.

"It was the only way to see Caroline and Anna," retorted Mary. "Given that you've got Anna on house arrest, and Caroline won't leave her."

"As I told you, she's wearing an anklet," said Jeffreys. "It allows her limited freedom. No doubt you need them alone for your nefarious purposes."

Simon on the sofa opened his mouth to inquire. Patrick, beside him, nudged his husband to leave it.

"All in good time," Mary smiled at them. "If my proposition works out, you will be the first ones we tell."

Simon relaxed, and his eyes fell on Arthur puffing away while he contemplated the bare Christmas tree in the corner. Simon turned back to Mary, looking mischievous.

"Did Jeffreys tell you that Arthur was shot by a poacher, after all? The man down in Devon confessed and surrendered his shotgun to the police."

"Oh," said Mary, looking at Arthur's grin.

"Seems Viktor had not yet gotten around to bumping me off," he said. "I see you've noticed our unadorned Christmas tree, Miss Wandwalker."

Around it there were cardboard boxes, some gaping open. Mary could see piles of tinsel and baubles all mixed up with glass stars. A few painted wooden animals looked forlorn on their backs or sides.

"Are those decorations new? Is the Christmas tree part of the family being back at Falconer House?"

Arthur laughed. "We've been wondering when you'd ask about the changes on the estate," he said, delighted. "Yes, Helga will help decorate the tree tonight. She found these traditional Hungarian carvings in Oxford. Good for the babies when they see them next year. Turns out there is a Hungarian community in the county who have befriended her. She's at therapy right now, of course."

"I'll be picking her up later," said Patrick. "In fact, I can give you a ride to the cottage on the way."

"Thank you," said Mary, noting the steady rain that was already crushing the daylight. "You're saying that Helga still lives here?"

"Yes, with three gay men," said Simon, grinning. "If it wasn't for the rain, we'd show you Patrick's new studio in the old stables. Soon it will be two couples, as Pa's Oxford friend is moving in."

"We're talking about getting married," said Arthur, taking the cigar out of his mouth and looking at it. He was flushed. Mary wanted to say something nice. While she was pondering, Simon chipped in.

"Yup, believe it or not, Ma's divorcing him at last," said Simon. "If I wasn't on the wagon, I'd offer everyone Champagne. She came for a visit, said, 'Thank God, Pa's sorting himself out at last.' Then she announced that she'd like to spend her remaining years married to a man who actually fancied her. There is one, apparently, an Estate Manager in Devon. We'll give them a permanent room here, of course. We hope he'll help with Falconer House paperwork."

"Don't forget we can't give away too many bedrooms," said Patrick. "Of course, your mother is welcome, and her new man, but to make ends meet we must accommodate a certain number of students."

Mary's jaw dropped. "You're carrying on with Viktor's ... Viktor's ...?" She could not find the words.

"Far from it," said Arthur, tapping out his ash. "You see, Miss Wandwalker, Patrick discovered that those slave-owning Falconers donated a lot of money to several very rich Oxford colleges. These days, they are short of rooms for students and keen to convince the next Labor Government that they care about recruiting from the whole spectrum of society. Jeffreys here has been splendid in helping us convince of the wisdom of our plan." He paused to tap out his cigar and grin at Mary. "Falconer House will offer room and board to students from poor backgrounds, paid for by those colleges. For my part, I plan to emphasize support to undergraduates from Afro-Caribbean communities."

There was a pause. Arthur's fierce blue eyes met Mary's comprehending gray ones. Pondering the new Falconer House incarnation gave her an idea.

"Speaking of deserving students from ethnic minorities," she began, "wouldn't it be great to have a nurse based here? Especially if he was also pursuing a medical degree."

"Jamie Sanders," said Patrick, clapping his hands. "Good old Cardinal took slave-related monies from more than the Falconers. Arthur could have a word."

"Delighted," said Arthur, thumping his stick on the grate next to his chair. "That young man was kind to our Perdita. We should have thought of him before. Another reason to be grateful to you, Miss Wandwalker."

Mary caught the approving wink from Mr. Jeffreys.

"And what about …" she began. It was a delicate subject.

"Naturally, we are continuing to support Viktor's erm … proteges," broke in Simon.

"Let's tell Miss Wandwalker about Helga and the twins," added Patrick.

"Saving the best news for last," beamed Arthur.

"I'm so happy, I could burst," said Simon. "You see, Miss Wandwalker, Helga's asked Patrick and I to adopt her twins." Simon grinned. "We are going to be fathers together. Pa's over the moon that he'll be a grandfather again."

Mary was stunned. Then her face sagged.

"It's okay, Miss Wandwalker," said Patrick, with a compassionate glance. "Arthur has the lawyers working on it. Helga will not be giving up her rights. She too will have a permanent home here at Falconer House. We're aiming for coparenting, with Helga free to do whatever she needs to do to recover. The adoption thing is so the twins can inherit the Falconer name and, eventually, the estate.

"Oh," said Mary with a glance at Mr. Jeffreys. He smiled, refusing to be drawn in. She sipped her coffee and considered the news. Simon fidgeted in his seat.

"Will you be seeing my wife's husband while visiting Oxford?" he said with his devastating lack of tact. Richard was the subject of Mary's concern. What about the questionable paternity of Helga's twins? However, she understood Simon's real question.

"I'm glad Richard has gone back to Belinda," she said firmly, as the rain spread tiny hands all over the window. "Going back to the marriage was the right thing, for both of them." She cleared her throat and reached for the coffee pot to pour a second cup.

"Don't worry, Miss Wandwalker," said Arthur. "We know that the twins could be Richard's and not Viktor's. The babies may not be Falconers by blood."

"You don't mind?" Mary was astonished.

"I think Simon is a bit bothered," replied his father, mischievously. "Patrick and I keep reminding him about the very odd ..."

"... and appallingly painted," broke in Patrick.

"Portraits in the attic," continued Arthur. "Quite a few times the Falconer heir developed an appearance shared with the coachman or the gardener."

"Some practice sketches of servants clinched it," contributed Patrick.

"Really?" queried Mary. "I thought that the lady of the house would be careful to produce an heir that resembled her husband."

"Well, that was the idea," said Patrick. "However, if no babies came, then the woman got the blame for being 'barren.' Horrible word. You'd expect a resourceful Lady Falconer would have her eye on a likely young man. A sensible husband knew how to turn a blind eye."

"'Service Through Family,'" said Mary, smiling. "Of course."

"Therefore," sailed on Arthur. "If the twins do turn out to be Bishops rather than Falconers — and we have a pact not to do DNA tests, or tell them anything, until they are 21 — then good for the line, I say." He chuckled. "Who'd have thought my wild son would turn out more of a snob than I."

"I've agreed," said Simon, shortly. "After all, I'm taking cooking lessons and going to Narcotics Anonymous in Oxford. So, I'm fully signed up to this crazy ..." he stopped and kissed Patrick's cheek, "and rather wonderful enterprise."

Before Mary could comment, footsteps could be heard on distant marble. Then there was a padding sound on the corridor's carpet.

"Come in," yelled Simon.

A red face topped with damp white hair peeked around the library door.

"Hiya, Patrick. Greetings Falconers," said Mike McCarthy. "Thanks for leaving the door unlocked. No, no coffee. I've got to speak to Miss Wandwalker in the lobby before I lose my nerve."

"Come with me," said Mary to Mr. Jeffreys.

"Naturally." He pulled himself up from the groaning chair.

"I bet you know what he's going to say," grumbled Mary as they followed Mike McCarthy down the drafty corridor to the even chillier marble lobby. The three sets of footsteps echoed over to stand beside the most recent Falconer portraits.

"I suspect you've worked it out for yourself," returned Mr. Jeffreys, as they arranged themselves around Margaret Falconer's portrait. Mary stared at Mike. He wriggled and looked away. She did not want to see it. He did not want to say it. Mr. Jeffreys gave that impatient cough that Mary remembered.

"Patrick says I have to tell you," began Mike McCarthy.

"No, really ..." began Mary. A look from Mr. Jeffreys shut her up.

"Begin with you were in love with Margaret Falconer," commanded Jeffreys.

McCarthy instantly relaxed. "I was very young, you see. She was 17 years older, so much a woman of the world, and yet actually quite vulnerable under that tough exterior. I know she regretted her rejection of you, Miss Wandwalker. That is, eventually."

"There was nothing about regret in her diary," Mary said stiffly. "Though she did mention you had been kind."

"Ah, the reticence of the upper classes," said Mike, easily. "She was a great lady. I know she would have come to appreciate you, Miss Wandwalker."

Mary scowled. Get on with it, she wanted to snap.

Mike spoke quickly. "Margaret welcomed art students who came to practice in the house and on the estate. I adored her. She knew, I thought. Anyway, I hoped she knew. Unfortunately for me she only had eyes for her husband, Sir Daniel. It killed her when he became infatuated with Rosalind Forrest. She was terrified he'd ask for a divorce." He swallowed. "I couldn't bear to see her in pain. She became like a ghost, with Rosalind sucking the life out her."

"So, what did you do?" asked Mary. I know what he did, she said to herself.

"Um … Well, you see we students discovered the magic mushrooms. I tripped over them while sketching in Falcon Wood. Put a handful in my backpack and tried them with my friends. Really wacko strong stuff. So, I went back for more. It was only supposed to be for fun. Taking whole mushrooms isn't dangerous. It never occurred to us to distill the liquid."

"And yet your innocent drug dealing became something more," said Mary. Her words sizzled like acid. It would corrode the marble beneath their feet. Mike McCarthy winced, took a quick look at Mr. Jeffreys's set face, and continued.

"Kyrill Solokov was always around in those days. He'd be shut up with Sir Daniel in the study for hour after hour. Everyone knew they were spies. It was Solokov who first brought Rosalind down. Officially she was getting some acting kudos at the National Theater."

Mary nodded, her expression stony.

McCarthy talked even faster. "Solokov was Rosalind's official suitor, giving her an excuse to descend for long weekends. Soon it was Daniel and Rosalind who would spend time alone. That's when Kyrill spotted what I was doing. He followed me into the wood and saw me eat a mushroom. By the time he caught up with me, I was high enough to tell him all about it. I didn't know that he began experimenting with the liquid."

"Psilocybin," said Mary. Her entire body had become very cold. "Distilled to a lethal strength. Is that all? It is enough." But she knew there was more.

"Wait a minute, Miss Wandwalker," said Jeffreys. "McCarthy, you're prevaricating. Tell her about that day when you gave Rosalind Forrest mushrooms. Her and ..."

"David Falconer," groaned Mike.

The three of them stood silent. Mary could not breathe.

Mike turned back to Mary, his eyes pleading.

"I could see what Rosalind was like: trained to please men and compete with other women. Badly educated and insecure, she was a typical product of Hollywood. I was a nothing art student. Sir Daniel was the one she really wanted. Yet even after the affair began, there were times Daniel had to be busy with Solokov and not her. For Rosalind's entertainment that left the two boys, young men really. Since Arthur was a nonstarter for women, she took to David as his father's favorite. The fact that he was in love with a woman his own age she regarded as a challenge."

"Get on with it," said Jeffreys curtly.

"Remember, this was for Margaret who was desperately unhappy. Oh, all right, Jeffreys."

McCarthy swallowed. "Miss Wandwalker, I took Rosalind and David on a picnic. I pretended to discover the mushrooms and suggested we swigged them down with Champagne. After they both ingested, they only had eyes for each other. I left them to it. It only happened once, I'm sure. Yet, this portrait ..."

He turned to look at the forlorn Margaret Falconer: betrayed wife, widow, and bereaved mother. "You see the resemblance?"

"Yes," rasped Mary. "I see it. I saw it the first time I came. I suppose I knew then what it meant."

That was a lie. It had taken days. Every time she passed the painting it reached out with that tug in the guts. They were going to make her say it, damn them.

"Viktor Solokov," she began. "As well as inheriting the Falconer blue eyes, Viktor resembles Lady Margaret. He has that jawline of hers. It means, it *has* to mean, he was David's son, not Sir Daniel's." Her throat dried.

"Worse than that for me," said disconsolate Mike McCarthy. "Patrick told me that psilocybin killed David, making him crash the car. Kyrill got magic mushrooms from *me*. If I had left the mushrooms alone, he might not have found them. He would have no idea what grows in English woods. Kyrill, the Kestrel, got his poison from me, and so did Rosalind. You know, don't you, that she eventually died of drugs in LA? My stupidity …"

"Stop. You've said enough. You didn't kill them," growled Mary. "It is not all about you, Mr. McCarthy. Not Rosalind, not even … David. You might have led Kyrill to 'shrooms, but you did not make him kill anyone with psilocybin."

"I really … am … sorry,"

Mike McCarthy hung his head. Mr. Jeffreys walked over to one of the lobby chairs and sat down. The creaking noise broke the tension.

It's done now, thought Mary, and I am still standing. David and I, what we had, does not have to be diminished by the revelation that he was human.

"All right," she said. "I appreciate you telling me, Mr. McCarthy."

"Mike," he said.

"Miss Wandwalker," said Mary.

Mr. Jeffreys grinned.

CHAPTER 46
THE DEPTH ENQUIRY AGENCY

An hour and a half later Mary kicked off her shoes and wriggled her damp toes at another wood fire blasting heat. She was in the gardener's cottage, facing another couple on another sofa. A pot of tea and a plate of homemade mince pies steamed on the table between them. Biting into the warm pastry, Mary's mouth watered at the fruity, spicy taste of Christmas. Comfort food can, she reflected, caress a bruised heart.

"It must have been a shock," said Caroline, cautiously, while pouring second cups of tea all around. "Hearing about David and Rosalind Forrest, Miss Wandwalker. Doesn't it make George and Viktor brothers?"

Looking simultaneously tired and rested, Caroline sat back and took Anna's hand. That perfectly made-up young woman stared at Mary. Anna positively glowed in a sky-blue jersey and impossibly skinny black jeans. How does she get to look that good in designer clothes when she's recently been in jail? wondered Mary.

"Half-brothers," said Mary, to Caroline's point. "I don't what to talk about it. If there is anything I've learned, it is that families are inescapable. Often they make no sense at all." She gave Caroline a crooked smile. "On the other hand, families can regenerate. That's the reason I'm here."

"You need us," Anna smiled with hideous complacency.

Mary wanted to snap back. Only her instinct for honesty saved her. She did not want her carefully crafted offer rejected before it could be understood. Anna was goading her, she realized. Mary took a deep breath.

"Yes, it's true. I need you both. You, Caroline, and Anna, may not be my blood relations, yet you're all the family I've got."

Caroline flushed with pleasure. She's different, thought Mary. She's become more composed. I can see the agony of losing George together with a kind of a peace in her eyes. That dark red dress over leggings fits her better. Mary suspected Anna's influence. That young woman had an answer for Mary.

"Not family. I have no family," Anna said.

It's a chess move, thought Mary. "Then think of what I'm offering as a job," she responded, tartly. "A job moreover that will give you freedom, not otherwise possible. You know what Mr. Jeffreys said."

Anna's black eyes flashed.

"Darling," said Caroline. "Remember what Miss Wandwalker told us on the phone. Mr. Jeffreys has done deals with all those nasty police agencies. After you debrief with their representatives in London, we three can live together. Miss Wandwalker wants to buy a house in Surrey."

Her glance at Mary was part anxiety, part gratitude. "Mary's cashing in her pension so that she can pay for the house. She'll become your legal guardian so we can set up the ... what was the name?" She appealed to Mary.

"The Depth Enquiry Agency," Mary replied. "Motto: 'We go deeper than the police.'" She clasped her hands and leaned forward.

"I've done investigations. Some to get the government out of a hole, some to look after people at the Archive when their lives went haywire. We three saw that the police don't always pursue crimes in the best way. Plus, some of the worst offences," Mary glanced at skeptical Anna, "may not contravene a law or look like the crimes they actually are." She banged a fist on the arm of her chair. "We're going to help people. In return, they'll pay us fees. It will be a business that could work for all three of us."

Anna snorted. "You have no idea ... what's out there."

"Then it's a good thing you do," countered Mary.

Would they go for it? Mary could not be sure. Why did she feel so ... so emotional about it all?

She leaned forward. "Caroline is going to be great with our clients, especially the vulnerable ones. I've got research skills, contacts, my famous intuition. You, Anna, have ... experience."

Anna laughed like an owl screech.

"Anna's a real witch with the internet," said Caroline eagerly. "That's so important these days." She turned to face her lover. "Darling, you will say yes, won't you? Otherwise ..." She looked falteringly at Mary.

Mary thought back to her last interview in Mr. Jeffreys's office. Sunset blazed behind him when she sat down. A horned moon rose before they completed negotiations over Anna. Finally, Mr. Jeffreys got out the whisky.

"There is no way she and Caroline Jones will last as a couple," he'd insisted, as they held the peaty nectar to their noses before drinking.

"Love or no love," he continued. "With Mrs. Jones's mental health problems, you can't expect the poor woman to hold onto a savage creature like Anna ... Vronsky, as she now wants to be called." He sighed, then added with grudging approval. "The only hope of keeping them together is a structure with you taking responsibility. This Agency you propose might work, I'll admit."

The Agency as a family, thought Mary to herself.

*****

That was two days ago. Now, in the stuffy cottage, Anna scowled at her current lover and her previous lover's birth mother. Another chess move, guessed Mary. Anna began to speak.

"Why Depth Agency? Why work for you, Miss Wandwalker? You say equal partners, but I know you will take charge. I know your type."

Mary paused. She was out of options. If this last card was thrown back in her face, she would have no choice. She would leave with nothing. Anna would return to custody, and Caroline would face a destructive second loss. How to make Anna care?

"I meant what I said about regenerated families."

She spoke directly to Anna while looping in Caroline with glances at her strained expression. "Both of you were loved by my son."

Caroline quivered. It had been an arrow to her chest, Mary could see. Well, I'm not sorry, she admitted. Falling for Anna is all very well, but George was only buried 10 days ago.

"You were there," Mary said, making her voice softer. "When he died, you were both there, and he said your names. He said your names to *me*."

Caroline and Anna took on identical expressions.

Mary calmed herself. "You see, I finally realized what he meant. He wants me to look after both of you."

She forced out the next words; they were all she had.

"A long time ago I refused to be George's family, to keep the baby and be a mother. My life has been poorer for it. With his dying breath, George offered me a chance to be your family."

Mary looked at her cold, reddened hands. The fire crackled. Caroline bent and added a few extra sticks.

"Yes," Caroline said. "Yes, Miss Wandwalker. I'm in."

Mary raised her head to Anna. Inscrutable as a statue, her eyes gleamed like black earth in the rain. Suddenly she stuck out her tongue at Mary.

There was a pause. Mary felt it stretch beyond her patience, beyond her hope.

"All right, I'll do it for George," Anna finally said. "But we get to choose the new house in Surrey. I mean *together*, Miss Wandwalker."

Relief flooded Mary. Her spirit ran barefoot from the cottage, leaping and dancing on her dead son's family ground. "Call me Mary," Miss Wandwalker said to Caroline Jones and Anna Vronsky. "Now move over so I can sit between you. I've brought my laptop to show you the properties in our price range. We need a home that *is* a nest and we're going to get one."

Mary Wandwalker's final final Falconer Family Tree
(motto: *Service through Family*)

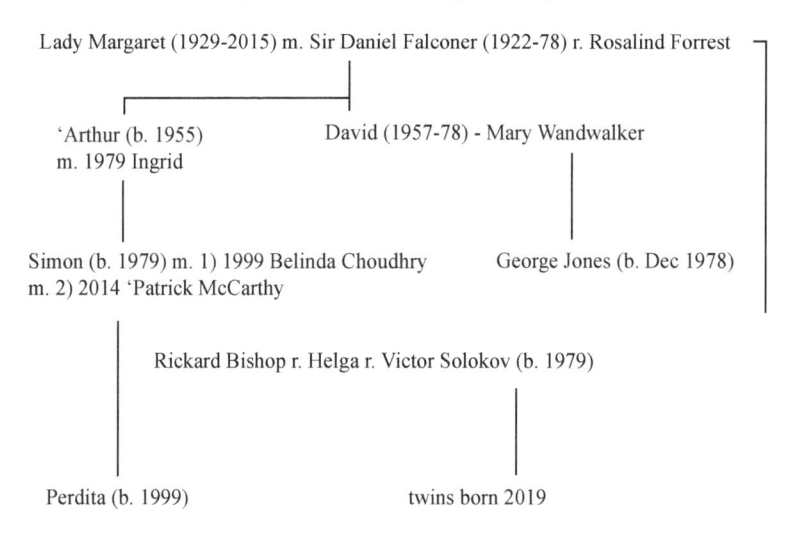

Lady Margaret (1929-2015) m. Sir Daniel Falconer (1922-78) r. Rosalind Forrest

'Arthur (b. 1955) m. 1979 Ingrid

David (1957-78) - Mary Wandwalker

Simon (b. 1979) m. 1) 1999 Belinda Choudhry m. 2) 2014 'Patrick McCarthy

George Jones (b. Dec 1978)

Rickard Bishop r. Helga r. Victor Solokov (b. 1979)

Perdita (b. 1999)

twins born 2019